Edward Marshall

**Oxford**

Edward Marshall

**Oxford**

ISBN/EAN: 9783744659697

Printed in Europe, USA, Canada, Australia, Japan

Cover: Foto ©ninafisch / pixelio.de

More available books at **www.hansebooks.com**

WYMAN AND SONS, PRINTERS,
GREAT QUEEN STREET, LINCOLN'S-INN FIELDS,
LONDON, W.C.

# CONTENTS.

## CHAPTER I.

INTRODUCTION. A.D. 634-1075.

Bishops in Oxfordshire—Bishopric of Dorchester—Division of the See of Wessex—Bishoprics of Sherborne and Winchester—Dorchester a Mercian See—Removal of Bishop's Throne to Lincoln—Architecture ... *Page* 1

## CHAPTER II.

INTRODUCTION CONTINUED. A.D. 1075-1500.

Organisation of the Church in Oxfordshire—Parishes—Archdeaconry — Peculiars — Deaneries — Suffragan Bishops — Visitations — University of Oxford — King Alfred not the Founder—Foundation of Merton College and University College—Jews in Oxford—Dominicans — Franciscans —Augustinians — Hospital of St. Bartholomew—Councils at Oxford, Woodstock, and Eynsham—Knights Templars—Knights Hospitallers—Alien Priories—Architecture ... ... ... 28

## CHAPTER III.

INTRODUCTION CONTINUED. A.D. 1500-1528.

Wolsey and Oxford—Suppression of St. Frideswide's Monastery—Foundation of Cardinal College—Foundation of King Henry VIII.'s College—Later Architecture ... ... ... ... .. ... .. 68

## CHAPTER IV.

HISTORY OF THE DIOCESE. A.D. 1528-1558.

Dissolution of the Monasteries—Foundation of the See of Oxford, with seat at Oseney—Removal to Christ Church—Suppression of the Chantries—Schools of Edward VI.—Oxford under Queen Mary ... *Page* 83

## CHAPTER V.

HISTORY OF THE DIOCESE. A.D. 1558-1660.

The Diocese under Queen Elizabeth—Vacancy of the See —Roman Catholics executed—Proceedings of Abbot —Estates of the See—Palace at Cuddesdon—Charge against Laud — Bishop Skinner — The Usurpation— State of Oxford—Extracts from Court Books... ... 108

## CHAPTER VI.

HISTORY OF THE DIOCESE. A.D. 1660-1715.

The Restoration—Bishop Skinner—Act of Uniformity and its results—Bishop Fell—Magdalen College—Bishop Parker—Bishop Hall—Nonjurors—Bishop Talbot ... 144

## CHAPTER VII.

HISTORY OF THE DIOCESE. A.D. 1715-1882.

Bishop Potter—Bangorian Controversy—John Wesley and Methodism in Oxford—Succeeding Bishops—Bishop Lloyd—Bishop Bagot—Addition of Berks—Bishop Wilberforce—Addition of Bucks—Wilberforce College —Bishop Mackarness ... ... ... ... ... 166

## CHAPTER VIII.

UNION OF BERKS AND OXON, WITH HISTORY OF THE ARCHDEACONRY OF BERKS, A.D. 705-1856.

Union of Berks and Bucks with the Diocese of Oxford—Early History of the Archdeaconry of Berks—Historical Events — Councils of Windsor and Reading — Coverdale at Newbury — Sufferers for Religion — Bishop Jewel — Dr. Twisse — Nonjurors — Wantage and Clewer—Endowment ... ... ... *Page* 192

## CHAPTER IX.

HISTORY OF MONASTIC AND COLLEGIATE FOUNDATION FROM A.D. 675.

Benedictine Order—Abingdon—Reading—Windsor ... 222

## CHAPTER X.

UNION OF BUCKS WITH OXON AND BERKS, WITH HISTORY OF THE ARCHDEACONRY OF BUCKS, A.D. 1075-1837.

Union with the Diocese of Oxford—Early History of the Archdeaconry — Sufferers for Religion — Hooker—Clergy during the Commonwealth — Extracts from Parish Register—The Restoration—Endowment ... 253

## CHAPTER XI.

HISTORY OF MONASTIC AND COLLEGIATE FOUNDATIONS FROM A.D. 1200.

Monastic and Collegiate Foundations—Prebend of Aylesbury — Bonhommes at Ashridge — Eton College — Conclusion ... ... ... ... ... ... 266

## APPENDIX.

A. List of Bishops in Oxfordshire ... ... ... *Page* 281
B. List of Bishops for Berkshire ... ... ... 283
C. List of Endowed Grammar Schools ... ... ... 284

# OXFORD.

## CHAPTER I.

INTRODUCTION. A.D. 634—A.D. 1075.

Bishops in Oxfordshire—Bishopric of Dorchester—Division of the See of Wessex—Bishoprics of Sherborne and Winchester—Removal of Bishop's Throne to Lincoln—Architecture.

FOR the earliest traditions of the diocese of Oxford, a reference must be made to another period than that of the existence of the present see, which was formed by King Henry VIII. There was a bishopric of much importance in Oxfordshire some centuries before this was established, to which the conversion of the kingdom of Wessex to the Christian faith was due. Though Oxford may have had a position of less relative influence, its name may yet be taken to include a high antiquity, when it is regarded in the Celtic form[1] of Ousen-ford, the ford across the water, which is still to be traced in Ousen-ey, or Oseney,

---

[1] "Proceedings of Oxford Architectural and Historical Society," New Ser., vol. ii., 1864-71, note by J. Parker, p. 93.

which intimates the existence of an island or eyot, in which it was situate. The name of Oxna-ford, or Oxene-ford, though still an early one, is yet, like the Oxford of to-day, a departure from its original intention, though it is not inappropriate in itself, and is in correspondence with the arms of the city, in which there appears the ox crossing the ford.

In the fifth century the British Church had its share in the great political change which ensued upon the departure of the Roman legions, and the subsequent influx of the English in A.D. 449, who brought with them the religion of their Teutonic ancestors in its primitive state, uninfluenced by the diffusion of the gospel, as it had become extended to the more civilised of the Roman provinces. The religious character of the district from which the see of Oxford was taken in later times soon felt the influence of this invasion, in the course which the English conquest and English settlements took. And when Britain had become English the heathen worship of the conqueror had left its mark in countless ways.

The mission of St. Augustine sought to re-establish the faith. Sent by Pope Gregory the Great, who had not forgotten what in early life he had observed of the Angles in the market-place at Rome, Augustine with his followers disembarked at Ebbsfleet, in the Isle of Thanet, in A.D. 597, when the political state of the kingdom was not unfavourable to his reception. For Æthelberht, the King of Kent, had married the Christian Bercta, the daughter of King Charibert, and the church of St. Martin, near Canterbury, had been assigned to her use. This became available for the purposes of the mission, which had its success, through which Æthelberht received baptism from Augustine. But it is to another mission that the conversion of the Saxons in the South beyond the boundaries of the kingdom of Kent is to be attributed. Nor was this long delayed. The kingdom of Wessex was still pagan on the death of Augustine; and now, with the fresh efforts which were made for the introduction of Christianity within its borders, the history of the diocese of Oxford, as the actual seat of a bishop, though with a see of a different name, will properly begin. The account of the conversion of the kingdom of Wessex is derived from Beda.[1] It apppears from his statements, that in the reign of King Cynegils, in A.D. 634, the West Saxons were visited by the mission of Birinus, which was unconnected with the previous mission of Augustine. Previously to setting forth Birinus, whose own origin is unknown, expressed in the presence of the Pope Honorius his intention to "scatter the seeds of the faith" in the remoter districts of the English where no preacher of the truth had been before. By his direction he received consecration from Asterius, Archbishop of Milan,[2] who was living at Genoa. No see was allotted to him, and he was free to choose his own field of labour. When he came into Britain he visited first the West Saxons, and found them the most utter pagans. Upon this he determined that it

[1] Beda, "Hist. Eccl.," iii., 7, compared for the date with the "Anglo-Saxon Chronicle," *ad an.*
[2] W. Bright, "Early Eng. Ch. Hist.," p. 146, n. 7. Oxf., 1879.

would be best to attempt their conversion, and seek no further for the subjects of his mission. His choice was wisely made. For soon after this the king was "catechised and baptised," with his people, whose conversion followed his own. Oswald, the King of the Northumbrians, was present at the time, and was his godfather. The two kings joined in making a gift to Birinus of the strong place by the water,[1] the city of Dorcic,[2] the Durocina of the Romans, the modern Dorchester, that it might become the seat of a bishopric. It was situated near the junction of the two rivers the Thame and the Thames; and the early importance of this site is denoted by the intrenchment extending across the angle which is formed by the conjunction of the two streams, and by the Roman way which led to it from the neighbouring town of Alchester. The narrative of the baptism of Cynegils is not without some points of interest. The express mention of his having been "catechised" before baptism implies at least the power on his part of returning an answer to the interrogation which was made before the administration of the sacrament, and suggests an idea of the care and order with which the preparation for the rite and the administration of it were attended. And then, too, as was so often the case, the conversion of the king to an acceptance of the faith is seen to have ensured the conversion of his subjects as well, as if their spiritual and temporal allegiance were equally involved in a loyal submission to the will of the king.

---

[1] Scil. "dwr," Welsh.
[2] Beda, "Hist. Eccl.," *u. s.*, iii., 7.

It is further stated, that St. Birinus built and consecrated churches in the immediate neighbourhood of Dorchester, and by his pious care invited many to the Lord. These churches attest the completeness with which the organisation of the mission was developed. In after-times three churches were supposed to have existed in Dorchester;[1] but there was no actual proof that such were identical in their sites with those which were constructed by Birinus, and which were possibly built of wood. The site of a bishop's palace was also shown?[2] The success which attended the early efforts of Birinus is further indicated by the baptism of the son of Cynegils, King Cwichelm, whose messenger had attempted the life of Edwin, when the faithful Ella interposed his body to receive the stroke which was intended for his king. Nor was this the only later royal baptism; for it was preceded by that of King Cuthred, whom the bishop himself "received from the font." Birinus died in the year A.D. 650, and was buried at Dorchester; but his body was in all probability removed to Winchester by Bishop Heddi. The canons of Dorchester, however, were unwilling to allow that that had lost the venerated body of the bishop, and maintained that it was another body[3] and not that of Birinus himself, which was then translated, as evinced by the miracles still performed at the original place of sepulture. Birinus is supposed to have placed a

---

[1] J. Leland, "Itin.," vol. ii., p. 28. Ox., 1768, 9.
[2] *Ibid.*, p. 39.
[3] Ralph Higden, in Gale, "Hist. Angl. Script.," t. i. p. 231. Oxon, 1691.

foundation of secular canons[1] in his cathedral church, who were replaced by Augustinian monks, when the abbey of Dorchester was reconstituted by Alexander, Bishop of Lincoln, in A.D. 1140. The church of the abbey still remains to testify in its present grandeur, what the magnificence of this foundation must once have been, when its state was unimpaired. It is now the best memorial of Birinus and his work, nor in the restoration of it which has been in progress so long, has this connexion been otherwise than religiously preserved. The painted glass in the lights under the canopies of the piscina and sedilia in the chancel represent important incidents in his life, and show how he received his mission to preach the gospel in these parts.

The influence which these memorials of St. Birinus were calculated to exert upon the mind of a thoughtful visitor to Dorchester, is thus described by the antiquary Thomas Hearne. "I know of no truly religious person," he writes,[2] "but what is affected with what remains of the historical painting in Dorchester windows, relating to Birinus's voyage thither, and his converting the heathen." These windows, it has been stated on high authority, are believed to be unique."[3] They are of the assigned date of *c.* A.D. 1370.

[1] The secular clergy were those who lived in the world, as the canons of cathedrals, or the parish priests. The regulars were those who, whether clergy or laymen, lived under rule in religious houses.

[2] In Will. of Newburgh, "Hist. Rer. Ang.," vol. iii., p. 773. Ox., 1719.

[3] J. H. Parker, "Introduction to the Study of Gothic Architecture," engraving, p. 182. Ox., 1881.

At a later period Birinus was recognised as a saint, and his memory is kept in the Roman calendar on the 3rd of December; there is abundant record from authentic sources to confirm the opinion of his merits which this title implies, in whatever manner it may have been conferred upon him, of which there is no record.

On the death of Cynegils the instability of the conversion of Wessex was but too plainly shown, for his son Kenwalch, upon his succession in A.D. 643, refused to embrace the faith. The danger of a relapse into paganism, however, was averted in the course of events. Misfortune produced in his case its best fruits, and the temporary loss of his kingdom, arising from the illtreatment which he received from his wife—the sister of Penda—was the cause of his baptism and conversion. In Anna, the King of East Anglia, with whom he took refuge for the three years of his banishment, he had the example of a good man, and of one who was happy in his family life, as he himself was not, and it was not in vain. After his restoration, in A.D. 650—the year of the death of Birinus, and during the vacancy of the see—there came into Wessex, from Ireland, a French bishop named Agilberht, who had been in that country for the opportunity of reading the Scriptures and of theological study, and who had remained there for some years, its collegiate and monastic institutions being in great repute. On arriving in his new country, Agilberht presented himself to King Kenwalch, and made an offer to serve him and preach the Word of Life to his subjects. It was accepted, as the king could perceive his learning and industry, and he desired him to occupy the see of Dorchester, and remain with him. He thus became bishop, and held the see for some years. But in process of time the king became weary of the "barbarous" tongue of Agilberht, being ignorant himself of any other language than his own; and in A.D. 660 he introduced into the diocese, without the consent of Agilberht, another bishop of his own nation, Wini, who, like his predecessor, had been consecrated in France. A place for his ministrations was to be found, and the king proposed to divide the see and create a new bishopric, of which Winchester should be the seat.

In the end there came a change of feeling towards Wini in the heart of the king, and he proved as unfaithful towards him as he had previously towards Agilberht. For some cause, which has not been ascertained, he became opposed to the bishop, who was expelled from his see, and who then took refuge with Wulfhere, King of the Mercians, "of whom," it is emphatically stated, "he purchased for money[1] the see of London," which he held for the remainder of his life.

At this early period there is found the existence of the fault which so often reappeared in later times; and when the scene was the bishopric of London, and the partner in the transaction the king himself, the difficulty which the spiritual power had to contend with in this respect appears at once in the strongest light. Wini himself, it has been supposed, became

---

[1] Beda, *u. s.*

convinced of his sinfulnesss, and it is recorded that he laid aside his state, as bishop, for three years, and lived a life of penitence, as a monk, at Winchester,[1] lamenting the simony of his earlier years, and ever ruminating upon those expressive words, "I have erred in youth, I will amend in old age."

On the expulsion of Wini, the kingdom of Wessex was left without a bishop, and so for a time continued. But the king was not insensible of the evil of this. He remembered his own exile, and his return after receiving the faith; and he feared the loss of the divine protection as the consequence of this wrong to the Church. He sent into France to Agilberht, and with all humility besought him to return. Agilberht, however, had now the tie of his own bishopric, which he felt that he could not in justice forsake. He adopted, accordingly, another course. In his stead, he recommended his nephew Eleutherius, or Lothere, as one who might occupy his place, if the king should think fit, for which his previous life had been no unfit preparation. This proposal was accepted, and Eleutherius was received with much satisfaction both by the people and the king. The see of Canterbury was held at the time by Archbishop Theodore, and the king applied for the consecration of the new bishop to him. This, accordingly, took place at Canterbury, and Eleutherius, "by synodical authority," as it is stated, held the bishopric of the West Saxons.[2]

---

[1] Rudborne, "Hist. Maj. Winton.," after Florence of Worcester, "Chron.," iii., 6, in H. Wharton's "Angl. Sacr.," tom. i., p. 192. Lond., 1691.

[2] Beda, "Hist. Eccl.," iii., 28.

In the same manner as in more modern times, the natural growth of the Church required the subdivision of the see. But it also became apparent that many causes, arising from various sources, may prevent the change from being at once effected. It was accepted as a possible result, that the dignity of a bishop might be lessened by the diminution of his see, and this was an effect which was not hastily to be produced.

In A.D. 673, on September the 24th, a council was held by Archbishop Theodore at Hertford, at which all the Anglo-Saxon bishops except the simoniacal Bishop Wini were present.[1] Eleutherius came to represent his see. It was agreed that decrees of former councils should be observed, and several questions relative to the time of Easter, the relation of bishops with each other and the rest of the clergy, the freedom of monasteries from episcopal jurisdiction, the annual synod at Clovesho,[2] and the subject of marriage and divorce were determined, in accordance with ancient canons on the different points.

After the death of Eleutherius, the see of Wessex in its undivided extent descended to Heddi, who became Bishop of Winchester, in A.D. 676, and who has by some authorities been identified with Ætla.[3]

---

[1] Beda, "Hist. Eccl.," iv., 3, and Haddan and Stubbs, "Councils and Ecclesiastical Documents," vol. iii., pp. 118, *seq.* Ox., 1869-78.

[2] Various conjectures as to this place have been offered, and among these it has been supposed that it is Abingdon.—*Ibid.*, *note e*, p. 122.

[3] Ætla is mentioned by Beda, "Hist. Eccl." (iv. 23), as Bishop of Dorsic, but his history cannot be determined with certainty. Haddan and Stubbs, *u. s.*, pp. 129-30, note *d*.

Like his earlier predecessor, St. Birinus, Heddi has been recognised as a saint, the day of his commemoration being the 7th of July. He obtained from the pope a confirmation of the removal of the see of Dorchester to Winchester, and at the same time a permission to translate the body of St. Birinus to it for the greater honour of his cathedral church.[1]

This respect for the relics of great and holy men was suggested no less by natural piety than the desire to preserve, as a sacred deposit, the remains of those whose name in the Church was of lasting esteem; and the custom may be traced to primitive times. In the authentic Acts[2] of the martyrdom of St. Ignatius at Rome, A.D. 107, it is recorded that, after he had been thrown to the beasts, "the harder parts of his sacred body, which alone could be recognised, were carried back to Antioch, and wrapped in linen—a treasure of inestimable value, as left to the Church by the grace with which the martyr was endued;" and these relics, in after-ages, were regarded with the same reverence as at the first.[3] In the course of time there was a further

---

Mr. Haddan suggests that "that there was an attempt to preserve the see of Dorchester, as well as that of Stow or Sidnacester," which may account for "the otherwise incomprehensible Ætla of Dorsic."—"Remains," p. 322, note *f*. Ox., 1876.

[1] Beda ("Hist. Eccl.," iii., 7) and Hen. of Hunt. (bk. iii., sect. 5, pp. 99, Lon., 1853) mention the translation.

[2] "Patr. Apost.," tom. ii., p. 552, ed. Jacobson. Oxon., 1840.

[3] S. Chrys., "Orat. in S. Ign., c. v., Opp.," tom. ii., p. 660. Par., 1718-38.

reason for obtaining the translation of the bodies of saints, arising from the reputation for miraculous effects which their presence conferred. The unwillingness of the canons of Dorchester to allow that the removal had actually taken place, and their appeal against the supposition, to which allusion has been made,[1] were not unconnected with this.

Heddi, as appears from the epilogue to the Penitential of Archbishop Theodore,[2] was in close friendship with that prelate, and he appears to have provided by a decree—of which, however, the authenticity is not ascertained, that the see of Wessex should not be divided before the bishop's death.[3] One who had laboured so faithfully and so successfully for his diocese was not to suffer in his own person any diminution of authority by a change in its extent. The see of Wessex was therefore left undivided by Archbishop Theodore, and remained in the same condition unto the death of St. Heddi. But in the preceding year its division was determined at a synod, of which the place is uncertain, and which apparently was one which was held from year to year.

The division of the great diocese of Wessex, which had been so often attempted and so frequently deferred, was destined at length, as in the instance of other dioceses, to have its accomplishment. Heddi died on July the 7th, in A.D. 705, and it was finally considered that the diocese was of too great

[1] *Supra*, p. 5.
[2] Haddan and Stubbs, *u. s.*, vol. iii., p. 127, note *a*.
[3] *Ibid*, p. 126.

extent to be governed by a single bishop, and the division was made after the question had been determined "by a council of the Fathers of the Church and the kings."[1] One part, which consisted of Hampshire, Surrey, and Sussex, together with Oxfordshire, was assigned to the see of Winchester, while the other, comprising Berkshire, Wiltshire, Dorsetshire and Somersetshire, the country to the west of Selwood, was allotted to Sherborne.[2] Bishop Daniel was the first to hold the new see of Winchester, while Aldhelm, the saint and scholar, was appointed to Sherborne. The king, under whose direction the disposal of these bishoprics was made, was the most famous of the early kings of Wessex. Ini had been successful in his attempts to extend his kingdom in the west. He had founded within his newly-acquired country the Abbey of Glastonbury, in a spot already consecrated by its earlier associations, and of which the large remains are of unfailing interest. And in his regard for the spiritual welfare of his fresh subjects he intrusted the diocese to one who was eminently fitted for his office. In the latter part of his long reign provision was made for the civil no less than the ecclesiastical necessities of the kingdom. Internal divisions, how-

[1] "Vita S. Aldhelm.," in Haddan and Stubbs, *u. s.*, vol. iii., p. 275.

[2] This is the division after William of Malmesbury and the "Anglo-Saxon Chronicle," in Haddan and Stubbs, *u. s.*, vol. iii., p. 276. But another distribution gives Somersetshire, Dorsetshire, and Wiltshire, with any undefined county in the West, to Sherborne, and the rest to Winchester.

ever, proved more formidable than the wars with the Mercians or Britons, and Ini was compelled to leave the kingdom, for which he had done so much. At the sight of the desolation of his home, which his enemies had plundered and defiled, his spirit failed. Equally with his queen, he became convinced of the passing fashion of the present world, and took refuge, as a pilgrim, in Rome, the "eternal" city, where he died about a year after his arrival, in A.D. 726. The substitution of the two sees of Sherborne and Winchester for the previous bishopric, which comprised the undivided see of Wessex, changed at once the condition of Dorchester as an ecclesiastical centre, which lost the distinction of having the bishop's throne located there. For the period, accordingly, which succeeded this, the history of the diocese of Oxford loses its individual character. It is to be sought in the histories of the two dioceses which came into possession of the privilege which was accorded to Dorchester, and which are now represented by the bishoprics of Salisbury and Winchester, until the former position which Dorchester held was regained.

It cannot be determined with certainty[1] at what time the district of Oxfordshire became part of the extended kingdom of Mercia. It may perhaps have belonged to Wessex up to A.D. 778, and the victory gained by Offa over the West Saxons at Bensington, near Dorchester, in that year; after which it may have become attached permanently to Mercia.[2] But, however this may have been, at the interval of a

---

[1] See Haddan and Stubbs, *u. s.*, vol. iii., p. 130, note *c*.
[2] Haddan and Stubbs, *u. s.*, note *e*.

century there is the re-establishment of a bishopric at Dorchester, as a Mercian see, having regained its privilege through the following course of events.

In A.D. 679, Archbishop Theodore made a division of the large Mercian bishopric,[1] in effecting which he obtained the assistance of the provincial bishops whose sees he was enabled to establish. Five bishoprics were formed—namely, Worcester, Lichfield, Leicester, Sidenacester or Lindsey, and Dorchester, over which a bishop named Ætla, a disciple of St. Hilda, is stated to have been placed. It has been already stated that it is not possible to account for his position with any certainty.[2] He has on the one hand been identified with Heddi, and on the other has been supposed to have been a separate occupant of the see for a short period, and then to have left it vacant for redistribution by an early death. But, independently of this question, a succession of bishops was established at Sidenacester, or at Lindsey,—for the names are both applied to it,—and at Leicester.

From the time when Totta, or Torthelm as he is also named, became Bishop of Leicester, in A.D. 737, to the time of Ceolred, the sixth in succession from him, the occupants of the see derived their title from the city of Leicester.[3] But their designation became changed, and they are known as Bishops of Dorchester from the time of Alheard, who succeeded Ceolred. The death of Alheard occurred during the three years of the great "mortality among

---

[1] Flor. of Worc., app. to "Chron.," *ibid.*, p. 128.
[2] *Supra*, p. 10.
[3] Haddan and Stubbs, *u. s.*, vol. iii., p. 129, note *d*.

cattle and among men," *c.* A.D. 897; and he is described as Bishop of Dorchester in the notices of it.[1] The removal of the bishop's chair from Leicester to Dorchester was not a mere arbitrary change of place; for "it was undoubtedly occasioned by the conquest of Mercia and Middle Anglia by the Danes, which took place in A.D. 874." Ceolwulf, the successor of Alheard, was not consecrated before A.D. 909, during which time the see must have been vacant. He is the bishop whose name appears as Cenulph in the alleged epistle of Pope Formosus, which professes to give directions for the filling up of seven vacant sees, but which is undoubtedly to be accounted a forgery.[3] Ceolwulf was followed by Bishop Winsy, whose successor, Oskytel, attained to great eminence. He was consecrated Bishop of Dorchester in A.D. 950, but did not die in possession of the see. He was translated to the archbishopric of York, and survived his removal from Dorchester for some years, and died in A.D. 971. His death is recorded in these terms:—" This year died Archbishop Oskytel; he was first consecrated Bishop of Dorchester, and afterwards of York; by favour of King Edred and all his witan he was consecrated archbishop; and he was a bishop twenty-two years; and he died on the massnight of All-hallows, ten days before Martinmas, at

---

[1] "Anglo-Sax. Chron.," and Flor. of Worc., *ad* A.D. 897.
[2] Haddan and Stubbs, *u. s.*, vol. iii., 129, note *d*.
[3] The letter is inserted by Will. of Malmesbury in his "Chronicle of the Kings of Engl.," bk. ii., c. 5, p. 127, Lon., 1856. It is refuted by Wharton, "Angl. Sacr.," *u. s.*, tom. i., p. 554.

Thame. And Abbot Thurkytel, his kinsman, carried the bishop's body to Bedford, because he was at that time abbot there."[1] A great change was effected in the condition of the bishopric by Leofwin, who succeeded him *c.* A.D. 956.

Bishop Leofwin, in A.D. 953, held the see of Sidenacester, or Lindsey, in which there had been a succession of bishops from the time of Bishop Eadhed in A.D. 678. Subsequently to his appointment to this see he first united the bishopric of Leicester with the see of Lindsey, which he previously held. At a later period, probably after the translation of Bishop Oskytel to the see of York, he formed a second union by joining these two sees with the bishopric of Dorchester,[2] *c.* A.D. 965, where he placed the bishop's throne. By this change of arrangement the see of Dorchester received a great increase of extent, and became the largest Mercian see.

Escwy, one of the successors of Leofwin, was recognised as a brave and skilful warrior; and, accordingly, when Æthelred the Unready, in A.D. 992, was called upon to oppose the threatened invasion of the Northmen, he had recourse to him for assistance.[3]

One of the successors of Escwy, Eadnoth was present at the battle of Assingdon in Essex, so fatal to Edmond Ironsides, in A.D. 1016; nor was he spared in the performance of the sacred office of

---

[1] "*Anglo-Sax. Chron.,*" *ad an.*
[2] Will. of Malmesbury, "De Gestis Pontificum Anglorum,' l. iv., sects. 176—7. 1870. Rolls' Ser.
[3] Florence of Worc., and "Anglo-Sax. Chron.," *ad an.*

saying mass for the safety of the English Crown. His hand was first cut off, for the sake of obtaining the pastoral ring which he wore, and he then was put to death.[1]

Another, Ulf the Norman,[2] has obtained notice for a different cause. Edward the Confessor, whose youth was passed in Normandy, and whose affections were given to the home of his earlier years, never lost the impressions which he had received. Upon succeeding to his kingdom he placed his Norman favourites in the highest offices of Church and State. And among the appointments of this class which he made was the nomination of his chaplain Ulf to the see of Dorchester, upon whom he "unworthily bestowed the bishopric."[3] Ulf was a man of no learning, and was entirely unfitted for his high office. The result was a great dissatisfaction and a consequent appeal to the pope, which was preferred under the following circumstances. After a short interval following his appointment, in A.D. 1050, Ulf was present at Vercelli, a town of northern Italy, to which he had apparently come for consecration or confirmation. An accusation was then brought which charged him with being so illiterate as to be incapable of going through the

---

[1] Hist. Eccles. Eliens., in Kennet's "Par. Ant.," vol. i., p. 65. Ox., 1818.

[2] E. A. Freeman. The authorities for this part of the history are arranged in Dr. Freeman's "History of the Norman Conquest," vol. iv., Ox., 1871; and the results of the conquest are stated in his "Short History of the Norman Conquest," Ox., Cl. Pr. Ser., 1880.

[3] "Anglo-Saxon Chron.," *ad an.* 1050.

offices which he had to say. The synod was on the point of deposing him, but the king's influence was sufficiently powerful to avert this disgrace, and he prevailed upon the pope, Leo IX., to preserve his bishopric. Accordingly, after a large expenditure of money on Ulf's part, his cause was successful. The staff which he had received, as the authorities state, was not broken, in sign of his deposition. It was restored to him and he retained his see.[1] He did not, however, die in the peaceable possession of it, for when Earl Godwine and Harold returned, with permission from the king, their united fleet sailed up the Thames, and filled with consternation all the Normans who were in and near London. Robert, the Archbishop, and Ulf "cut their way out of the city, slaying as they went."[2] By this course, however strange a one for prelates of the Church to adopt, they saved their lives. Both crossed the sea and never returned. The bishopric of Dorchester, in consequence, became practically vacant. But Ulf was never formally and canonically deposed, nor the legitimate vacancy of the see announced.

Wulfwy succeeded, in A.D. 1053, and met with no opposition on account of the circumstances through which the see had to be filled up. At a later period, in A.D. 1061, he was successful in an application which he made to Pope Nicholas II. He obtained a bull[3] of some importance in determining the extent of the jurisdiction of his see. The Archbishop of

---

[1] Freeman, *u. s.*, vol. iv., p. 117.
[2] Freeman, "Short Notice," *u. s.*, p. 40.
[3] Wilkins, "Conc.," vol. i., p. 315. Lon., 1737.

York had advanced a claim from time to time in respect of certain places in the northern part of the diocese; but the bull confirmed the privileges of the see of Dorchester, specially mentioning the district of Lindsey, and the Church of Stow, with Newark and its dependencies, which had been unjustly visited by Archbishop Alfric. Wulfwy was the last Bishop of Dorchester who lived and died in possession of the see, with the bishop's throne in the accustomed place.

The next who succeeded, and who closes the line of the Bishops of Dorchester, has a place of more importance in general history from his connexion with Duke William, and from the change which he effected in his diocese, extending over so large a part of England. The policy of the Conqueror in reducing the kingdom to obedience was, at no long interval, manifested here. In transferring the chief offices in Church and State upon every vacancy to his Norman followers, he found an early occasion to carry into effect his purpose in this see. Wulfwy died in A.D. 1067, and his successor was found among the ecclesiastics who had come from Normandy. The almoner of the Abbey of Fécamp had rendered the Duke great service. When "he sailed from St. Valery to Pevensey"[1] one of the ships of his fleet had been fitted out by Remigius, who held that post, and furnished with a complete equipment. Nor was this an act of disinterested service. He made a compact to receive a bishopric in return, if the expedition was successful.

[1] Freeman, *n. s.*

The Conqueror was true to his engagement, and Remigius obtained the see of Dorchester, which was one of the richest in England. He thus became the first Norman promoted by William to an English bishopric. The circumstances of his consecration, however, were not happy. He applied for it to Stigand, who had intruded into the see of Archbishop Robert, who was neither lawfully deposed nor deprived, and this made the consecration liable to the charge of being uncanonical and schismatical. Remigius entered, indeed, upon the see without opposition, but he was not permitted to remain in undisturbed possession. He was accused for this reason to the pope, Alexander II., and not for this only, but for the simoniacal contract which he had made with William. To answer this he was compelled to appear in Rome, and he made his journey with Lanfranc, Archbishop of Canterbury, and Thomas, Archbishop of York. On his cause being heard the bishop defended himself by alleging that he only applied to Stigand, as being actually his metropolitan, without knowing the character attaching to his acts, a defence which is scarcely to be credited as true. He was on the point of being condemned, and having his staff of office broken, but he was saved by the intervention of Lanfranc, to whom he proposed submission. The accusation of simony had also very nearly succeeded, but Lanfranc was again able to prevent his condemnation. Accordingly, Remigius was confirmed in his possession of the see, but not without incurring a large expenditure, as his predecessor Ulph had done before.

There was a further question to be determined, upon which the provincial relations of the see itself depended, and the settlement of which has preserved to the diocese of Oxford its present position, as dependent upon the metropolitical see of Canterbury, and not of York. The Archbishop Thomas claimed the bishoprics of Dorchester, Lichfield, and Worcester, in right of the see of York. And this the pope was not inclined to decide. It was to be heard and determined in England by an ecclesiastical council of the bishops and abbots of the realm.

The three prelates returned, and the case was heard for the first time at the council held at Winchester, at the time of Easter, on April the 12th, A.D. 1072.[1] This was an ecclesiastical assembly. But the case was heard a second time, in the season of Pentecost, at a more general gémot of the whole realm, at Windsor. The laity were now present, as well as the bishops, and abbots, and other ecclesiastics. The king presided, while the papal legate, Hubert, was also present. The king recommended them all to decide according to right, and the decision was in favour of Canterbury, the Humber being fixed upon as the future boundary line between the two provinces. This, accordingly, was not a convocation, but a parliament, which adjudged a point respecting the two sees,[2] and which made the ecclesiastical division of England, in respect of the two provinces, what it now is.

Remigius entered upon his bishopric with every

---

[1] Freeman, *u. s.*, vol. iv., p. 358.
[2] *Ibid.*, note 2.

desire to effect great things;[1] but an important change was impending by which his plans were to have another sphere of operation than Dorchester. It had been determined, at a synod held in London in A.D. 1075,[2] that the decrees of the Popes Damasus and Leo, and of the councils of Sardica and Laodicea, forbidding that the bishops' chairs should be placed in the smaller towns, should be observed in respect of certain sees which were named, while in the case of others it should be deferred. The bishopric of Dorchester was not specified, but it was probably[3] in consequence of the decision of the council that Remigius took occasion to change the seat of his bishopric. The situation of Dorchester was not such as to render it a convenient place for the bishop's throne of so large a diocese, extending from the Thames to the Humber. The bishop himself also had never been satisfied with his seat in so small a town,[4] which was far from meeting the claims which he conceived himself to have. He was a man of unbounded energy, and would rejoice in the opportunity of making his influence more widely felt. Accordingly, this "man of small stature but of lofty soul removed the seat of his episcopal see to the lordliest spot within the diocese. He forsook the old home of

---

[1] Will. of Malmes., "De Gest. Pontif." l. iv., sect. 177, u. s., p. 312.

[2] Wilkins, "Conc.," u. s., vol. i., p. 363.

[3] J. Brompton, ap. Twysd., "Script. Dec.," p. 995, Lon., 1652; Flor. Worc., in "Mon. Hist. Brit.," p. 644, Lon., 1848, Record Publ.

[4] Hen. of Hunt., "Chron.," l. vi., *ad fin.*; Mat. Par., "Hist. Maj.," p. 12, Lond., 1640.

Birinus, by the winding Thames, guarded by its Roman dykes, and looking up to the hill fort of Sinodun.[1] He placed his church and throne among yet prouder relics of earlier times, side by side with the castle which was already rising to curb the haughty burgher of wealthy and famous Lincoln."[2]

The authority which the king exercised in effecting the removal of the bishop, may be learnt from the following statement, which is contained in a royal grant[3] from Richard II., confirming certain rights of the Bishop, and the Dean and Chapter of Lincoln, and is the recital of a previous grant from the Conqueror, which runs thus :—

"William, King of the English, to the sheriff T., and to all the sheriffs of the bishopric of Remigius greeting: Know ye that I have transferred the seat of the Bishopric of Dorchester to the City of Lincoln, with the counsel and advice of Alexander the Pope, and of his legates, and also of Lanfranc, the Archbishop, and of other bishops of my realm, and have given land there free and quit of all customary services, sufficient for the erection of a mother church for the whole diocese and of the buildings of the same."

While he was resident in Lincoln, Remigius was enabled to conceive, and nearly complete, a most important work for the diocese. Not without some

---

[1] "Wittenham."

[2] Freeman, *u. s.*, vol. iv., p. 421.

[3] Pat. 2, Rich. II., pt. i., m. 5, reciting an Inspeximus charter of Edward III., in which the recital in the text is comprised, in the Public Record Office.

opposition, arising from the claim of the Archbishop of York to the district of Lindsey, he raised a new minster, described as "the Church of the Blessed Mary of Lincoln," on the site of an earlier church, with a foundation of secular canons. The day for the consecration was fixed, in A.D. 1092, the king was present, every preparation was made that the ceremony might be most august and imposing; but on the very day before—or possibly a few days earlier[1]—the bishop died, and the dedication of his church was postponed. This was the origin of the Cathedral of Lincoln;[2] and some portions of this earlier church are still visible in the west front.

After the removal of the bishop's chair from Dorchester to Lincoln, the privilege of containing within its extent the seat of a bishopric was not regained by Oxfordshire until a considerable part of the sixteenth century had elapsed. For this period, accordingly, the general course of diocesan history is to be sought in the annals of the see of Lincoln.

The architecture of the period which has been under review, or, to speak more correctly, of the latter part of it, is well represented in the diocese. Without entering upon the question of the supposed Anglo-Saxon work, as in the churches of Caversfield and Wickham, there are numerous and fine examples of Norman work from the time of the Confessor to Henry II. There is the plain and massive Norman

[1] Will. of Malmes. ("De Gest. Pontif.," *u. s.*, p. 312) has "pridie," but other authorities have "four days."
[2] Sir C. H. J. Anderson, "The Lincoln Pocket Guide," pp. 97-8. Lond., 1880.

church at Crowmarsh Gifford, and the works of Robert D'Oyley, who was appointed Constable of Oxford by the Conqueror. Reference is made to some of these in another place;[1] but there may be mentioned here the Tower of St. Michael's Church, which was undoubtedly built by him, as was the Tower of the Castle.[2] These retain some of the characteristic features of what has been deemed to be Anglo-Saxon style. There is "a curious and fine Norman church" at Avington. The crypt[3] of the church of St. Peter in the East, in Oxford, with its provision for the inspection of the relics which were placed there, has been assigned to a date c. A.D. 1150. The rich and beautiful church at Iffley,[4] with the church at Stewkley, which so much resembles it, may be considered to be of the date of c. A.D. 1160. The church of St. Frideswide, which is now the cathedral, was consecrated in A.D. 1180, but it had been in the course of construction during the preceding twenty years, as the confirmation of the charter, granting the monastery to the Norman monks,[5] was granted by Pope Hadrian IV., in A.D. 1158. The Norman portion still remaining is a fine example of late and transitional Norman work. In Dorchester Church there is also, as it has been described, "a great deal of building remaining,[6] of which the archi-

[1] *Infra*, p. 30.
[2] J. Parker, in "The Visitors' Guide to Oxford," pp. 66, 131.
[3] *Ibid.*, p. 16.
[4] J. H. Parker, "An Introduction to the Study of Gothic Architecture," pp. 59-63. Ox., 1881.    [5] *Ibid.*, p. 97.
[6] J. Parker, in "Proceedings of the Oxford Arch. and Hist. Soc.," *u. s.*, New Ser., No. XXII., p. 195.

tecture must undoubtedly be assigned to the time of Henry II."

There are two Norman leaden fonts, at Dorchester and at Warborough, while there is one of similar, but of later work, at Long Wittenham, while another leaden font at Childrey, with twelve small figures of bishops, holding a staff in one hand and a book in the other, is possibly of the thirteenth century. The church at Frilsham, in Berkshire, has the dedication of St. Frideswide, the Oxford saint.

It will be observed that this notice of the early architecture of the diocese has carried on the subject to a later date than that assigned to the chapter of which it forms part. The several stages of Romanesque architecture in England, its ruder character, the introduction of better Norman work in the time of Edward the Confessor, the further improvement and development of the style after the arrival of the Conqueror, and its transitional character, in the latter part of the twelfth century, are essentially connected with each other, and their relation is preserved by this arrangement.

## CHAPTER II.

INTRODUCTION CONTINUED. A.D. 1075–A.D. 1500.

Organisation of the Church in Oxfordshire—Parishes—Archdeaconry—Peculiars—Deaneries—Suffragan Bishops—Visitations—University of Oxford—King Alfred not Founder—Foundation of Merton College—Jews in Oxford—Dominicans—Franciscans—Augustinians—Hospital of St. Bartholomew—Councils at Oxford, Woodstock, and Eynsham—Knights Templars—Knights Hospitallers—Alien Priories—Architecture.

THE bishop's throne having now been transferred from Dorchester to Lincoln, the parishes comprised within this county, which had previously been under the eye of the bishop, lost the advantage of his personal presence; but from the character of their diocesan they were not left destitute of a fatherly care for their spiritual welfare. The energy and zeal, and the capacity for administration, features so remarkable in the character of Remigius, had now a wider sphere for their development; nor did he fail to avail himself of his fresh opportunities.

In A.D. 1086, the year preceding the departure of Remigius from Dorchester to Lincoln, the "Domesday Survey" was completed, and in this unique and priceless record the place names are found so dispersed over the whole surface of the country, that there could have been no locality in which the inhabitants could not easily have been discovered and identified by any one to whom the spiritual charge of a district was intrusted, however large a one it might have been. And these names correspond very nearly with the present names of parishes, so that their site can be readily ascertained. The churches, however, then in existence in Oxfordshire are not mentioned except in a few instances, and the number cannot be determined. But it is evident, from a comparison with those which are enumerated in the next authentic ecclesiastical record in A.D. 1291, that they could not have been built at the time in many of the places which are named, for they are not found mentioned even in this later survey.[1] A further comparison with the present names of parishes may serve to show how the formation of such parochial relationships was arranged. In the "Domesday" record the same name is found to be applied to a district which afterwards became divided, on which a characteristic appellation was imposed for distinction on the separate parts. This will explain the reason for the occurrence of a single name in adjacent parishes with some epithet to distinguish the one from the other. The repetition arose from a natural desire to retain the former associations attaching to the name, although a severance of local interests had taken place.

The population of the county of Oxford, as it is enumerated in "Domesday Book," with the exception of Oxford itself, the inhabitants of which were not

---

[1] "Taxatio P. Nich. IV., *c.* A.D. 1291," *infra.* p. 35.

reckoned, amounted to six thousand seven hundred and seventy-five.[1] The churches are not enumerated, but a few are incidentally mentioned, as St. Mary's, St. Michael's, St. Peter's, St. Ebbe's, and St. Frideswide's, in Oxford. Some of these, at the least, had fallen into a ruinous state at the time of the Conquest, for Robert D'Oyley the Elder, the builder of the castle, on his recovery from a dangerous sickness,[2] c. A.D. 1066–1087, evinced his penitence "by rebuilding, at his own cost, the parochial churches which were in ruins, both within and on the outside of the walls of Oxford." The plunderer of churches and of the poor had become the restorer of the one and the comforter of the other, and the performer of many good works. There can be no reason for questioning that the old tower of St. Michael's church, with its so-named Saxon work, was part of the church above mentioned, as existing with this dedication; and the remains of Norman work in other churches may perhaps be referable to him as the builder, as well as this.

The course which was adopted by Remigius upon his accession to the see of Lincoln, for the administration of his large diocese, appears the wisest that he could have selected. He proceeded at once to place his seven archdeacons over the several counties which were comprised within his bishopric; and, consequently, upon this appointment the Arch-

---

[1] Sir H. Ellis, "Introduction to Domesday," vol. ii., p. 477. Lond., 1833.
[2] "Chron. Mon. de Abingd.," vol. ii., pp. 14, 15. Lond., 1858. Rolls' Ser.

deaconry of Oxford was assigned to Alfred,[1] who is described as being "a famous rhetorician," and who was instituted to his office A.D. 1078.

The emoluments of the office at first probably consisted of the usual fees and payments in this instance. But in course of time, at a period between the years A.D. 1225 and 1279, an important addition was made by the acquisition of the impropriate Rectory of Iffley,[2] which had previously belonged to the Priory of Kenilworth. The practice of appropriating the tithes of a parish to a religious institution was an abuse which largely prevailed, and became a source of revenue of the highest value. In order to effect an appropriation, it was necessary in the first place to obtain the patronage of the Church. But before the arrangement could be completed the permission of the pope, as well as the licence of the king and of the bishop had also to be obtained. The consent of the patron was at the same time implied. As an appropriation was originally made to a spiritual corporation alone, this provided the services of an officiating minister, who acted as chaplain, and was removable at will. There was found, however, as was likely in such a provision, a frequent source of abuse, and it was enjoined by

[1] Henry of Huntingdon in his "Letter to Walter," al. "Chronicle," bk. viii., *u. s.*, p. 305. There are no documents in the Registry of Lincoln so early as this appointment, nor any previous to the episcopate of Oliver Sutton in A.D. 1280; by favour of W. Moss, Esq., of the Diocesan Registry, Lincoln. Canon E. Venables, however, states that there are records earlier than of A.D. 1280.

[2] See E. Marshall's "Account of Iffley," p. 60. Oxf., 1874.

statute that a proper maintenance should be secured to the minister, and the permanence of his appointment ensued;[1] and further, that he shall be one of the secular clergy,[2] it having been too frequently the practice that the offices of the Church were performed by some one deputed for that service, as a member of the religious foundation to which the church belonged, and resident in the convent. When the appropriation had once been made, it was only by some accidental and unforeseen occurrence that the act could be reversed, and the divided interests reunited. It is not, however, so unfrequent an arrangement that a portion of the rectorial estate is reunited to the vicarage, or perpetual curacy, under the authority of the ecclesiastical commissioners. This has been effected in the parish of Iffley, the patronage of which is vested in the Archdeacon of Oxford, to whom it had belonged from early times, being the only benefice to which he presents by virtue of his office.[3]

The list of the archdeacons during the removal of the bishop's throne contains some names of eminence. Of the thirty-eight archdeacons in succession eight became bishops in two instances of the see of Lincoln itself, and three were made deans. Two are known as the celebrated writers, Walter Map and William Lindwood; while a third, Lionel Woodville, who was promoted to the bishopric of Salisbury, was brother-in-law of King Edward IV.

The form in which the institution of one of the

---

[1] 15 Ric. II., c. 6    [2] 4 Hen. IV., c. 12.
[3] See E. Marshall's "Account of Iffley," *u. s.*, p. 60.

archdeacons is recorded, will serve to illustrate the results of a practice which required the intervention of the legislature to preserve from the papal encroachments the supremacy and other rights of the Crown. Upon a vacancy occurring by death in the archdeaconry of Oxford in A.D. 1313, a foreign ecclesiastic received the appointment, and his admission to the office is described in these terms:[1] "Gailhard de Mota, a Roman Cardinal, was admitted by papal provision." He held the office in A.D. 1345, when the king issued a precept to the Barons of the Exchequer to release him, with other cardinals in possession of ecclesiastical benefices, from the payment of the king's tenth.[2] In this brief he appears to have been in possession of several preferments, for he is described as Archdeacon of Oxford and of Ely, Precentor of Chichester, and Prebend of Melton, in the church of Lincoln. This abuse became so inveterate, that various statutes[3] were passed for its repression, and the possession of benefices by aliens was further restrained by limiting the exercise of the king's licence for holding them.[4]

The institution of a peculiar jurisdiction with the privileges and exemptions attached to it was another proceeding which infringed the rights which the bishop had in the diocese. An abbey for Augustinian canons had been built at Dorchester *c.* A.D.

---

[1] Le Neve, " Fasti Eccl. Angl.," vol. i., p. 65. Ox., 1854.
[2] Rymer, " Fœdera," vol. v., p. 442. Lon., 1708.
[3] 25 Ed. III., st. 5, c. 22, and st. 6; 38 Ed. III; 13 Ric. II., st. 2, c. 2; 2 Hen. IV., c. 3.
[4] 7 Hen. IV., c. 8; 3 Hen. V., c. 4.

1140, by Alexander, Bishop of Lincoln, in honour of St. Peter, St. Paul, and St. Birinus.[1] The endowment provided for it consisted of several churches in the adjoining portion of the diocese, which were rendered from the ordinary jurisdiction of the bishop, and together formed the Peculiar of Dorchester. These were nine in all.[2] But, besides this group of churches, there was one other peculiar benefice, which belonged to the Archbishop of Canterbury, whose advowsons were in all cases entitled to this privilege; and one other, which belonged to the Bishop of Lincoln. The Peculiars were once nearly three hundred in number. They were for the most part of papal introduction; and seem to have had for their chief object the abridgment of the legitimate authority of the bishop in the diocese; and this could not be without a great injury to ecclesiastical jurisdiction. They are now practically abolished by recent legislation.[3]

The peculiar benefices in the diocese of Oxford are now absorbed into the deaneries in which they are locally situated, and are made subject to the same jurisdiction with the other parishes.

Another diocesan institution is also found to have been matured during the period which has been now under review. There is mention of the existence of rural deans in a canon of the Council of Oxford in

---

[1] Dugd., "Mon.," vol. vi., p. 323; *supra*, p. 6.

[2] See the return from the Bishop of Oxford in the year 1814, in "Val. Eccl. Hen. VIII.," vol. ii., app. p. 510., *Infr.*, p. 83.

[3] Sir R. Phillimore, "Eccl. Law of England," vol. ii., p. 1203. Lond., 1873.

A.D. 1222;[1] and the grouping of the several parishes in their respective deaneries is shown to have been universal in the archdeaconry of Oxford, as in other archdeaconries, when the general survey was made,[2] about the year A.D. 1291. Pope Nicholas IV. had granted to King Edward I. a tenth part of the ecclesiastical revenues of England and Wales, for the purpose of defraying the expenses of an expedition to the Holy Land; and it was therefore necessary that a fresh survey of the property, subject to the impost, should be made on the part of the king, that it might be assessed at its full value. The churches of Oxfordshire are seen to be distributed into nine deaneries, which are very nearly identical with those which now exist. But the exact date of the formation of the rural deaneries is a question which cannot be determined with certainty.[3]

In the same document the number of the parochial churches and principal chapels appears to amount to one hundred and eighty-eight, which leaves a large deficiency, before the total sum of those which are enumerated at the present time is reached. It is seen, however, that the work of church building had made so remarkable a progress; and the evidence is so far more complete than that of Domesday Book to

[1] Wilkin's "Conc.," *u. s.*, vol. i., p. 588.
[2] "Taxatio Eccl. Angl. et Wall. auct. P. Nich. IV., *c.* A.D. 1291." Lond., 1802.
[3] It is most probable that the word "episcopi" in the title "Decanus episcopi," in early editions of the laws of Edward the Confessor (xxxi.), is not a part of the original text. It is not in the text printed by Thorpe, "Ancient Laws," vol. i., p. 454. Lond., 1840. Record Publ.

show that few of the inhabitants could have been far removed from free access to the means of grace. The number of parishes was not greatly increased in the course of the succeeding half-century. For when the new survey[1] was made, in order to ascertain the exact value of the ninth of corn, wood, and lambs which was granted to Edward III., in A.D. 1340, it was found that the parishes were one hundred and ninety-four in number. The principal church would in each case be represented in such parishes; but, to many of them dependent chapels would be attached.

An additional measure which the Bishops of Lincoln adopted for the due administration of their extensive diocese was the appointment of suffragan bishops, with either a permanent title and position, or a temporary delegation of authority. The lists of these for the various dioceses are incomplete. But there are several whose names are recorded in connexion with the diocese of Lincoln. Two of these appear to have their sphere of duty in Oxfordshire.[2] From A.D. 1506 to 1514, John Thornden, Bishop of Sirmium or Cyrene, was commissary at Oxford; and Robert King, who had been consecrated Bishop of Rheon, in the province of Athens, in A.D. 1533, was appointed Suffragan of Lincoln in 1535. As he was at first Abbot of Thame, and afterwards of Oseney, his relations with the diocese arose in the earlier part of his life, and he has even been called " Bishop of

---

[1] See "Nonarum Inquisitiones in Curia Scaccarii temp. Edw. III.," pp. 132–142. Lond., 1807.

[2] Stubbs, " Registr. Sacr.," app. v. Oxf., 1858.

Thame." His name will appear with further information respecting his life in the sequel.

It appears to have been the practice in this part of the diocese, from its distance from the seat of the bishop, to allow the consecration of new churches and chapels to be deferred for an indefinite period, until there should occur the occasion of an episcopal visit. Several churches in the neighbourhood of Oxford were in such a state in A.D. 1273; in which year an Irish bishop, Reginald, Bishop of Cloyne, was deputed to such as a temporary suffragan, in the archdeaconries of Oxfordshire and Buckinghamshire. And a record is preserved in the register of the Bishop of Lincoln of the churches which were consecrated by him in his visitation tours at this time.[1]

Another form of episcopal relief was also available from time to time for a more limited portion of the archdeaconry. From the situation of the royal castle at Woodstock there were frequent visits of bishops in attendance on the Court. The parochial chapel of New Woodstock, with the adjoining cemetery, is found to have been in existence[2] in A.D. 1279. But it was not yet consecrated; and accordingly a licence was granted to the inhabitants by the Bishop of Lincoln in A.D. 1337, enabling them to dedicate and consecrate their chapel with the adjoining cemetery by any Catholic bishop.[3]

---

[1] Extracts from Lincoln Registers, in Kennet's "Par. Ant.," *n. s.*, vol. i., pp. 393-5.

[2] "Rotuli Hundredorum," vol. ii., p. 841. Lon., 1812.

[3] Extract from the Register of Bp. Burghersh, at Lincoln, f. 354 b.

There would be also the metropolitical visitations of the archbishop of the province at long and uncertain intervals, as well as the ordinary visitations of the bishop of the diocese. St. Hugh had visited the archdeaconry of Oxford in A.D. 1191 and 1194,[1] but subsequently the practice appears to have fallen into disuse, for, when Bishop Grosseteste determined to visit the diocese[2] on his accession to the see of Lincoln in A.D. 1236, he was met with the charge of doing something "new and unheard of." He replied that, although anything were new, if it were for the good of man it was, nevertheless, a blessed thing; and he not only held the visitation, but took every means to prevent extortion on the part of his successors in the procurations which they might claim. It is stated that he confirmed during his visitation tour, and took with him two confessors for the benefit of his clergy. Other forms of supervision than those now practised would also demand attention. In the second of the two visitations by him, which have been mentioned above, Bishop Grosseteste excommunicated an adulterous wife who resisted his admonition at Oxford; and in the former, upon coming to Godstow, he manifested his indignation on witnessing in the chapel of the convent the honoured tomb of Rosamond Clifford. In like manner, in the visitation of A.D. 1236, he deposed the Abbot of Dorchester and the Prioress of St. Frideswide's, and appointed

---

[1] "Magna Vita S. Hug.," lib. iv., c. 6, p. 181. 1864. Rolls' Ser.

[2] See Wharton, "Angl. Sacr.," *u. s.*, vol. ii., p. 347, for Bp. Grosseteste's statement.

others in their place.¹ The excesses which were committed in the various parishes on the occasion of the visitation itself, as well as at other ecclesiastical functions, prove sufficiently the need of reform in the manners of the clergy. And no less are the persistent efforts, which were required before such reform could be effected, an evidence of the difficulties through which alone the change could be produced.

Apart from the account which has been already given of the organisation of the Church in Oxfordshire during the period of the removal of the bishop's chair, there are certain events occurring in the course of the general history of the time to which reference may be made, as illustrative of various phases of religious life.

It is not proposed to insert a detailed account of the origin and progress of the University of Oxford, but some notice of so integral a part of the diocese is requisite. The alleged foundation, or restoration, of King Alfred may be set aside as belonging to what has been termed "the mythical history of Oxford." The growth of the legendary story has been traced from its earliest known occurrence in the "Chronicle of John Brompton," through its introduction into the evidence in favour of the claims of William, of Durham's College, the precursor of University College, in the reign of Richard II., and its insertion in the rolls of Parliament, until it is found, at length, to be interpolated in Asser's "Life of Alfred,"² at the

---
¹ Ann. de Dunst. in "Ann. Monast.," vol. iii., p. 143. 1864-9. Rolls' Ser.
² See in "Mon. Hist. Brit.," pp. 489, 490.

beginning of the seventeenth century, and it is pronounced to be entirely unworthy of acceptance.[1]

The college, which is entitled, upon documentary evidence, to be considered the earliest foundation, is undoubtedly Merton College, which is founded by Walter de Merton, Bishop of Rochester, who in A.D. 1268 transferred to Oxford the college which he had founded at Maldon in Essex; and for which, on its removal, he obtained a charter under the name of "the house of the scholars of Merton."[2]

The statutes which Walter de Merton provided for the government of his college, and which he finally settled in A.D. 1274, supplied the model for similar foundations, both at Oxford and Cambridge. The corporate body was to consist of a warden, chaplains, and so many scholars as the revenues of the college might be able to maintain.

But although Merton College may, for the reason alleged, be considered the earlier foundation, if the rudimental state of the foundation is taken into account, University College may claim to have an earlier origin. William of Durham, who died at Rouen in A.D. 1249, bequeathed money to trustees for the maintenance of a body of masters in the Uni-

---

[1] For proof of the statements in the text see "Monumenta Historica Britannica," Pref., pp. 72–9, Lond., 1848; W. W. Shirley, on Asser's "Life of Alfred," "Proceedings of Oxf. Arch. and Hist. Soc.," New Ser., vol. i., pp. 313–21, Ox., 1864; J. Parker, "On the History of Oxford, A.D. 912–1100," pp. 5, *sqq.*, Ox., 1871.

[2] Wood, "History and Antiquities of Colleges and Halls," pp. 3, *sqq.* Ox., 1786.

versity who were to be natives of Durham. With this benefaction certain halls and other tenements were purchased, and a small society was formed wich received its statutes in A.D. 1280. This is now represented by University College, which has succeeded to its position.[1]

For different reasons, Oxford was a place of considerable importance even before this period; and naturally enough it attracted the attention of the Jews, who were desirous of improving their position in the country as a place of settlement. They obtained permission to establish themselves here in the reign of King William II., and in process of time were possessed, together with other property, of three halls, or lodging-houses, for the accommodation of students, while they themselves taught Hebrew to Jewish and Christian scholars alike.[2] The Church was not unmindful of the duty which, under these circumstances, she owed them. The Dominican or Preaching Friars,[3] known from their distinctive habit as the Black Friars, whose order, instituted by the famous St. Dominic, had been introduced into England in A.D. 1221, had obtained on their first establishment a settlement in the same part of the town,

---

[1] Wood, *u. s.*, p. 40.

[2] Milman, "History of Latin Christianity," *u. s.*, bk. xv., vol. iii., p. 231. Lond., 1864.

[3] "The difference between monks and friars is this :—monks had nothing in proprietorship but all in common; friars had nothing in proprietorship or in common, but, being mendicants, depended on charity."—H. Goodwin, "Engl. Arch. Handb." Oxf., 1867. The cells, which they at first possessed, had large revenues attached to them by successive benefactors.

which was known as the Jewry; and it is doubtless to the effect of their preaching that the conversions which ensued were to be attributed, and that the king, Henry III., was induced to give them important assistance by his patronage. He had already built a house for the converts from Judaism in London, in which they might live together under rule, and might be maintained for the remainder of their lives without the necessity of practising usury, as they had done before. And he now proceeded to found a similar institution in Oxford, with an especial regard to the wants of those who were either strangers or infirm.[1] This is the more worthy of notice in a history of the diocese, inasmuch as besides the one mentioned as existing in London, and another at Bermondsey, no other place of refuge of a similar kind is known to have been established.[2] In process of time the Jews became a numerous and powerful body, and there were frequent interruptions of the peace between the scholars in Oxford and themselves. It was so in A.D. 1244, when certain "clerks" of the University broke into the houses of the Jews and obtained plunder of great value. The magistrates of the city imprisoned the offenders; but they were released by the order of Bishop Grosseteste on failure of the proof of felony.[2] In this instance the members of

---

[1] Mat. Par., *u. s.*, p. 393. *ad* A.D. 1233; Wood, "Hist. et Ant. Univ. Oxon.," tom. i., p. 132, Ox., 1688. A print of the "Domus Conversorum," as the house was named, is given in W. H. Turner's "Records of Oxford," p. 436. Ox., 1880.

[2] Milman, who cites Wikes, "Chron.," ad A.D. 1244, in "Hist. of the Jews.," bk. xxv., vol. iii., p. 255. Lon., 1866.

the University were the aggressors; but the Jews, on the other hand, were the first to offend upon a memorable occasion in A.D. 1288. It was Ascension Day. Prince Edward was in Oxford on a visit, and the chancellor and the whole body of the University were going in procession to the relics of St. Frideswide, when the Jews offered a deliberate insult to the Cross, for which they had to make a just reparation.[1] Previously to this time the Jews had obtained considerable property and large influence in Oxford, for, in A.D. 1265, Walter de Merton purchased of them the ground upon which the front of Merton College now stands.[2] In another part of the county there arose a feeling of a different kind towards the Jews. The charge which was so often made against them, was preferred in respect of an act alleged to have been committed at Woodstock, for it is recorded that in A.D. 1179 a boy was martyred there.[3] The popular report in this, as in other cases, was doubtless raised without a minute inquiry into its truth or falsity.

At no long interval after the arrival of the Dominican Friars, the Franciscans, or Grey Friars, obtained a position in the same part of Oxford.[4] In A.D. 1224, fifteen years after the establishment

[1] Milman. *u. s.*, p. 256; Wood, *u. s., ad an.* 1288.

[2] Bp. E. Hobhouse, "Sketch of the Life of Walt. de Merton, p. 30. Ox., 1859.

[3] Mat. Par., *u. s.*, p. 137, *ad* A.D. 1179.

[4] The authority for the history of the Franciscans in Oxford is the account of Thomas de Eccleston in the "Monumenta Franciscana," edited by J. S. Brewer, pp. 1, *sqq.*, 1858. Rolls Ser.

of their order, and two years before the death of their great founder, St. Francis of Assisi, a company, consisting of four clerical and five lay members, landed at Dover in the month of September, to establish themselves in England. After a short stay of two days at Canterbury, they proceeded to London, where they were hospitably received by the Dominicans, their great rivals in the future. As soon after their arrival as the 1st of November, two of the clerical brethren, Richard of Ingearth and Richard of Devonshire, both Englishmen, came to Oxford, where they, too, received great kindness from the Dominicans, who provided them with a lodging in their own house for eight days. They then took up their abode in the parish of St. Ebbe, where a house was let to them by Robert le Mercer, and where they afterwards obtained a site for their residence by the gift to the community of Thomas le Muliner.

It was in accordance with their principles and with their general practice to select such a low and unhealthy district of a town as this must have been, that they might bestow their service where it was most needed, and might bring the gospel where the necessities of the people from their poverty and ignorance most of all required it. And they shrank from no condition of poverty and hardship for themselves. When the first purpose of their mission was accomplished, the two brethren who came first removed to Northampton, and left charge of the community at Oxford to William de Esseby, who thus became the first warden of the brethren in Oxford, although at the time of his appointment to the office he was a mere novice.

The care of the poor was not the only object of the Franciscans. They were great promoters of learning; and their presence at Oxford, as in other Universities, was signalised by their efforts to enlarge the sphere of education, and to effect a systematic study of theology. With this view their first provincial in Oxford established a school in the vestry, and induced the famous Grosseteste to read lectures there.[1] Other prelectorships were instituted with a similar purpose, and among their learned teachers were Adam of Oxford and Adam Marsh. In the midst of this the Franciscans lived in a state of great poverty, wearing no shoes and using no pillows for their rest, the only remission of their austerities being due to sickness. In the description of the characteristic features of the several provinces in England, a devotion to study is stated to have marked their condition in Oxford, a want of money in Cambridge, a zeal for poverty in York, and the affection of mutual charity in Salisbury.[2]

The abandonment of the receipt of money for themselves individually, or for their order collectively, did not, however, prevent the establishment of a large foundation at Oxford by the Franciscans, with a magnificent church of 316 feet in length, and a proportionate breadth, and with ten chapels on the north side.[3] The site of the monastery is still determined

---

[1] "Monumenta Franciscana," *u. s.*, p. 37.

[2] *Ibid.*, p. 37.

[3] Ingram, "Mem. of Oxf.," vol. iii., St. Ebbe's, p. 16.

by the name of Paradise Gardens, which formed part of the precincts. The two neighbouring foundations of the Dominicans and Franciscans, the Black and Grey Friars, at the time of the dissolution, were sold together to the same purchasers, R. Andrews and J. How, for the sum of £1,094.[1]

A company of Augustinian Friars, or Friars Eremites, as they were also called, was sent into England by Lanfranc of Milan, the first general of the order, c. A.D. 1251. Some of those who then came obtained the patronage of Sir John Handlow,[2] of Boarstall, in Buckinghamshire, who urged the foundation of a settlement in Oxford, and purchased a site for a convent on the ground which is now occupied by Wadham College, in A.D. 1269, which he presented for a place of residence. The branch of the order which was thus established in Oxford took a prominent part in the studies of the place, and became celebrated for its success in teaching theology and philosophy. In the course of time, indeed, its influence became so great that the form of holding disputations "apud Augustinienses," "doing Austins," as it was commonly termed, became so connected with the routine of University life, that it outlasted the removal of the order; nor was it abolished before the passing of the new statute for examinations at the beginning of the present century.[3]

The Hospital of St. Bartholomew,[4] described as on

---

[1] Ingram, "Memorials," *u. s.*, vol. iii., St. Ebbe's, p. 10.
[2] Kennet, "Par. Ant.," *u. s.*, vol. i., pp. 381, *sqq*.
[3] Ingram, *u. s.*, vol. ii., Wadham Coll., pp. 1, *sqq*.
[4] The authorities for the statements in the text are principally

the outside of the East Gate, and well known from its present chapel, which was given by King Edward II. to his new foundation of Oriel College for a place of retirement during the prevalence of sickness, shows the provision which was made by such donations to preserve the health of the residents in the University; as the state of neglect into which it was then found to have fallen, "through the failing or carelessness of the masters," proves the danger of decay to which such institutions are liable, although established from the purest motives of charity, which, in this instance, was the maintenance of infirm lepers, for twelve of whom, with a chaplain, it had been originally founded by King Henry I.[1] And the mediæval, or true leprosy, by which such misery was once caused, and which such hospitals were intended to alleviate, was a much more formidable disease than the forms of leprosy which are mentioned in the Bible, except, possibly, in the instance of Job. Nor, again, is it devoid of interest to notice, as showing the difficulty of adjusting conflicting claims, that a series of lawsuits between Oriel College and the City of Oxford began in the reign of Richard II., and has been continued to a very recent date. The chapel to which allusion has been made is a building of the fifteenth century, with insertions of earlier work.

Another feature in the ecclesiastical history of this

given in "The Town Clerk's (G. P. Hester's) Report respecting St. Bartholomew's Hospital." Ox., 1845.

[1] Wood, "Hist. of City of Oxford," by Peshall, p. 273. Ox., 1773.

period in connexion with Oxfordshire is the occasional assembling of a council at Oxford, or in the neighbourhood,[1] for the settlement of some urgent question affecting the interests of the Church. Of these the councils which are now to be mentioned appear to have been the most important. The first which comes under review[2] is the Council of Oxford in A.D. 1160. This was convened upon the introduction into England of a foreign heresy. The Publicans, as they were termed by a corruption of their name,[3] were the inheritors of the opinions of the Paulicians, and had propagated their views in the south of France. They were accused of a want of faith in the Holy Trinity, and certainly rejected the sacraments and sacramental rites. There were at this time about thirty representatives of their number in England, who had arrived under the leadership of a German named Gerhard. The king, Henry II., who was unwilling either to condemn them without a hearing, or to give

---

[1] The Council of Kyrtlington in A.D. 977, which is commonly stated, as by Wilkins ("Conc.," *u. s.*, vol. i., p. 262), to have been held at the village of that name in Oxfordshire, was in reality held at Kyrtling, in East Anglia. So Florence of Worcester remarks, "A very numerous synod was held at a vill called Kyrtling, in East Anglia" (*u. s.*, p. 106). It is also doubtful whether the Council of Ænham, in A.D. 1008, was held at Eynsham, as Wilkins shows (*u. s.*, p. 285). Both of these are therefore omitted.

[2] Wilkins, *u. s.*, p. 438; Harduin, "Conc.," tom. i., p. 11, col. 1583. Par., 1715.

[3] "Publicani, *i. q.* Populicani, haeretici Manichaeorum sectarii, qui Graecis Παυλικιανοί Latinis scriptoribus Pauliciani." See Ducange, s. vv., "Publicani," "Poplicani," "Populicani," ed. Migne, Par., 1866.

them their liberty, took this step in order to ascertain what their peculiar tenets were. The accusation respecting their want of faith in the Holy Trinity was not substantiated, but the rest of the allegations were proved against them. They refused, however, to retract their opinions, remaining firm in the profession of their belief, and joyful in being thought worthy to suffer persecution for it. Upon this refusal they were delivered to the secular magistrates, and, by the king's command, were branded, scourged, and driven from the town, with a strict injunction that no one should afford them relief. It was the inclement season of winter, and they all sank under the cruel treatment which they received.

Another council was held at Woodstock in A.D. 1170, this being a royal seat, at which the two kings, Henry II., and his recently crowned son, were present with the Archbishop Thomas Beket and seven of his suffragan bishops. It was an unwonted thing for an Englishman to occupy the see of Canterbury, and there would be an occasion for reconciling the feelings of the higher and of the lower clergy, under such a presidency, even if the occasion of the council were so ordinary a one, as the election of a bishop for the see of Norwich, and the nomination of successors in some vacant abbacies.[1] At a similar council, which was convened at Eynsham, in A.D. 1184, the excellent choice was made of St. Hugh, the Prior of the English Carthusians, for the bishopric of the diocese, which was vacant by the translation

---

[1] Wilkins, "Conc.," *u. s.*, vol. i., p. 482.

of the bishop, Walter de Coutances, a former Archdeacon of Oxford, to the archbishopric of Rouen.[1]

There was yet another purpose for which a council was convened at Oxford by Stephen Langton[2] in A.D. 1222. In the long succession of prelates who have occupied the see of Canterbury there has not been one who has had a more constitutional idea of the position of the archbishop in maintaining the liberties of the people against the encroachments of despotic power. For the part which he took in the contest between the king and the barons he was suspended from the functions of his office, and was compelled to make a visit to the court of Rome. The pope confirmed his suspension; but he was shortly afterwards released from it on the condition that he did not return to England before that peace was restored.[3]

After the death of King John and the establishment of his youthful successor upon the throne, Langton was permitted to return and to resume his office as archbishop. His attention was then directed to the restoration of discipline in the Church, of which there was the greatest need. In pursuance of his design he summoned a council at Oxford in the year which has been already stated, A.D. 1222. Fifty canons were published at its close, and were directed against the most prominent of the abuses which were prevalent. They pronounce a sentence of excommunication against all who should encroach upon the

---

[1] Magna Vita, S. Hud., *u. s.*, l. iii. c. 1. p. 102.
[2] Wilkins, "Conc.," *u. s.*, vol. i., p. 585.
[3] Mat. Par., *u. s.*, p. 279.

rights and privileges of the Church, or disturb the public peace, or should give false testimony, or promote false suits. They protect the patronage of the Church from abuse, and confine bishops, archdeacons, and deans, as well as other clergy, to a strict performance of their respective duties, and the proper celebration of the offices of the Church. They specially provide that mass shall not be said by any priest more than once in the day, except at the greater festivals of Christmas and Easter, or at funerals; that sermons shall be preached frequently; that care shall be taken of the ornaments of the Church; and that no priest shall take part in a cause of blood. They forbid the improper resignation of a benefice for a mercenary cause, and ensure the rights of perpetual vicars, and their sufficient maintenance, and secure for the larger parishes an adequate number of clergy. They direct that there shall be public confessors for those of the clergy who may dislike to confess to the bishop. They regulate the expense at the visitation of the archdeacon, and forbid the taking of fees for burials and the administration of sacraments. They enjoin further that Jews shall not have Christian servants, and that they shall wear a distinctive mark in front of their garments. These canons also regulate the dress and manners of the clergy, and prescribe sumptuary enactments for monks and nuns.

A deacon was presented at this council on account of his apostatising to Judaism out of love to a Jewess. For this he was condemned to be burned; and it is probably the first instance of capital punishment in

England on the ground of religion,[1] preceding, as it does, by so long an interval the well-known statute for the burning of heretics.[2] A peasant was also presented for falsely pretending to have imprinted on his body the marks of the five wounds, and he was condemned to a life-long imprisonment with bread and water for his fare.[3] Or, perhaps, his punishment was a more summary termination of his life, for it has been stated, that he was crucified at Adderbury.[4]

It will illustrate the influence of the papal legate, and his power of summoning the English bishops to consult with him, if reference is made to a council of the bishops, not, however, of much importance in itself, which was not, indeed, held at Oxford, but which arose out of the circumstances attending a fatal quarrel, of which Oxford was the scene, and which forms an incident in the history of one of its two great abbeys. Otho, the papal legate, came to Oxford in A.D. 1238, and took up his quarters at Oseney.[5] His arrival had been expected and the clerks of Oxford had sent presents for his table, and came after dinner to offer to him their respects. The porter received them rudely and refused to admit them. Upon this they tried to force their way in, and a general fight took place. While this was going on, a certain poor Irish chaplain, who was

---

[1] Lingard, "History of England," vol. iii., ch. vi., p. 247, note *n*. Lond., 1855.

[2] 2 Hen. IV., c. 151; see *infra*, p. 59.

[3] Wilkins, "Conc.," *u. s.*

[4] 7 Hen. Knighton, "Chron.," in Twysd., *u. s.*, col. 2430.

[5] Mat. Par., *u. s.*, pp. 469, 470, *ad* A.D. 1238.

standing by, asked for relief; upon which the chief cook threw some boiling water over him. His cause was taken up by a Welsh cleric, who drew his bow, and killed the man who did the wrong, who happened to be the brother of the legate, and called them all to arms. The legate was amazed, and as much frightened as a man of courage could be, and put on his canonical robes and took refuge in the tower. But not satisfied with this, as he was earnestly sought for, he thought it the safest course to effect a retreat, and made his way to the king, who was then at Wallingford, and lamented bitterly with tears and sobbing the ill treatment to which his household and he himself had been subjected. The king upon this sent Earl Warren with a body of soldiers to Oxford. A lawyer named Otho and thirty others of the offenders were captured and taken to Wallingford, where they were imprisoned in the castle. The legate, on his part, after consulting with such bishops as were present, placed Oxford under an interdict, and excommunicated all those who took part in the offence. He himself went to London, where the prisoners were forthwith carried. He then summoned to his councils the Archbishop of York, and the bishops of England, that they might deliberate upon the state of the Church and the perils of the clergy. They exhorted the legate to abstain from any precipitate action, and suggested that a due submission should be made to him and his forgiveness asked on the part of the Oxford scholars, in St. Paul's Church; which accordingly was done, and the interdict was then removed.

Some points in this story are interesting as illustrative of the manners and history of the time. It seems strange that the brother of the legate should have held an office in his kitchen; but the explanation which is given of this is that he lived in the constant dread of poison, and felt obliged to have one who was nearly related to himself, and in whom he for that account could place confidence. The fact that a papal legate, claiming to exercise a spiritual authority of the highest kind, should have been compelled to take such precautions for his personal safety, is not an insignificant one. If it arose from the fear of what an Englishman might do, it may intimate his own sense of the insecurity of his position as an uncongenial one to the English mind. Again, it is a circumstance which recalls the Oxford of the past, that the assembled bishops alleged as a reason for extending mercy to the offending clerks, that "the clerical order of the University, as of a second church, might be preserved."[1] It is indeed a subject for hope that such a reason may never fail to have due weight. But it is equally certain that a different theory has prevailed, which disregards the clerical character of Oxford, and regards it as a national institution. It is therefore as the result of other causes that the position of the

---

[1] "Ut salvaretur status clericalis Universitatis, veluti secundae ecclesiae," Mat. Par., *u. s.*, p. 470. In A.D. 1257, the liberties of the University were defended by the Masters of Arts before the king at St. Albans against the Bishop of Lincoln, on the ground that Oxford was, after Paris, "schola secunda ecclesiae." —*Ibid.*, p. 945.

clergy in the University exists in its present state, and that the majority even, at the present time, consists of members of the English Church. The religious character of Oxford in the future will depend upon the convictions of individuals, and not upon external guarantees and public recognition. And, lastly, when the situation of Oxford is described as a three days' journey from London, there is a reminiscence of the old London road, and a signal illustration of the altered conditions of modern life.

It may be mentioned as an evidence of the general condition of the diocese at this period, and of the prevailing corruption of manners, that in the sermon which Bishop Grosseteste preached before the pope and the cardinals assembled, at the Council of Lyons, in A.D. 1250, while describing the state of the Church and the great need of reformation, he made no exception in favour of his own diocese.[1] But, then, the evils which he complained of are precisely those which the canons of the Council of Oxford, as previously noticed,[2] were designed to prevent. It is to be supposed, therefore, that it could have had but little effect in arresting the evils from which the Church was suffering.

The occasion for holding the next Council at Oxford arose out of the foreign relations of the Church and kingdom. Pope Clement V. had removed the papal chair from Rome to Avignon, where French influence was paramount; but upon

---

[1] See E. Brown's "Fasciculus Rerum Expetendarum," vol. ii., pp. 250, *sqq.* Lond., 1690.
[2] *Supra*, pp. 50, 51.

the death of Gregory XI., in A.D. 1378, there was a loud outcry raised for a Roman, or at least an Italian, pope. After the election of Urban VI., in the Roman interest, Robert of Geneva was also elected in the same year, and assumed the title of Clement VII., so beginning the schism which ensued upon the rival claims of the pope and anti-pope. In consequence of this, and as France and Spain alone adhered to the new pope, the king of France, Charles V., addressed a formal document containing the declaration of his clergy in favour of Clement, and bearing the seal of the University of Paris, to Richard II., in order that he might advise with his clergy in a case of so much doubt. Upon this, the king convoked a council of the more learned theologians at Oxford, to consider the application which had been made to him. The decision was in favour of Pope Urban. Nor was there an omission to make the declaration from Oxford as formal a one as that which had been received from France; for it was confirmed by the seal of the University and of the king, and was transmitted to the French king at Paris. An adherence was manifested to the traditional principle of opposition to the French, and nothing further ensued, " either pope maintaining his claim under the shelter of the prevailing schism." [1]

The Council at Oxford, which is the last to be noticed, was called into existence by the altered con-

---

[1] Hen. Knighton, ad an. 1395, in Twysd., *u. s.*, col. 2742. Wilkins ("Conc.," *u. s.*, vol. iii., p. 224) places this council in A.D. 1395; but Urban VI., in whose favour the Oxford theologians decided, died in A.D. 1389.

dition of the English Church itself. Near the close of the fourteenth century, when the state of England had been lowered by inglorious wars and other causes of decline, Oxford had become the centre of a great religious movement. The opinions of Wycliffe had first been broached at Oxford, and their tendency, being for a time unperceived, had been suffered to take deep root without opposition. From his zeal against the Mendicants and other religious orders, whose inconsistency he exposed, Wycliffe had become an acknowledged leader in the University and in the Church, and had attained a high position. His good fortune, however, became changed, and the result of the meeting of the convocation, which accompanied the Parliament at Oxford in A.D. 1382, had been the retirement of Wycliffe from Oxford, the scene of his influence, to his living of Lutterworth in Leicestershire. His retreat was not long, for he died in A.D. 1384. But Oxford remained the stronghold of his followers' faith after his death. And, as their doctrines excited a not unnatural indignation in the clergy throughout the land, the authorities of the University were called upon to suppress them. They were unsuccessful in their attempts, and accordingly, in A.D. 1408, Thomas Arundel, the Archbishop of Canterbury, determined to exercise his jurisdiction as visitor of the University, and devise some adequate remedy. He came for this purpose with a large and splendid retinue, and upon his approach was met by the heads of houses, who refused to admit the archbishop as visitor in no very courteous terms. It was not the first time that he had been foiled in such an attempt, and, as before, he appealed to the king. The king declared in his favour, and the decision was confirmed by Parliament, while the archbishop took the additional step of procuring a bull from the pope revoking the exemption which had been granted to the University by a former pope. The bull, however, was in a short time recalled. The controversy at length being closed, submission was made to the archbishop, and his claim allowed. The final result was that a council [1] of all the bishops of the province was held at Oxford [2] to inquire into the charge of heresy. The bishop of the diocese was Philip de Repingdon, who was a cardinal, and was chancellor of the University as well. The decrees of the council were contained in thirteen chapters, and were to the following effect. None of the regular, or of the secular clergy, unless authorised by law or privilege, were to preach in any church without an examination by the bishop; nor was any one to be permitted, under pain of an interdict, to preach in a church without proof of his authority. Preachers were to adapt their sermons to the requirements of their hearers, enforcing respectively the duties of the clergy and laity. No preacher, nor any schoolmaster, was to contravene the doctrine of the Church. No book of Wycliffe's, nor any other without examination, was to be read

---

[1] Wilkins, "Conc.," *n. s.*, vol. iii., p. 314.

[2] This is sometimes described as the Council of London: " In variis MSS. nunc Oxoniense nunc Londinense dicitur, eam unam ob causam quod et Oxonii anno 1408 celebratum, et Londini anno 1409 promulgatum sit."—Cossart, in Hard., " Conc.," *n. s.*, tom. vii., col. 1948.

within the precincts of the University, a copy of the original also being first deposited in the chest. No unauthorised person was to translate the Scriptures. No one was to maintain any proposition of an apparent evil tendency. No one was to presume to question the decrees of the canon law in any article of belief, or of the religious customs therein enjoined. No clerk was to remove to any part of the province and officiate there without letters dismissory from his diocesan. Every head of a college or hall was to inquire at least once a month if there were any Lollards among his students. Those who broke the above-named constitutions were declared incapable of preferment for three years.

It appears that, besides the bishops who were summoned to the council, other clergy were present; but the legislative power is shown by the form of the archbishop's mandate for publishing the constitutions to have resided in the archbishop and his suffragan bishops alone, and not in the clergy of the lower order with them.[1] It belongs to general history to relate the severity of Archbishop Arundel towards the Lollards in adopting the Act of Henry IV., by which the secular arm was authorised that it should "them before the people in a high place do to be burnt."[2] But it may at least be observed how great is the contrast to be found in the present treatment of Wycliffe's memory by the reproduction of the Wycliffe versions of the Bible at Oxford. An edition of the "Holy Bible in the earliest English versions,

---

[1] Collier, "Eccl. Hist.," vol. i., p. 627. Lond., 1708-14
[2] 2 Hen. IV., c. 15 *ad fin.*

made from the Latin Vulgate by John Wycliffe and his followers," was issued by the University Press [1] in 1850, and a reprint of the Revision of Wycliffe's Version, by John Purvey,[2] appeared in 1879, while a portion of the Old Testament from the Wycliffite version in the same edition was reprinted in 1881.[3] A selection from his English works had been published in 1869.[4]

There is a passage of history during this period in which the religious interests of some parts of Oxfordshire, and of the other counties within the present diocese of Oxford, were concerned. The Knights Templars, arising from a very humble origin, had become a corporate body of great power and influence. As a community which was half military and half monastic, it required of its members the observance of the three monastic vows of poverty, chastity, and obedience, but allowed them, at the same time, to take their place in the stirring scenes of life, and exercise their special calling in feats of arms and on the battle-field. The successive privileges which the order obtained from papal grants had given it a singular independence. There were two preceptories belonging to the order in Oxfordshire, with the same number in Berkshire, and one in Buckinghamshire. The

---

[1] Edited by J. Forshall and Sir F. Madden, in four volumes in 4to.

[2] Edited by Professor W. W. Skeat, in 8vo.

[3] "The Books of Job, Psalms, Proverbs, Ecclesiastes, and the Song of Solomon, according to the Wycliffite version, made by Nicholas de Hereford, about A.D. 1381, and revised by John Purvey, about A.D. 1388," 8vo.

[4] Edited by T. Arnold, in 3 vols., 8vo.

first of these in its relative importance was the one existing at Sandford-on-Thames, which, before its removal from the original site at Cowley, received a grant of lands from Matilda, the wife of King Stephen,[1] which was also confirmed by him. The Knights Templars at the later period now under review were subjected to the gravest charges against their good fame and reputation. In France the king, Philip IV., had determined upon the suppression of the order; nor was this change of fortune to be confined to its existence in France. So determined, indeed, was the king to accomplish his purpose of destruction, that he made use of his influence with his son-in-law, King Edward II., to induce him to adopt a similar course of proceeding in England, and his reluctance was finally overcome by a fresh bull from the pope, Clement V., which reversed altogether the policy of his predecessors. Accordingly, in A.D. 1309 and 1310, a process of inquiry was conducted with much severity, in order to ascertain whether the charges which had been made against the order could be sustained,[2] and in not a few instances this was followed by imprisonment in the Tower. The final result of the movement was the dissolution of the Order of the Knights Templars by a decree of Pope Clement at the Council of Vienne, on April the 3rd, A.D. 1312. A further step was subsequently taken in England in A.D. 1323, in which year an Act was passed [3] which transferred the possessions of

---

[1] See Wilkins, "Conc.," *u. s.*, vol. iii,. pp. 347 *sqq.*
[2] 17 Ed. II., s. 3.
[3] Dugd., "Mon.," vol. vi., p. 843.

the Templars, which had been resumed by the king and other lords of the fees, to the brethren of the Hospital of St. John at Jerusalem, for that this order "was likewise ordained, instituted, and canonised for the defence of Christians and the Holy Church." The knights of this order had commonly the name of Hospitallers, from receiving and entertaining the pilgrims to the Holy Land at their hospital in Jerusalem.[1]

The preceptory at Bisham, in Berkshire, formed an exception to the general transference of the estates of the Knights Templars within the present diocese of Oxford, as the lands belonging to it had been previously sold by the Templars themselves.[2] William de Sautre, too, the preceptor of Sandford, on his part, was fortunate in obtaining a pension, small as it was, of five marks.[3]

At a later period the Knights Hospitallers experienced in their turn a similar change of fortune. In A.D. 1541 this order also was dissolved, when the estates became vested in the king,[4] the prior receiving the large annual pension of a thousand pounds, and the subordinate members proportionate sums. The knights were temporarily reinstated by Queen Mary in A.D. 1554 as the Knights Hospitallers of St. John

---

[1] Gibson's "Codex Jur. Eccl.," tit. lii., ch. iv., note *g*, p. 1241. Lond., 1713.

[2] "The Knights Hospitallers in England; being the Report of the Prior Philip de Thame to the Grand Master for A.D. 1338." Camden Soc., No. 65, p. 213. 1857.

[3] *Ibid.*, p. 206.

[4] 32 Hen. VIII., c. 34.

of Jerusalem in Clerkenwell. The first and only prior who was appointed after the restoration was Sir Thomas Gresham, as " their nests were plucked down before they were warm by the coming in of Queen Elizabeth."[1] In his capacity of prior, however, Sir Thomas Gresham was summoned by writ to the Queen's first parliament; but "he had hardly sat down in his seat before he was raised up,"[2] his order, in common with the other restored orders, being at once dissolved. The action taken by the Queen appears to have been by the prerogative of the Crown, and not by statute.

In the succeeding century a further intimation was given of the fate awaiting monastic foundations in no distant future by the dissolution of the alien priories; and in this, too, the three counties of the present diocese had their part. These institutions were of two kinds. Some were merely the cells, or detached houses, of foreign foundations, dependent on them for their administration, and owing to them a simple obedience. But others were possessed of a certain independence, being conventual in their character, with the liberty of choosing their own prior. And this distinction was recognised by the legislature as a sufficient reason for a different mode of treatment.[3] Such establishments, and especially the former of the two divisions, could not but share the general dislike

---

[1] Fuller's "Hist. of the Holy War;" Suppl., bk. v., c. viii., p. 242. Lond., 1651.

[2] Fuller, Hist. of Abbeys, in "Church Hist.," bk. vi., p. 359. Lond., 1655.

[3] See *e.g.* 1 Hen. V., c. 7.

and suspicion which attached to the position of foreign ecclesiastics. The first of the kings, however, who invaded their possessions was Edward I., who seized the alien priories in A.D. 1295 as being prejudicial to the interests of the Crown; and subsequently to this the same course was taken by Edward III. But it was not until the permission was granted by the parliament which was held at Leicester, in the second year of Henry V., that the alien priories became legally vested in the king,[1] to the number of one hundred and ten. An exception, however, was made in favour of such as were of a conventual character, these having become priories denizens by naturalisation, with the right of electing their own superior.[2] The greater part of these foundations, in whatever way they had been seized, were regranted by Richard II. and his four immediate successors for religious uses. Of such institutions there was one in Berkshire,[3] two in Buckinghamshire, and four in Oxfordshire. In the disposition of these, which are comprised in the present diocese of Oxford, the principal grant to be noticed is that of the Priory at Steventon to the Abbey and Convent at Westminster, to which body it was regranted by

---

[1] In A.D. 1414, "Rolls of Parliament," vol. iv., p. 22. This is recited in the Letters Patent of June 26, A.D. 1415, granting a rectory lately appropriated to the alien Priory of Wells, and pensions from certain churches formerly belonging to the Abbey of St. Stephen at Caen. Rymer, *u. s.*, vol. ix., p. 280.

[2] 1 Hen. V., c. 7, *u. s.*, p. 63.

[3] Dugdale ("Mon.," *u. s.*, vi., p. 1044) makes two in Berks; but he erroneously places Strathfieldsaye in that county.

Henry VIII., and the grant of the priories of Cogges and Minster Lovell to his new foundation of Eton College by King Henry VI.

With this notice the review of the historical association of the archdeaconry of Oxford during the interval between the removal of the bishop's throne from Dorchester and the creation of the bishopric of Oxford by King Henry VIII., may be closed.

As at the close of the former period, the architecture during the time which has been under review requires a brief notice. In the course of this part of the history there have been the origin, progress, and decline, of Pointed Architecture, in its three successive characters, the Early English, the Decorated, and the Perpendicular styles. The three counties of the diocese, in comparison with some other parts of England, are not remarkable for the size and magnificence of the parish churches, considered as a whole. But it would not be easy to find a locality in which a greater variety in the objects of architectural interest exists than in Oxford and the adjacent county. Only a few of the churches can be selected, in which the features which require attention are most distinctly to be traced. The church of St. Giles in Oxford is a good example of very late transitional work, for, while the lower part of the tower is of the date, *c.* A.D. 1120, the chancel and nave are a century later, *c.* A.D. 1200–1220.[1] The chapter-house of the cathedral, to which, however, there is an entrance by a Norman doorway, is an example of

[1] J. H. Parker, "Introduction," *u. s.*, p. 98; J. Parker, "Visitors' Guide," *u. s.*, p. 114.

the Early English style in its best period. It has lately been restored, as a part of the work which has so long been in progress at Christ Church. The chancel of Stanton Harcourt Church, in which the early wooden screen has been preserved, is another instance of good Early English work. The church of Uffington in Berkshire, the chancel of Chetwode Church in Buckinghamshire, and the tower and other parts of Aylesbury Church, are also examples of this style.

The rise of the next style can be equally exemplified. The chapel of Merton College, which is also the parochial church of the parish of St. John the Baptist, was built *c.* A.D. 1280–90, at the expense of the executors of the will of Walter de Merton.[1] The tower and spire of the church of St. Mary the Virgin are about ten years later in date : and then succeeds the south aisle of the church of the church of St. Mary Magdalen with its characteristic tracery ; and, a few years later than this, there is the beautiful spire of Bloxham Church. The use of the ball-flower ornament, which is so commonly found in the work of this period, may be illustrated from the sedilia at Chesterton, *c.* A.D. 1326, and the Jesse window in Dorchester Church, in which the genealogy of our Lord is indicated by the ramifications of the tracery extending from the mullions over the whole window, and surmounted by a hood moulding with this flower. In Berkshire there is a fine church of this style, the church of Shottesbrook, which has been designated

---

[1] J. H. Parker, "Introduction," *u. s.*, p. 193.

by Rickman "a miniature of a cathedral," which was built[1] in A.D. 1337; and in Buckinghamshire there is the church of Olney, a name familiar from other religious associations.

Near the close of the fourteenth century, the flowing tracery of decorated work began to pass into the straighter lines of the perpendicular style. This is represented in a variety of instances. The chapel of New College was built in A.D. 1380–86. The transepts of Merton College Chapel were completed in A.D. 1424, to which the tower was added in A.D. 1450. The chapel of All Souls' College, of which the fine reredos has lately been discovered and renewed, was consecrated by the founder, Archbishop Chichile, in his old age, in A.D. 1442. The chapel of Magdalene College, which was built in A.D. 1475–81, has a tower, of work a few years later in date, having been constructed in A.D. 1492–1508. Very fine and remarkable parish churches of this style exist at Ewelme and at Minster Lovell in Oxfordshire. In Berkshire there is the church of St. Helen at Abingdon, where the tower, however, is earlier, and the chapel of St. George at Windsor, the finest building of the period in England. In Buckinghamshire there is the church of Maids Moreton, the chapel of Eton College, and, late in the style, the church of Hillesdon, the early delight of Sir G. G. Scott.

[1] "Ecclesiastical and Architectural Topography," pt. ii., Berks, No. 109. Ox., 1849.

## CHAPTER III.

INTRODUCTION CONTINUED. A.D. 1500—A.D. 1528.

Wolsey and Oxford—Suppression of St. Frideswide's Monastery—Foundation of Cardinal College, and of King Henry VIII.'s College—Later Architecture.

AT the beginning of the sixteenth century, a period of more than four hundred years had elapsed from the time of the removal of the see of Dorchester to Lincoln ;[1] and for so long an interval the county of Oxford had lost from within its extent the bishop's seat. But the course of events in the English Church was now leading by various steps to the re-establishment of the former position of the county in this respect, under new conditions. The earlier proceedings in the religious movement of the reign of Henry VIII. did not affect the county of Oxford, nor the extensive see within which it was comprised, in any special manner, with the exception that Wolsey became the Dean and Bishop of Lincoln before his promotion to the archbishopric of York. From the time, however, that Colet, Erasmus, and More, had been present together at Oxford as the representatives and promoters of the new learning, there had been within the University a growth of fresh principles and new ideas, which were to be

[1] *Supra*, pp. 23-25.

developed and made permanent for the future by the great institution of which Wolsey was the founder; which was destined to occupy so prominent a place, and exercise so large an influence in the ecclesiastical affairs of the diocese.

Wolsey had found an early patron in Richard Fox, the Bishop of Winchester, who proved himself the wise and prudent, no less than the generous, founder of Corpus Christi College. For, after his work had been begun, he did not refuse to listen to the advice of Hugh Oldham, the Bishop of Exeter, who, in this instance, was more far-sighted than himself; for, when he proposed to become a benefactor to the college, it was upon the condition that he abandoned the design of making it a home for a company of monks whose end and fall they themselves might live to see, and made it a college for secular students who, by their learning, might do good to the Church and Commonwealth. And so it is a sign of the progress of the times, and not only of personal co-operation, that the portraits of the two bishops hang opposite to one another at either end of the college hall. By the introduction to court which Wolsey had received in the reign of Henry VII. through the patronage of so able a politician, as well as so distinguished a prelate, as Fox, he had found free scope for his singular abilities, and had attained by successive steps to his high promotion. Having been appointed papal legate jointly with Campeggio by Leo X. in A.D. 1518, by the subsequent grants of Adrian VI. and of Clement VII. he obtained the renewal of his office for successive periods, became sole legate on the departure of his colleague, and finally legate for life in A.D 1523. Ambitious of succeeding to the papacy on the death of Clement VII., and failing in the attempt, he had a narrower sphere for his great designs and high aspirations. They must find their exercise within the limits of the English Church. In accordance with this was his desire to effect a reformation of ecclesiastical abuses, and raise the clergy to a higher standard in their life and character. Concurrently with it was an equally strong wish to promote the growth of the new learning. And the natural course to adopt was to begin with the education of the clergy.

The attention of Wolsey had been directed to Oxford by an incident which occurred some time previously.[1] The king and queen were at Abingdon in A.D. 1518, and the queen desired to visit the popular shrine of St. Frideswide, and to see the University itself. Wolsey accompanied the royal party, and remained at Oxford after the departure of the king and queen. Upon this occasion he made a speech before the governing body of the University, and declared his intention of establishing fresh lectureships, and of using his interest with the king in its behalf. The statutes and charters were placed in his hands, with a view to such improvements as he might think fit; and shocked at the declension from their original purpose, which a comparison with the existing state of things revealed, he resolved to reform the abuses which cast a shade upon the place

---

[1] Wood, "Hist. of Univ. Oxford," vol. i., p. 666. Oxf., 1792-6.

of his early studies. In pursuance of this object he interceded with the king in the interest of the University, and created seven new professorships, which subsequently, upon his fall, reverted to the king.

But about this time another project took possession of his thoughts, and this in a few years was to induce a greater change, and enable him to promote with authority the reforms which he desired to effect. In contemplating the new foundation which he proposed to establish, Wolsey could not but remember the bishops who had preceded him as founders of existing colleges, and the benefits which they had conferred upon the nation at large, no less than the grateful recollection which they had secured for themselves. And it would have been an act not unworthy of his largeness of heart and high purpose to give effect to his own ambition by the same means, as well as in the same spirit with them. But his personal splendour and manner of life have rendered possible another view, in which self-aggrandisement and the love of power appear as the leading motives of what he did. Nor did this escape observation at the time. A contemporary writer,[1] who, however, was no friend to the cardinal, has averred, that "turning his mind to vast and immense designs, he proposed to found two colleges for students, one, that is, at Oxford, and another at Ipswich, a humble place, where he himself was born—for vain glory, rather than the advancement of religion and learning. And seeing that he was not influenced by a true piety and

[1] Polydore Vergil, "Hist. Angl.," lib. xxvii., p. 77. Lugd. Bat., 1651.

liberality, he was willing, from the spoils of one altar, as the common proverb is, to clothe another." But however questionable may have been the course which he took in despoiling the monasteries to procure the necessary funds, he has found a zealous defender of his motives in one of the most recent examiners of his life.[1]

To render possible the result of so large a conception as Wolsey had formed, a greater provision than any private means could supply was required; and, accordingly, the suppression of several monasteries was an integral part of his plan. In furtherance of this object he had received a special authority for the visitation of such foundations as papal legate, upon which he had acted by instituting an inspection of them in various dioceses, and calling a meeting of bishops and abbots in A.D. 1519. The largest of those which it was proposed to suppress, that their revenues might be appropriated to the new college, was the Benedictine monastery of St. Frideswide in Oxford, on the site which is now occupied by Christ Church. The origin of this foundation has much of a legendary character attached to it; but it is not required to attempt to divest it of the accretions which have been formed around the nucleus of simple fact. In its traditional form it offers an explanation of the esteem in which the name of St. Frideswide was held, and of the devotion which was attracted to

---

[1] See Rev. J. H. Blunt, "Reformation of the Church of England, A.D. 1514-47," Lond., 1879; in which the chief authorities for this portion of the history may also be found enumerated.

her shrine. She is represented to have been the daughter of Didan and his wife Saffrida—Didan being an under-king in Oxford and its immediate neighbourhood, about A.D. 726. As she grew up in a religious frame of mind, her high birth, her wealth, and beauty, so far from being impediments to her piety, proved incentives to it, creating in her the fear that through these attractions she might be the more easily seduced by the vanities of the world and the temptations of life. And therefore, in compliance with her wish, her father prepared her a place for religious retirement at a distance from his court. Being sought in marriage by Algar, a Mercian lord, she with difficulty concealed herself and escaped from his suit; and when he entered the town in search of her, and was punished with blindness for his presumption, it was only at her intercession that his sight was restored. She afterwards found a safer place of refuge at Binsey, near Oxford, where she died in peace, when her body was removed for burial to the church dedicated to St. Mary, which became so famous in after-time for the devotion which was paid at her shrine.

The home which her father's care had provided for his daughter and her companions was replaced by a foundation of secular canons; and some "inns,"[1] it is stated, were provided by the king for those who sought the benefit of their learning and piety. These may not unreasonably be supposed to be an early anticipation of the future student life of Oxford.

[1] Scil. "diversoria religioni aptissima," for the connexion of which with the halls of the future see Ingram's "Memorials of Oxford," *u. s.*, Christ Church, p. 10.

This church has some historical associations of its own. In A.D. 1002, when a peace had been purchased from the Danes at a high price by Æthelred, its conditions were treacherously broken. The West Saxons rose on St. Brice's day,[1] and massacred those who on the faith of the engagement were dwelling among them in peace and security. The Danes in Oxford took refuge in the town, and it was burned with them to the ground.[2] In after-ages the relics of St. Frideswide were treated with every mark of veneration, and were from time to time translated to a place of higher honour within the church. Such a translation[3] occurred in A.D. 1180, and again in A.D. 1289, on which occasion the Bishop of Salisbury, the Earl of Cornwall, and other persons of note were present.[4] The ancient "altar or reliquary" of St. Frideswide is considered to be still in existence, embedded in the masonry of a buttress of the chapel attached to the south transept.[5] And the Latin chapel on the north side of the cathedral contains what is supposed to have been the watching chamber of the monastery, forming the place of retirement for the monk whose duty it was to guard the treasures, while he was engaged in this office.

About the year A.D. 1480 a shrine of a more elaborate character than the former one was constructed.

---

[1] "Anglo-Sax. Chron.," *ad* A.D. 1002.
[2] William of Malmes., "Chron.," *u. s.*, bk. ii., ch. 10.
[3] T. Wykes, Chron. *ad an.* in "Ann. Monast.," *u. s.*, vol. iv., p. 39.
[4] Ann. Osen., *Ibid.*, p. 38.
[5] Ingram, *u. s.*, p. 31, with wood engraving.

This also was removed in A.D. 1539, when the offerings were transferred to the king's treasury. Catherine, the wife of Peter Martyr, was buried near the spot upon her death in A.D. 1552. But her body was exhumed by the visitors of the University at the instance of Cardinal Pole, to whom an account of the proceedings was transmitted for his approval; the reason alleged for this act being that, as she was a nun before her marriage, she had become unworthy, from forsaking her vows, of resting by the side of the Virgin St. Frideswide. After the accession of Queen Elizabeth, authority was granted for a search to discover her remains, in A.D. 1561, the result of which is described by an eye-witness, John Calfhill,[1] in a letter addressed to Grindal, who was Bishop of London. It is stated in this letter that the remains were discovered in a dunghill, and that upon his suggestion when the supposed relics of St. Frideswide had been brought in, enclosed in the silken wrappers in which they had been found,[2] the two were placed together and inseparably mixed. It was thought that by this the later indignity offered to the dead, and the former superstition connected with the saint, would be effectually remedied. And in this manner the dust of them both reposes beneath the pavement of the cathedral church.

[1] J. Calfhill, "Hist. de Exhum. Katterin. nuper Uxor. Petr. Mart.," ad calc. C. Hubert., "de Vita Bucer. et Fag." Argent., 1561.

[2] "Binis manticis sericis texta et involuta," *ib.*, p. 202; but Mr. Froude has "a box," "Hist. of Engl.," vol. vi., p. 468. 1864.

In pursuance of the scheme which he had formed, part of which was the appropriation of the revenues of this house to the new college, Wolsey brought about the surrender of it to the king by John Burton,[1] the prior, in A.D. 1524. By this step any resistance on the part of the convent was prevented. And accordingly the foundation which had been in existence more than eight centuries was prepared for its suppression. And this was effected in the same year[2] by means of a bull from Pope Clement VII., which authorised this act and the annexation of the estates. The preamble of the bull, which is cited at length in the letters patent of Henry VIII., sets forth that, "whereas by the study of letters men are formed in good manners, the humble are raised up and the studious inspired with a spirit of wisdom and understanding, and are rendered more apt and able for counsel and advice of others, it is expedient that the college should be founded;" and it is afterwards alleged that the object of its foundation is "partly the profession of the liberal arts and partly the due performance of divine offices in that place." The bull is dated on April 3rd. On May the 16th the king's assent to the suppression of the monastery and the institution of a college of secular canons is conveyed in letters patent granted to Wolsey,[3] by which accordingly the foundation of the college was duly authorised.

In the following year there was a licence from the king by which Wolsey was empowered to found and

---

[1] Wood, "Hist. of Coll. and Halls," p. 420. Oxf., 1786.
[2] Rymer, vol. xiv., p. 15.    [3] Rymer, *ib.*

make perpetual his college upon the site of the suppressed monastery, "for the continual observance by honest and good men of good studies and divine worship." Wolsey had become seised of the site by other letters patent of July 1st in the same year. Nothing could have been better than the proposed object. It was intended for the instruction of the youth of England with a view to the advantage of the State from their earliest years. The range of subjects over which their studies was to extend was a very wide one. It was to take in theology, and the canon and civil law, the liberal arts, medicine, humanity, and other like studies, with the further purpose of the maintenance of divine worship. The foundation was to be known as "the Cardinal College," and was permitted to hold estates of the yearly value of £2,000.

The favour of the pope, combined with Wolsey's influence at Rome, led to the acquisition of further privileges and immunities by the new foundation. A bull of Clement VII., in A.D. 1528, authorised the retention of the revenues and estates of the suppressed monasteries which had come into possession to Wolsey before he had applied for the papal letters mentioned before;[1] and this was followed by various others which conferred exceptions and indulgences in respect of visitation, and the confirmation of privileges, with a further right of annexation. John Higden, the president of Magdalen College, was the first dean.

---

[1] Rymer, *u. s.*, vol. xiv., p. 251.

In all this, whatever was done was with the full sanction of the pope as well as of the king ; nor does anything appear to have been effected without deference to ecclesiastical authority. It was a part of Wolsey's great plan for the reformation of the monasteries, by which the use was retained for the furtherance of his own designs, while the inmates themselves were expelled. But he did not exercise his authority with due regard to existing rights. Little or nothing was given to alleviate the distress to which many of those who were expelled must have been subjected, with the exception of the pension which some of the chief among them obtained. In any case the loss of the corporate life, which had been enjoyed in the ancient foundation, must have been to the aged and the weak, and those who had given up their self-dependence, not easily to be regained, a simple desolation of heart. Nor was the proceeding acceptable to the nation at large. A letter of the king to Wolsey is preserved in which he states that there is "great murmuring at it throughout the realm."[1] And, for his own feeling as to the charges which were brought, he adds: "It grieveth me to hear it spoken of him whom I so entirely love." Besides this, the invasion of the monastic property on this occasion formed a precedent of no good omen for the future.

In order that the purposes of his new foundation might be effectually accomplished, an invitation was given by Wolsey not only to the learned of his own

---

[1] The original letter is printed in Wood's "Hist. and Ant. of Coll. and Halls," *u. s.*, p. 417.

University, but of Cambridge as well. They came to it imbued with the new learning and with the spirit of progress; and a founder has no means of controlling the events of the future, nor of regulating the course of thought in those to whom he has given power and influence. And Wolsey must have felt how different was the result from that which he had endeavoured to produce, when the doctrines of Lutheranism found a place within his own college. In order to procure a supply of well-educated students, it was a further part of Wolsey's design to establish another foundation at Ipswich, on the same enlightened principles. In pursuance of this he obtained, in A.D. 1528, certain other bulls[1] for the suppression of several monasteries and the annexation of some churches, with the appropriation of their revenues, for the foundation of a college in that town.

On the attainder of Wolsey on October 28th in the following year, all the estates and revenues in his possession reverted to the Crown. The foundation of Cardinal College had not been completed, and its property shared the common fortune of the forfeited estates. After an existence of only four years in its original state, it passed, with much of the property of the suppressed monasteries, into the hands of favourites of the king. And a miserable condition of things within the walls of the college was a natural result. So much so, indeed, was this the case that a petition from the members of the former foundation was presented to the king, who refounded it in his

---

[1] Rymer, *u. s.*, vol. xiv., pp. 240, 1, 4, 6, 7.

own name by letters patent, dated on July 18th of the same year.[1] Upon this it received the name of "King Henry VIII.'s College"; and it was permitted to hold property to the same amount as the previous foundation. The same dean was reappointed, with a distinguished body of canons.

The notice of this college must now be discontinued, until in the course of the diocesan history it is required that it shall be resumed.[2]

As the effects of an exhaustion of the knowledge of the true principles of Gothic architecture were felt within the diocese, of which a singular instance was the demolition of the church of Banbury at the close of the eighteenth century, so in like manner there appeared in it from time to time the forerunning signs of the revival which has been seen in the present century; for the earliest of the societies which have formed to advocate this movement was the "Oxford Architectural Society," which was founded in A.D. 1839. Some few instances in this progress will alone be mentioned, which are selected in a great measure from the associations of the names of founders or benefactors, which they introduce.

Many of the buildings of the University, as the old schools which were rebuilt A.D. 1613–1618, and of separate colleges, as the choir of the chapel of Wadham College of the same date, and the chapel of Lincoln College, which was consecrated in A.D. 1631, are of this higher character. In Christ Church, again, there are to be noticed the staircase to the

---

[1] Pat. 18 Hen. VIII., p. 1; Wood, *u. s.*, p. 428.
[2] See *infra*, p. 94.

hall of the date of A.D. 1640, and the tower of Tom Gate, the upper part of which forms the completion of Wolsey's work by Sir Christopher Wren, *c.* A.D. 1682. Connected with Christ Church, as being from a design by Dean Aldrich, is the church of All Saints, in Oxford, which was erected in A.D. 1706-1708.

The porch of the church of St. Mary the Virgin, with its curious history, is noticed in another place.[1] It is sufficient to mention that this ensured its preservation when it was proposed to remove it a few years since. A different future has attended the chancel of Islip Church, which was built by the celebrated Dr. South in A.D. 1660, for it has been reconstructed. The nave of Littlemore Church, with its exquisite proportions, the first stone of which was laid by the mother of Cardinal Newman, during his incumbency in St. Mary's in A.D. 1846, is now part of an enlarged parish church. The church of St. Barnabas, at Oxford, was erected at the expense of Thomas Combe, the successful manager of the University Press, and the donor of the chapel at the Radcliffe Infirmary in A.D. 1868. It forms a good specimen of a Basilican church.

In Berkshire, the church of St. Mary at Reading has this description: "It is said[2] to have been rebuilt, in A.D. 1551, of materials brought from the ruins of the Abbey and Friary, and the singular mixture of good and bad Gothic seems to verify this account."

[1] In the account of Archbishop Laud, *infra*, p. 123.
[2] "Arch. and Hist. Topogr. of Engl.," *u. s.*, Berks, No. 98.

The supposed work of Bishop Jewel at Sunningwell is mentioned in another place.[1] The church at Theale was built in a costly manner by the late President of Magdalen College, Dr. Martin Joseph Routh, and his widowed sister, Mrs. Shepherd.

There remains to mention, in Buckingham, the chapel which was built on the north side of the church of Chenies, in A.D. 1556, which contains monuments of members of the family of Russell, whose burial-place it is. There are several tombs of the Dukes of Bedford in successive generations from the sixteenth century. At Penn-street, there is a church which was erected at the expense of Earl Howe in A.D. 1849.

While these pages have been passing through the press a font has been placed within the cathedral of Christ Church, for the first time, it is stated, in the course of its long history.

[1] *Infra*, p. 216.

## CHAPTER IV.

### History of the Diocese of Oxford.
### A.D. 1528—A.D. 1558.

Dissolution of the Monasteries—Foundation of the See of Oxford, with seat at Oseney—Removal to Christ Church—Suppression of the Chantries—Schools of Edward VI.—Oxford under Queen Mary.

The progress of the ecclesiastical reforms affected the diocese in yet another but not very different manner from that which was described in the preceding chapter.

An immediate effect of the new legislation was to cause an important addition to accrue to the revenues of the Crown by an act annexing the first fruits and yearly tenths from all ecclesiastical benefices to the Crown.[1] And, in order to ascertain the exact value of this fresh source of emolument, a new survey of the ecclesiastical property was required, which was entered upon at once, and was completed without delay in the same year, A.D. 1535. The report which the commissioners returned into the Exchequer forms a record of the first importance,[2] to which, under the title of the "Valor Ecclesiasticus of King Henry VIII.," a

---

[1] 26 Hen. VIII., c. 3.

[2] This was published by the Record Commission in six folio volumes in 1810-1834. Oxfordshire and Berkshire are comprised in vol. ii., and Buckinghamshire in vol. iv.

reference in these pages is so frequently made. A commission to institute a general visitation to inquire into the state of the monasteries was issued in the autumn of the same year.

In pursuance of this first visitation all the religious houses "which had not in lands, tenements, rents, tithes, and other hereditaments, above the clear yearly value of £200" were to be suppressed,[1] and this was effected accordingly in A.D. 1535. By the same act a general power to accept the resignation of religious houses was conferred upon the king. Among the 376 religious houses which were suppressed, the smaller foundations of the three counties forming the present diocese of Oxford had, indeed, their common share in the general misfortune; but no act of importance in connexion with the formation of the bishopric was the result of their dissolution.

The effect of the second attack upon the monasteries was very different in its relation to the diocese, the interests of which were largely involved in its results. Soon after the dissolution of the smaller houses, the foundations which had been spared at first were sought by Henry and Cromwell as a further spoil. When the rebellion in the North, which had revealed the opinion of the people, had been put down, in A.D. 1537, and twelve abbots had been hanged and quartered for their part in it, a fresh visitation was appointed. And the instructions were even less favourable than in the former instance. There was not, as there had been, a pretence of reformation.

---

[1] By 27 Hen. VIII., c. 28, s. 1.

The commissioners, so far as is known, were men of no personal repute. But they had the recommendation of a great faculty for inquiring into the vices supposed to be prevalent from their former practice in the ecclesiastical courts, to which the cognisance of such cases belonged. Their object was not a simple one. The former act had provided for the voluntary surrender of any religious foundation; and, besides securing fresh evidence to be available in the future, they were to procure, whenever practicable, such resignation to the king, who was desirous of maintaining the appearance of justice. For this purpose all available means were employed. Persuasion and threats; the encouragement of quarrels; the introduction of emissaries with the basest designs; the offering of bribes; the alliance of the secular clergy; the use of the pulpit; all these were employed on occasion to induce a surrender on the part of the abbot and convent. As there was no authority to proceed to suppression, it was the only step which the commissioners could take in furtherance of their ends. Many such surrenders were actually obtained, while in some instances they were forged, and even the former were doubtful in law from the compulsion under which they were made. In these cases there followed at once the seizure of any valuable property and spoliation of the house. Immediately after the commission of inquiry, in A.D. 1539, an act[1] for the dissolution of these greater religious houses was passed; and it is curious to observe how the preamble recites in total disregard

[1] 31 Hen. VIII., c. 13.

of the truth that "divers and sundry abbots and other ecclesiastical governors and governesses of divers monasteries ... of their own free-will and voluntary minds, good-wills and assents, without coaction or compulsion of any manner of person or persons ... had their several houses under their convent seal renounced and forsaken;" after which there follows a confirmation of all such surrenders as had been made since the last act; and it is enacted that the king shall have these "in as full and ample a manner" as their late owners had held them. And a similar provision is made for any future suppression or renunciation.[1] All the revenues accruing from this source were to be under the survey of the king's Court of Augmentations of the revenues of the Crown,[2] which had been specially formed for their cognisance. As in the former act, there is a reservation in respect of founders and donors.[3] But there is no similar provision for the maintenance of the former state and occupation on the part of the grantees.[4]

The immediate consequence of the passing of this act was the suppression of 186 foundations in A.D. 1539. The preceding inquiry had been directed towards the moral character of the monks and nuns, and had been conducted by commissioners who, as represented by Leigh, and Layton, and London, could not have ventured to undergo a personal examination themselves. And their evidence is open to the same, or even weightier, objections than in the former instance. The king was in the utmost want of money

[1] Sec. 3.
[2] Sec. 4.
[3] Secs. 4, 15, 26.
[4] See 27 Hen. VIII., c. 28, s. 9.

at the time; and, although the evidence may have been true in the most important particulars, it will not be denied that it was obtained in accordance with a foregone conclusion. Certainly good and pious men had anticipated the downfall of monasticism, as unsuited to the requirements of the times. But if the system had, indeed, fulfilled its primary purpose, and had become effete, and therefore disentitled to its former place in public esteem, these were but concurrent causes for its change with the prospect of relief which the wealth of the monasteries offered to the king. And this, no doubt, was the strongest motive in Henry's mind.

The religious houses in the three counties of the present diocese, rich and numerous as they were, held an important place in the dissolution. If there are taken the mitred abbeys of the Benedictines at Abingdon and Reading, the houses of the Bonhommes at Ashridge, the Augustinians at Notley, at Dorchester, and at Oseney, the Cistercians at Thame, and the Benedictines again at Eynsham and Godstow, it will be apparent that every part of the diocese, as it now exists, must have felt the common misfortune. Though pensions were granted to the inmates who were dismissed from their homes, these were too small to afford compensation even in ordinary cases for the loss of the familiar life; while the aged, and weak, and friendless must in the change of their accustomed habits have felt the extreme of bitterness.

Among the dissolved foundations there is one towards which, more than any other, the diocesan interest converges, as being destined to become the original seat of the newly created bishopric of Oxford. The expectation on the part of the king of obtaining a large increase of revenue must, in a great measure, have been disappointed, for in the disposition of the estates which reverted to the Crown he appears to have retained in the end a far less proportion than he was led to anticipate. The pensions which were granted to the several inmates, and the estates which were transferred to his favourites at a low rate of purchase, tended to diminish very considerably his own share of the spoil. However, in the dispensation of such of the revenues as he could command, the king was not unmindful of the use to which they might be applied for the public benefit. Six new bishoprics were at once created, two of which were taken from the large diocese of Lincoln, while five others were likewise contemplated. For the new see of Oxford, which was to comprise the old archdeaconry of Oxford, which was conterminous with the county, the abbey of Oseney was selected to furnish the site of the cathedral and bishop's throne. It was well adapted to become the seat of the bishop from its rich endowment, and extensive buildings, as well as from its convenient position. It stood on the low ground, at a short distance from the west end of the church of St. Thomas the Martyr, and it contained a chapel of such a character, from its size and grandeur, its noble campanile and far-famed ring of bells, as to be well suited for a cathedral church. It was, too, a foundation of high antiquity in its associations with the past, having been first established in A.D. 1129, by Robert d'Oyley the younger, the nephew of the Norman follower of the same name, upon whom in reward for his faithful service the Conqueror had bestowed the barony of which Oxford formed part. The estates belonging to it had been returned of the annual value of £654 10s. 2d. No vestige of it, however, now remains to mark the actual place where it stood, although in the map,[1] published by Agas, of the date of 1578, there is a small view which shows a ruined tower and line of wall. A portion of the abbey mill is the only part of the dependent buildings which is left at the present time.

The steps which were taken by the king for the establishment of the bishopric may be collected from the letters patent,[2] which were issued for its creation in A.D. 1542. Though Wolsey himself had passed away, this procedure on the part of the king was in reality a fulfilment of the intention of the cardinal in his great designs for the reformation of the Church; a part of whose purpose had been the formation of some new sees. And indeed, in A.D. 1528, he had applied in the king's name for papal bulls to authorise the suppression of as many as twenty-one monasteries for the endowment of the bishoprics proposed.[3] But the design of necessity failed of its accomplishment; for the decline of the king's favour had already begun, displeased as he was at the grandeur of the new

---

[1] This has been reproduced under the superintendence of the Ordnance Department.

[2] Pat. 34, Hen. VIII., pt. 6, m. 1; Rymer, *u. s.*, vol. xiv., pp. 754-759.

[3] See J. H. Blunt, "Hist.," *u. s.*, ch. ii., p. 69.]

college, and offended at the cardinal's arms being placed above his own over the gateway at the entrance,[1] and the disfavour became complete on the forced retirement of the cardinal to Esher in A.D. 1529. By the resignation of the Abbot Robert King, the king had obtained possession of Oseney, and nothing remained but the creation of the see by letters patent. Those which have been already noticed, as issued on September the first in A.D. 1542, were to this intent.—That whereas the king is in possession of the monastery by the surrender of the abbot, and desires nothing more than that the true religion and worship of God should not only be maintained but promoted, and reformed according to primitive rule and form, after the correction of the enormities of the life and profession of the monks: and that considering also that the site of the above monastery, being near to the town of Oxford, is a place apt and convenient for the institution of a bishop's seat and a cathedral church for a bishop, a dean, and six prebendaries who are priests, he has decreed that the said monastery shall be so constituted to the honour and glory of Christ and of the blessed Virgin: and that the town of Oxford and the college, named Gloucester College in the parish of St. Nicholas in the suburbs shall be now and for ever named "the city of Oxford": and that the see shall be for ever separated from the jurisdiction of the Bishop of Lincoln, and limited to the Bishop of Oxford and his successors, of which Robert King, the

---

[1] [Is. Wake's] "Rex Platonicus," pp. 44 [Oxon., 1607] in Fuller's "Church Hist.," cent. xvi., bk. v., *u. s.*, p. 169.

Abbot aforesaid, shall be the first bishop, who shall have, moreover, Gloucester College for his palace: and that John London shall be the first dean: and that the dean and chapter shall be a corporate body annexed for ever to the bishopric, in the same manner as the Dean and Chapter of Lincoln are to that see, and shall have the estates of the monastery, with the two closes of the extent of nineteen acres reserved to the use of the bishop: and that there shall be also an archdeaconry of Oxford, in like manner separate, with the same privileges and jurisdiction which the archdeaconry of the same name formerly enjoyed: and that the Bishop of Oxford shall have and exercise the same jurisdiction with that which was exercised by the bishop of Lincoln.

The effect of the letters patent accordingly was to establish the bishopric of Oxford with the authority and jurisdiction of an independent see, and with a cathedral and its chapter at Oseney, and a palace for the bishop's residence at Gloucester Hall. From the notices of the several parishes of the diocese in the "Valor Ecclesiasticus,"[1] it appears that the division of parishes, and the erection of churches within their boundaries had progressed since the time when the previous survey of them was made. The existence is recorded of two hundred and thirty-four churches or chapels in Oxfordshire, three of which, however, are described as destroyed, and one as desecrated. The town of Oxford at the creation of the bishopric received also an accession of dignity in its civil

---

[1] See *supra*, p. 83.

capacity. Like the other towns in which the new bishops were placed by Henry VIII., it gained by a clause in the patent the title of a "city." From thus becoming the centre of the newly-created bishopric, Oxford itself gained an accession of dignity to which the town of Cambridge never attained. The near proximity of the cathedral town of Ely, in which the bishop's throne had been placed upon the earlier separation of the diocese of Ely from the see of Lincoln, rendered it unnecessary that a new bishopric should be formed, with the bishop's chair at Ely. With such an arrangement there would arise a claim to the title of a city, on the principle that in the other instances of the creation of a new diocese the king had caused this privilege to be conferred by his letters patent. Nor, again, independently of this, had Cambridge the advantage of such a patron as Wolsey, who could advance its interests by identifying them with his own. The first dean of the cathedral of Oseney was Dr. John London, who had been warden of New College, and who has been already mentioned[1] as one of the commissioners on the occasion of the second visitation of the monasteries. He did not, however, long hold this preferment, for "he died in the Fleet Prison in London,[2] having been committed to that place for perjury in A.D. 1545."

Bishop King had previously been abbot of Bruerne

---

[1] *Supra,* p. 86.

Wood, "Fasti Oxon," t. 1, c. 660, Lond., 1691, where it is also stated that Foxe, in his "Acts and Monuments," "loads his name with a great deal of ill language."

and of Thame, as well as of Oseney, and has been mentioned among the suffragan bishops of the diocese of Lincoln.[1] His episcopate illustrates the continuity of the English Church amid the changes through which it passed in the sixteenth century from the sentiments of the reigning sovereign. He held his see during three reigns, and he is not unfrequently called the first and only Bishop of Oseney; but this title does not appear in the patent of creation.

The new see was not destined to continue long in this condition, nor was the bishop himself to retain his cathedral and his palace. In A.D. 1545, a commission was authorised to accept the surrender of the king's college, and of the new foundation of Oseney from the respective deans and chapters on the king's behalf. And the surrender was made on the 20th of May.[2] The bishop joined in the resignation; and this act deprived him of the ordinary jurisdiction of the see, which had been surrendered with the estates. And accordingly, to provide for the exercise of his office, as diocesan, he received from the king on the 2nd of June[3] a renewal of his authority, without which the affairs of the diocese could not be administered, pending the settlement of the new scheme for the bishopric. By this surrender the estates of the college and of the chapter, and, indeed, of the see itself, became vested in the king, and subject to a fresh disposal at his pleasure. And it is found in the course of events that the history of the Monastery

---

[1] *Supra*, p. 36.
[2] Wood, "Hist. of Coll. and Halls, *u. s.*, p. 429.
[3] Rymer, *u. s.*, vol. xv., p. 75.

of St. Frideswide, which was interrupted[1] for the description of the new bishopric, is resumed. By the new arrangement the separate foundations of St. Frideswide and of Oseney are brought into connexion with each other for a common purpose. But the diocesan associations, which belong to the actual site of the bishop's throne, pass away from the latter, and become attached for the future to the former of these two foundations.

The preparation for the change having thus been made, and every obstacle removed, letters patent[2] were issued on the 4th of November, in A.D. 1546, by which the transference of the seat of the bishopric to St. Frideswide's was fully authorised. And the site of this foundation, with the conversion of the chapel into the cathedral of Christ Church, was to become the central spot of the diocese, the chapter being reconstituted under a dean and eight canons, with the subordinate officers. The foundation was completed by other letters of the 11th of December. So far as the interests of the chapter were concerned an endowment was then secured. It was also provided that Bishop King should continue to occupy the see, and that Dr. Richard Cox, the successor of Dr. London at Oseney, should be the first dean of the new cathedral. At an earlier period he had removed from Cambridge to Cardinal College, at the instance of Wolsey, and was one of those whose progress of opinion belied the expecta-

---

[1] *Supra*, p. 80.
[2] Pat. 38 Hen. VIII., pt. 5; see Wood, "Hist. of Coll. and Halls," *u. s.*, p. 431.

tions of the founder. He had afterwards a varied and eventful life, being at one time tutor to Prince Edward, and then imprisoned on the accession of his successor; but, being released, he retired to Strasbourg, and was subsequently invited to Frankfort, where he was able to oppose successfully the extreme Puritanism of the English exiles. He became in the end Bishop of Ely.

Soon after his removal to Christ Church, Bishop King was a witness to a great change in the internal administration of the churches of his diocese, and the condition of a large proportion of the clergy attached to them. This was caused by the king's attack upon colleges and chantries, and other similar foundations, in the year preceding his death. An Act was passed for their suppression,[1] with the exception of such as were declared exempt from its operation, by which reservation the Universities were saved. The dissolution of these foundations, so far as it was incomplete at the time of the king's death, was finally accomplished on the accession of King Edward VI.[2] The chantries, which were then swept away with the fraternities attached to them, had undoubtedly become subject to much abuse. The priests who officiated at their altars formed a class by themselves, whose office it was to offer the sacrifice of the mass for the souls of those by whose benefactions they were supported, with no other duties incumbent on them. Their office was, in its exercise, a great departure from the practice of the early Church in

[1] 37 Hen. VIII., c. 4.   [2] 1 Ed. VI., c. 14.

its custom of offering prayers for the dead. The supposition that a payment in money could ensure a mitigation of the consequences of an evil life, made the sin which could be thus atoned far less an object of fear. Nor could it fail to place in a painful contrast the opportunities of the rich and the poor. Upon the question of the suppression of these foundations, and the appropriation of their revenues, if diverted to a legitimate purpose, there is no reason to think that the interference of the Crown was uncalled for. But the acquisition of the revenues was again a leading purpose, and not the mere substitution of a better object, though in some measure this was not overlooked. Several grammar schools—in all, fifty-three—were founded by the king after the passing of the Act for converting Chantries in the first year of his reign; of these the schools at Chipping Norton and Buckingham are within the present diocese of Oxford.[1]

The interests of the see were consulted in letters patent which were issued in the first year of King Edward VI. An endowment had been provided for the chapter,[2] but no similar provision had been made for the bishopric. To remedy this, a grant of a sufficient revenue for the see by the conveyance of various estates was secured by these letters,[3] but at the same time the former palace at Glou-

---

[1] "Report of Schools Inquiry Comm.," vol. i., Ap. iv., pp. 44, 46. 1868. See *infra*, Appendix C.

[2] *Supra*, p. 94.

[3] See in Br. Willis, "Survey of Cathedrals," vol. iii., p. 417. Lond., 1730.

cester College was reserved to the Crown. Bishop King was in consequence deprived of his episcopal residence; and it is supposed that he occupied from this time a house in the parish of St. Aldate, still known as "Bishop King's house," situate near the Trill Mill stream, with the front in Rose Place.[1] His arms occur several times in the ceiling of the room on the ground floor, and it is traditionally stated to have been built by him.[2] Bishop King died at the latter end of Queen Mary's reign, in A.D. 1557, with the reputation of a quiet and peaceful man of much gentleness, who was adverse to the religious persecutions of his time, "not caring to have anything to do with those who were called "heretics."[3] This did not, however, prevent him from subscribing and affixing his seal of office to the commissional letters by which the three bishops were placed on their trial within his diocese. He was buried in his cathedral, and a monument, removed from the north aisle in which it was first placed, still preserves the memory of the first bishop of the see[4] in the present site below the painted window containing his figure. This, again, is not without an interest of its own. It was taken down by a member of the family of the bishop in A.D. 1651, to save it from the threatened

---

[1] Ingram, *u. s.*, Parish of St. Aldate, p. 10, and for a view the house, p. 12.

[2] Wood, "Ath. Oxon.," *u. s.*, t. i., c. 586.

[3] Strype, "Life of Cranmer," vol. i., p. 481. Oxf., 1812.

[4] The inscription is:—"Hic jacet Rob. Kyng, S. T. P., et primus episcopus Oxon. qui ob. iv$^{to}$ die Dec. A.D. 1557." Wood, "Hist. of Coll. and Halls," *u. s.*, p. 466.

destruction, and was replaced after the Restoration in A.D. 1661.

The visitation of the University by Cardinal Pole has been mentioned.[1] But the chief event in the troublous scenes of the reign of Queen Mary with which Oxford is associated is the imprisonment of Cranmer, Ridley, and Latimer, and their cruel death. The closing scene of their lives is inseparably connected with the city of Oxford, its ancient prison and bastioned wall, the opposite college and the intervening ditch; while some of the incidents preceding this equally belong to its noblest and most famous church.

On the 8th of March in A.D. 1554, Archbishop Cranmer, who had refused to leave the kingdom on Mary's accession, and his fellow-prisoners, Bishop Ridley and Bishop Latimer, were removed from the Tower and brought to Oxford, and were confined in the common prison of Bocardo, which was over the city gate, near St. Michael's Church.[2] On Saturday, the 14th of April, the representatives of the lower house of Convocation, with the prolocutor, Dr. Hugh Weston, the Dean of Westminster, with the delegates of the two Universities, went in procession to the church of St. Mary the Virgin, where they took their places in front of the high altar. After the formal opening of the proceedings, by their direction Cranmer was introduced. Subjected to a lengthy examination, he

---

[1] *Supra*, p. 75. The visitation was in A.D. 1557.
[2] The site is not always correctly described. It is marked in the map of Oxford by Ralph Agas, *u. s.*, in 1578, as "Northgate and Bocardo," adjoining the west side of the tower of St. Michael's Church, which was in the line of the city wall.

so conducted his case as to win their approval of his demeanour, and even to touch their hearts. On Sunday he sent his answer to the charges against him in writing, and on Monday a public disputation was held in the Divinity School on the subject of the Holy Sacrament, at the close of which the persons present were invited to raise their united shout of "vicit veritas."

On Tuesday, Latimer was brought before the Commissioners, when he pleaded that his age and failing memory unfitted him for dispute, and was returned to his dungeon as obstinate and incorrigible in his misbelief. On the next day, Ridley was summoned before them, when he proved a more formidable opponent than the other two had been. His friends were elated at what appeared to them to be his success; but on this occasion also a similar cry of "victoria" was raised, as if he had been a defeated disputant. On Thursday, Cranmer was cited to appear in the same School as an opponent to Harpsfield, chaplain to the Bishop of London, who had preached the sermon at St. Mary's on the previous Sunday, and who was now to perform an exercise preparatory to his degree.

On Friday, the three prelates were taken to St. Mary's Church, where they were invited to sign the articles which had been drawn up in condemnation of the opinions which they had proposed. When it was averred that they had been vanquished in a fair discussion, Cranmer protested that the whole proceeding had been most unfair; and when his protest was disallowed, appealed to the just judgment of

God. For himself he also appealed to the queen; but, as he imprudently intrusted his letter to the Prolocutor Weston for delivery, it was opened on the way and returned. With the sentence of condemnation which was passed upon the three, this the first trial was closed. But it was not considered advisable that their execution should follow. The Privy Council was not prepared for such a step. The papal authority had been abolished in England, and the principles of the Queen interfered with her acting, as Head of the Church; nor had there been any trial before a competent tribunal to justify the delivery of the prisoners to the secular arm. Accordingly there is a minute of the 3rd of May, to the effect "that the judges and the Queen's Highness' learned counsel should be called together and their opinions demanded what they think in law her Highness may do touching the cases of the said Cranmer, Ridley, and Latimer, being already by both the Universities of Oxford and Cambridge judged to be obstinate heretics, which matter is rather to be consulted upon, for that Cranmer is already attainted."[1] The life of the archbishop had been forfeited upon his attainder on account of his part in the attempt to place Lady Jane Grey on the throne; but as the three had been convicted of heresy no distinction could be made. Cranmer accordingly was respited with the others; and indeed a different sentence from that of death at the stake would have awaited him as a traitor. The three were therefore remitted to their prison.

[1] "Privy Council Registers," vol. ii., p. 112, in W. H. Turner's "Records of the City of Oxf.," p. 118. Ox., 1880.

Soon after this the Queen was married to Philip of Spain, and Cardinal Pole returned to England, with authority, as legate from the pope, to reconcile the kingdom, and remove the guilt of heresy and schism. It is incidentally mentioned that the imprisonment of the bishops was considered to do harm to the cause of their persecutors in the neighbourhood of Oxford. Sir Henry Bedingfield, who had the custody of the Princess Elizabeth at Woodstock, in his letter to the Council on the 4th July, adds in a postscript that it has come to his knowledge, "that the remaining of Cranmer, Ridley, and Latimer at Oxford in such sort as they do, hath done no small hurt in these parts, even among those that were known to be good afore."[1] It was the common effect of persecution for conscience sake; the injury recoils upon those who practise it. Bedingfield proved himself a watchful keeper to his royal prisoner, but he could not hinder her communication with Ridley, to whom she sent alms, by which he "was enabled also to minister to his distressed brethren and companions in prison."[2] They had at least this proof of sympathy.

After the arrival of the cardinal, and the reversal of the attainder to which he had become subject in A.D. 1539, the proceedings against the reformers were resumed in all their severity, and, accordingly,

[1] C. R. Manning's "Bedingfield State Papers," p. 68, n. d., reprinted from "Reports of Norfolk and Suff. Arch. Soc.," vol. vi., pt. ii.
[2] Coverdale's "Letters of the Martyrs," fol. 73. Lond., 1564.

a fresh commission was issued for the trial of the three prelates in A.D. 1555; but on account of the higher dignity of Cranmer, as an archbishop, he was to be separately tried. The result of this new trial, in respect of Ridley and Latimer, was that they were burned at the stake on October the 16th. The place where they suffered was not far from the prison in which they had been confined, and in which their fellow-prisoner still remained, who was a witness, it has been said, of their execution, and who must certainly have seen some of the attendant incidents. Cranmer prayed in all earnestness for their faith and constancy, not unaware that this was a prelude to his own death. For his trial was past some time before, and its course had been such as to destroy any reasonable hope of life.

The commissioners had met on the 12th of September in St. Mary's Church, where they took their seats on a scaffold erected in front of the high altar, the same position which had been occupied before. The chief of those who were then present was Dr. Brooks, the Bishop of Gloucester, who represented the absent commissioners appointed by the pope; and there were also two civilians, Dr. Martin and Dr. Story, who acted for the king and queen. These the archbishop saluted with deference, while at the same time he refused to recognise the authority of the papal see in the person of the bishop. The accusations against him were read, and he was permitted to make his defence, having been reminded by Martin that it was only by the authority of the pope whom he condemned that an attainted traitor was permitted even then to be alive. The archbishop offered his protest against this. He was also charged with the violation of the oath taken at his consecration, which he also repelled. At the last, sixteen articles embodying his alleged errors were produced, after which some questioning ensued concerning his marriage. With the production of the witnesses who were to be examined the proceedings of the day closed.

On the next day the depositions of the several witnesses were taken, when the trial was brought to an end, and an official report transmitted to Rome. Previously to this, however, Cranmer had received a formal citation to appear before the pope within eighty days. He himself addressed a letter to the queen, to which an answer was returned by Cardinal Pole. In the meantime the two bishops were put to death.

On the 29th of November the term of eighty days, within which the archbishop was to appear at Rome, expired; and on the 4th of December he was deprived of his archbishopric, to which Cardinal Pole was appointed on the 11th of December. Within three days afterwards the letter from the pope, which authorised his degradation and his delivery to the secular arm, arrived. On the 14th of February in the following year the pontifical mandate was put in execution. Thirlby and Bonner, the Bishops of Ely and London, were at Oxford to complete the work which had been thus far advanced. The court sat in the cathedral, and Cranmer was summoned to appear before the commissioners. After a recital of the commission, the usual form of degradation was adopted.[1] The archbishop was dressed in episcopal habiliments made of canvas, with the semblance of a crosier in his hand. The robes were stripped off. The pall was removed. His hair was clipped by a barber, and the tips of his fingers were scraped by Bonner. A threadbare gown was then thrown over him. Thirlby, indeed, showed some sympathy in the midst of all, and a stranger restored his clerical gown on the way to prison, and afterwards supplied the refreshment, of which, from the excitement of the day, Cranmer felt the most urgent want. And now it was that his spirit failed. Four different forms of recantation were signed in the short space of two days. After this Cranmer was invited to Christ Church, to exchange the misery of his cell for the amenities of social life, but at the same time to suffer temptation in a too seductive form. And here he was induced to make a fifth recantation, which was followed on the eighteenth by a sixth. On the twentieth he was visited by Dr. Cole, the Provost of Eton, who made close inquiry into the firmness of his adhesion to the recent profession of his faith.

On the 21st of March Dr. Cole returned, and on this occasion placed fifteen crown pieces in Cranmer's hand. It was customary to distribute alms at the time of execution, and this accordingly was a sign which could not be mistaken of the approaching end. Friar Garcina also came, and tendered a transcription

---

[1] The form of degrading an archbishop in the "Pontificale Romanum" is compared with the ceremonies used at the degradation of Cranmer, by Foxe, "Acts and Mon.," vol. viii., pp. 77-9. Lond., 1843-9.

of one of the previous papers, which was subscribed, but in all probability with a different motive from that which the friar conceived. Between the hours of nine and ten in the morning of the same day, the preparations for his death, and the preservation of the public peace, were completed. It was a wild and stormy morning, and, accordingly, the sermon which was to have been preached by Dr. Cole at the stake was transferred to St. Mary's Church. There Cranmer was placed on a scaffold, or platform, in front of the pulpit, which was then of stone, attached to one of the pillars on the south side of the nave; and with every appearance of deep sorrow, and with much solemnity of demeanour, he listened to the discourse and awaited its close. Then, after kneeling in prayer, his spirit renewed and his weakness overcome, to the amazement of all he made a full and free confession of his faith, expressing his deep abhorrence of the want of constancy and truth which he had shown. Hurried to the place of his death, and rejecting the last attempt to shake his firmness on the way, he fulfilled his promise of placing first in the flame the hand which had committed the unworthy acts of signature, and, repeatedly praying that the Lord Jesus would receive his spirit, thus died with patience and in hope.

Twice in later and more peaceful times the memory of the former scenes was revived near the spot where the three prelates were put to death. In A.D. 1841, the Martyrs' Memorial was raised after a public subscription, commemorating, by a cross of a similar design with the crosses in memory of Queen Eleanor, their sufferings and death; and at the same time the Martyrs' Aisle was added to the north side of the adjoining church of St. Mary Magdalene, in which was placed the door of the prison in which they had been confined with its lock and key, the prison itself having been demolished in A.D. 1771. At a later period, on the three hundredth anniversary of the death of Ridley and Latimer, a commemorative sermon was preached in St. Mary Magdalene Church by Canon Miller, who was then the incumbent of St. Martin's Church in Birmingham.

The latest act of Queen Mary, in which the diocese of Oxford had a special interest, was the nomination of Dr. Thomas Goldwell, the Bishop of St. Asaph, to the see of Oxford, which was then vacant from the death of Bishop King.[1] He received the custody of the temporalities of the bishopric[2] in the month of November in A.D. 1558, and he was, without doubt, indebted in this transaction to the good offices of Cardinal Pole, having been employed by him a few years before in communicating his sentiments to the queen respecting the ecclesiastical arrangements upon which she felt doubts in the early part of her reign. He was a zealous Romanist.[3] On the death of Queen Mary, which occurred within the space of a few days, and before he obtained possession of the see, he lost the occasion of being instituted to the bishopric, and left England. He was present at the Council of Trent in A.D. 1562, and was also commissioned by the pope to baptize the Jewish con-

[1] *Supra*, p. 97.    [2] Rymer, *u. s.*, vol. xv., p. 492.
[3] Wood, "Athen. Oxon.," *u. s.*, vol. i., col. 605.

verts in Rome, and to confer holy orders upon any English refugee. His learning and general usefulness entitled him to much respect, and he died in Rome at the age of eighty, with the character, it has been said,[1] of one "who was more conversant in the black art than skilful in the Scriptures."

[1] Will. Harrison's Description of Engl., in Holinshed's "Chron.," bk. ii., c. 2. See Wood, "Ath. Ox.," *u. s.*, col. 586.

## CHAPTER V.

HISTORY OF THE DIOCESE. A.D. 1558—A.D. 1660.

The Diocese under Queen Elizabeth—Vacancy of the See—Roman Catholics Executed—Proceedings of Abbot—Estates of the See—Palace at Cuddesdon—Charge against Laud—Bishop Skinner—The Usurpation—State of Oxford—Extracts from Court Books.

ON the accession of Queen Elizabeth, the see of Oxford was vacant in consequence of the death of Bishop King, and the incomplete appointment of Bishop Goldwell. For, unable to conform to the new state of ecclesiastical opinion, he had left the kingdom, and the bishop's throne remained without an occupant. This afforded an occasion for the revenues to be seised into the hands of the queen, while other provision was made for the administration of the affairs of the diocese. It does not appear, from the diocesan registers,[1] that there was any ordination of clergy during this vacancy, but there were numerous institutions to benefices in the ordinary course. These were principally made by the Archdeacon Walter Wright,[2] who was appointed to the custody of the spiritualities, and who appears to have derived his authority from the Archbishop of Canterbury,

---

[1] By favour of Thomas Marriott Davenport, Esq., of the Diocesan Registry.

[2] *Supra*, p. 91.

for there is a frequent statement in the diocesan registers of the archbishop's "having as much ecclesiastical jurisdiction in the diocese when the see was vacant as when it was full." This, it would seem, was derived from the authority which he possessed as metropolitan. Walter Wright had held the archdeaconry for a long period, being nominated to it while it was still a part of the diocese of Lincoln, and before the see of Oxford had been formed from it, although he was never installed under the former relation. Amid the various changes which ensued he continued to retain his preferment undisturbed. And, therefore, he was able to act as one of the visitors of the University under Cardinal Pole, and of Magdalen College under Bishop Gardiner, and to show his zeal in behalf of the then existing conditions of the Church; while his previous conduct did not prevent him from adapting his sentiments to the requirements of the succeeding reign. This was brought into prominence by the circumstances attending his death, for after making some reflections upon the pope's supremacy, in a sermon preached at Oxford, he was seized with a sudden fit of illness, and died in about eight days, in A.D. 1561. Attention has been directed to the state of mind in which he died, both by his friends and enemies, either party expressing an opinion according to their prepossession in his favour, or the reverse.[1] He appears, indeed,

---

[1] See the opinion of Ric. Saunders in his "De Vis. Mon.," l. vii., p. 690, Wirceb., 1592, with his severe strictures; and the remarks of Fuller, "Ch. Hist. Cent. XVI.," bk. viii., *n. s.*, p. 7 for the defence.

as one of the ecclesiastics of the time, whose change of conviction, however wrought, enabled them to act without scruple in accordance with their present interests.

The vacancy of the see continued to A.D. 1567, in which year a *congé d'élire* was issued, empowering the dean and chapter of Christ Church to proceed to the election of a bishop, the see being declared to be vacant by the death of Bishop King.[1] This was duly made in favour of Hugh Curen, or Curwen, who obtained the restitution of the temporalities of the see on the 3rd of December. The new bishop had succeeded in gaining the favour of the Court at an earlier period, in a manner which is, at least, open to question. As a doctor of the civil law, he had promoted the king's marriage with Anne Boleyn in A.D. 1532, and had found an occasion of commending the action of the king to public approval in the following year.[2] When Friar Peto, who was chaplain to Queen Katherine, had condemned the marriage in a sermon which was preached before the king at Greenwich, he defended it in terms equally strong with his on the next Sunday; and expressed his astonishment that any subject could conduct himself with so much effrontery before the king's face. Subsequently, being one of Queen Mary's chaplains, he was appointed to the archbishopric of Dublin, to which see he was consecrated in London at St. Paul's Cathedral in A.D. 1555. But in the course of years he became sensible of the advance of old age, and

---

[1] Rymer, *u. s.*, vol. xv., pp. 670-672.
[2] Wood, "Ath. Oxon.," *u. s.*, vol. i., col. 587, 597.

felt the burden of such an office to be too great. Accordingly, desiring to pass the remainder of his life more quietly, he requested that he might be allowed to exchange the archbishopric for the see of Oxford, in A.D. 1567. The permission was granted, and he obtained the restitution of the temporalities of the see at the date which has been already stated.[1] It was, however, but for a short time that he retained possession of it, for he died in the following year at Swinbrook, near Burford, a parish within the diocese in which he had resided, as there was then no episcopal palace belonging to the see. He was buried in the chancel of the parish church on the 3rd of November. Upon his death there was no immediate appointment of a successor, and the queen adopted the same course which she had taken on the previous vacancy. The revenues of the see were again taken into her hands, but on this occasion she retained them for a still longer period than before,—no appointment being made to the bishopric for the succeeding twenty-one years.

During the period which was occupied by the events that have been last described, a cause of offence of a different kind is found to have made its appearance at Oxford, and within the very precincts of the deanery. Thomas Sampson, who had been Dean of Chichester in the time of Edward VI., and who had been distinguished by his extreme Protestant sentiments, had left England, on the accession of Queen Mary, to join his fellow-countrymen who were in

---

[1] Rymer, *u. s.*, vol. xv., p. 672.

exile at Strasburg. On his return after her death, he had been installed as dean of Christ Church at the close of the year A.D. 1561. His previous opposition to the ecclesiastical habits had been confirmed by his residence abroad, and he had subsequently attained a high reputation as a preacher of ability at Oxford; as also had Laurence Humphrey, the president of Magdalen College, whose Calvinistic opinions were in agreement with his own. On account of his vehement opposition to the use of the ecclesiastical dress, Dr. Sampson was cited before the Court of High Commission at Lambeth, where a long series of questions was proposed to him, to which he returned an elaborate reply. But in this he failed to obtain a successful result, and, in the issue, was deprived of his deanery by the definitive sentence of Archbishop Parker. However, notwithstanding his continued nonconformity, he obtained some smaller preferments, and held the mastership of a hospital at Leicester, at the time of his death in A.D. 1589. His persistence in the objections which he felt, combined with his high moral character, and his suffering in the cause which he maintained, made him, with Laurence Humphrey, the leader of a popular party. And the result of the contest in which he was engaged is found to have an influence still. It was in consequence of the dissensions which were then so prejudicial to the interests of the Church, that Sir William Cecil addressed a "Queen's Letter" to Archbishop Parker to urge uniformity by putting in force the existing laws. And the directions which he issued in compliance with this have proved fertile in argument as to what in reality is to be esteemed their character and value. Nor can it be said that there is even yet an agreement in opinion as to the original character of the advertisements of A.D. 1566, whether they are to be taken, or not, as issued by the authority which was conferred upon the queen by the statute, and by virtue of which she was empowered to make alterations in the provisions of the rubric in the manner which was therein defined. The legal and historical conceptions cannot certainly be deemed to coincide; nor can the decisions of the ultimate Court of Appeal be said to meet with a general acceptance.

At the time when this vacancy drew near its close, in A.D. 1589, there was a prevailing excitement from the defeat of the Spanish Armada in the previous year, and a violent hostility against Roman Catholics. Immediately upon the victory, to satisfy the religious emotion of the people, or her own sense of duty, the queen had begun to put in execution the statutes which were enacted in the earlier part of her reign in reference to them. Following upon others[1] which were passed to restrain the queen's subjects in their due obedience, there was one of extreme severity[2] against Jesuits, seminary priests, and other disobedient persons, under the provisions of which any priest born within the dominions of the Crown, who should come from beyond sea, except from stress of weather, for a reasonable time, or who should remain three days without conforming and taking the re-

---

[1] 13 Eliz., c. ii., and 23 Eliz., c. i. [2] 27 Eliz., c. i.

quired oaths, should incur the penalty of high treason. This placed a formidable weapon in the hands of the queen, and Oxford presently witnessed the relentless cruelty with which it was capable of being used. In the year mentioned above, George Nicols, a native of Oxford, who had been resident abroad, came from the English college at Rheims, with Richard Yaxley, a priest and fellow-student, to execute his mission in the city and neighbourhood, with which he was familiar. They were shortly afterwards apprehended, in the middle of the night, at the St. Catherine's Wheel, where they lodged with Thomas Belson, a gentleman who had come for spiritual advice, and their servant Humphrey Prichard. Being brought before the vice-chancellor, they freely acknowledged that their mission was to preach the Catholic faith; and, after the fruitless visit of a divine who was sent to reason with them, they were notified to the Queen's Council. Upon this they were summoned to London, where Walsingham's argument was, "If you are a priest, then you are a traitor." They were then, on refusing submission, sent again to Oxford for their trial at the assizes, and, being found guilty, the four were hanged and quartered within the walls of the castle upon the 5th July. Their hostess at the St. Catherine's Wheel was subjected to the loss of her goods and perpetual imprisonment.[1]

After the see had remained vacant for a period of twenty-five years, it was thought fit that a bishop should be once more given to it. This was done at

---

[1] Bp. Challoner's "Martyrs to the Catholic Faith," 1577 1684, vol. i., p. 159. Edinb., 1878.

the instance of the secretary, Sir Thomas Walsingham, through the influence which he had with the queen. It is only in accordance with what is known of his policy and statesmanship that this should be stated to proceed from no desire to do justice to the claims of the diocese, but from "devotion to the leases that would yield good fines,"[1] and that upon this inducement "he recommended Dr. Underhill to the place, persuading him to take it in the way to a better."[2] Dr. John Underhill was a native of Oxford. He became the rector of Lincoln College, one of the vicars of Bampton, and the rector of Witney. He was appointed to the see at the close of the year A.D. 1589,[4] and held it to May, A.D. 1592, when he died, "in much discontent and poverty,"[5] without obtaining the preferment of which he had virtually received a promise. He was buried in the choir of the cathedral.[6] It is obvious to remark that this episcopate could have been productive of little good, for there is a note in the diocesan registers to the effect that there was no ordination during Bishop Underhill's occupation of the see, for he never came into the diocese after his acceptance of it.[7]

Although it may be considered to belong to the history of the University of Oxford rather than of the diocese, to show the state of feeling which prevailed, a

---

[1] Sir John Harington, "Brief View of the state of England," p. 148. Lond., 1653.     [2] *Ibid.*
[3] Wood, "Athen. Oxon.," *u. s.*, vol. i., col. 609.
[4] Rymer, *u. s.*, vol. xvi., p. 30.     [5] "Brief View," *u. s.*
[6] Wood, "Hist. and Ant. of Coll. and Halls," *u. s.*, p. 507.
[7] By favour of T. M. Davenport, Esq.

reference may be made to the method which was adopted in order to check the manifestation of sentiments opposed to the form of Protestantism which it was thought desirable to maintain. Dr. George Abbot, the subsequent Archbishop of Canterbury, was appointed vice-chancellor in A.D. 1600. In the same year he caused various superstitious pictures to be burned in the market-place at Oxford, and among them there was one in which the figure of the Father was placed over a crucifix, as ready to receive the spirit of the divine Son. It also occurred that certain young men were observed to kneel and beat their breasts before a painting of the Crucifixion in a window of Balliol College, which was removed by the master and fellows, and was replaced by one of plain glass at the instance of Abbot. In the same year a reference was made by the citizens of London to the two Universities respecting the cross in Cheapside, which had been taken down for repair; and he was able to refer to his action in the previous instance, which was accepted as a sufficient precedent for substituting a cross for the crucifix, which had previously been the characteristic form.[1] This in turn was destroyed during the Civil War.[2]

The sermons which Abbot preached in St. Mary's Church were deservedly well attended, and his influence in determining the state of religious feeling in Oxford was predominant. But it did not remain

---

[1] See Hook's " Lives of the Archbishops," *u. s.*, vol. v., p. 248. Lond., 1875.

[2] On the 2nd of May, 1643. Evelyn, "Diary," vol. i., p. 39. Lond., 1850.

unchallenged. A young man who was then only rising into notice, but who was to occupy a prominent place in the future, made use of his position in Oxford to vindicate the doctrine and constitution, and to maintain the perpetual visibility of the Church. William Laud's views were directly opposite to those which were entertained by the Calvinistic and Puritan party in Oxford, of which Abbot was the acknowledged head. For this he incurred his severe displeasure, from which he was never afterwards free. The resistance offered to him was further provoked by a sermon which he preached at St. Mary's Church in A.D. 1606, and for which he was submitted to questions by the Vice-Chancellor, Dr. Henry Airay, and subjected to the charge of Romish error by Abbot. No immediate result, however, ensued beyond an increase of the suspicion which attached to his proceedings.

Upon the death of Bishop Underhill, mentioned above, the see of Oxford had again been allowed to remain vacant, but not for so long a period as followed the death of Curwen. The same provision had also been made for the care of the diocese as on that occasion, for the Archbishop of Canterbury granted a licence to ordain clergy in the University and diocese to an Irish bishop in A.D. 1597, and to Dr. Henry Robinson, the Provost of Queen's College, and newly appointed Bishop of Carlisle, in the following year. The neglect of residence within his see in the past had proved, as was only to be expected, most prejudicial to its interests, and this was emphatically noticed while the facts were recent. A writer already

mentioned[1] could express it in such terms as these:—
"After Bishop Underhill was laid under the earth, I think, the see of Oxford would have been drowned in the sea of oblivion if his Majesty had not supplied it with the good father that now holdeth it, Dr. John Bridges, a man whose volumes in prose and verse give sufficient testimony of his understanding." Dr. Bridges was Dean of Salisbury at the time of his appointment to the bishopric, and his election was confirmed[2] in the January of A.D. 1604. Upon his accession he discovered that the see had suffered loss, and become impoverished during the previous reign; so much so, indeed, that the patrimony of the bishopric is described[3] as having been "much dilapidated and made a prey for the most part to Robert, Earl of Essex, to whom it proved miserably fatal." The Queen, indeed, had suffered the diocese to remain without a head for so long a period in all as forty-one years, which comprised nearly the whole of her reign, and had disposed of the revenues of it at her pleasure. The administration of the see on the part of the Crown had by this means been rendered subservient to reasons of state policy; and the will of the sovereign, irrespectively of the rights of the Church, had been held supreme.

The course which Elizabeth adopted was to take away the best of the estates which had been assigned under the letters patent of King Edward VI.,[4] and to

---

[1] Sir J. Harington, *u. s.*, p. 150.
[2] Rymer, *u. s.*, vol. xvi., p. 564.
[3] Wood, "Athen. Oxon.," *u. s.*, vol. i., col. 609.
[4] *Supra*, p. 96.

confer certain impropriations in their stead. It does not, however, appear that any immediate loss of income was incurred by this exchange; for, while some of the ancient property of the see was alienated from it, other estates were conferred in the place of it, which continued to belong to the see up to the recent changes effected by legislation.[1] The Rectory of Hook Norton, which formed a part of the exchange, and was so long the property of the Bishops of Oxford, has a history of its own of some interest.[2] It escaped from the spoliation of A.D. 1546 as being the subject of a long lease, but was granted by Edward VI. to the Duke of Northumberland; it was restored to the see by Queen Mary upon his attainder; it reverted to the ecclesiastical commissioners of England and Wales with the other estates of the bishopric, and has not been re-granted to it; but the right of presentation to the vicarage remains vested in the bishop. At this early period in the history of the see the general patronage of the bishop was very small. He had only the right of presentation to twelve vicarages or perpetual curacies, of little pecuniary value, with the nomination to the archdeaconry, which was referred to at an earlier stage.[3]

There is to notice in the episcopate of Dr. Bridges

---

[1] The estates which were taken were of the annual value of £193. 16s. 9½d., while those given instead were of the value of £201. 11s. 6d. These comprised the impropriations, or the prebends, of Stanton Harcourt, Cuddesdon, Culham, Banbury, Cropredy, Burford with Fulbrook, and Ambrosden. Browne Willis, *u. s.*, p. 417.

[2] See *Ibid.*   [3] *Supra*, pp. 31, 32.

the recurrence of an incident which proves the continuance of the penal statutes against the Roman Catholics in their full severity. George Napper, who had been a member of Corpus Christi College, had resided for a time in an English college abroad, where he had acted most courageously in his attendance upon the other students during a contagious epidemic, from which he also subsequently suffered. Returning to England, he had taken up his abode in Holywell Street, in Oxford, where he executed his mission as a seminary priest. He was seized at Kirtlington in the same county, and committed as a prisoner to Oxford Castle. Having been found guilty at the assizes of high treason under the statute,[1] he was reprieved. But, having subsequently converted a condemned felon to his own faith, he found public opinion excited against him; and he was summoned to appear before the vice-chancellor, to whom he did not hesitate to profess that he had "only done his duty." After a visit from the celebrated Dr. Hammond, to try his constancy by argument, he was hanged, drawn, and quartered in the castle-yard, on the 9th of November in A.D. 1610, as an example to others of his faith in Oxford. He behaved through his last trial with an exemplary calmness. "His limbs were placed on the four gates of the city, and his head on one of the towers of Christ Church or the steeple of the cathedral." The quarters, however, were secretly removed and buried in the old chapel of the preceptory of the Knights Templars at Sandford-on-Thames,

---

[1] *Supra*, p. 113.

His death under such a sentence, at an advanced age, and after a blameless life, was the cause of much regret.[1]

Unlike his immediate predecessor, Dr. Bridges resided within the limits of his diocese, and occupied a house at March Baldon, at which place he died in A.D. 1618. His two immediate successors were Dr. John Howson and Dr. Richard Corbet. The former of these, while he held the office of vice-chancellor at Oxford, was distinguished by his zeal in counteracting the efforts of the Puritan and Calvinistic party in the University, and by the sermons which he preached in St. Mary's Church, in order to prove that St. Peter had no "monarchical" authority over the rest of the apostles. After he became bishop, the sermons were published by the king's command, that he might escape the charge of favouring popery, to which he at that time was exposed.[2] When Archbishop Abbot was suspended from the exercise of his metropolitical functions by what can only be deemed an usurpation of ecclesiastical authority on the part of the king, Dr. Howson was one of the five bishops to whom a commission was granted, to act in his place within the province of Canterbury.

Dr. Corbet, the successor of Bishop Howson, was a determined opponent of the same party. But he was at the same time a man of a large mind, and was celebrated for his liberal and noble spirit, "being ever ready to express himself generous in public

[1] See Wood, "Hist. of the Univ.," *u. s.*, vol. ii., p. 105; and Bp. Challoner, *u. s.*, p. 31.
[2] Wood, "Athen. Oxon.," *u. s.*, vol. i., col. 481, 2.

designs."[1] After he had ceased to be Bishop of Oxford, he was a sufferer for his loyalty, and was deprived of the diocese of Ely to which he had been translated, and was condemned to an imprisonment of many years in the Tower of London.

The successor of Dr. Corbet in A.D. 1632, Dr. John Bancroft, became very soon after his appointment a great benefactor to the see. It has been mentioned,[2] that the Bishops of Oxford lost the palace at Gloucester Hall, which was originally granted for the residence of the bishop; and Dr. Bancroft at once took measures to supply this want. When the vicarage of Cuddesdon became vacant, having the right to present to it,[3] he collated himself, and caused it to be consolidated with the rectory, and annexed it in perpetuity to the bishopric.[4] He also obtained a grant of timber from the royal forest of Shotover, and built the new palace at the then large cost of £3,500. He procured also from King Charles I. an annual rent-charge of £100, secured on the forests of Shotover and Stowood. In A.D. 1635 he received Archbishop Laud at Cuddesdon, who had lent his assistance in furtherance of the plan, and who had paid a visit to Oxford as chancellor.[5] Dr. Bancroft lived in troublous times, and had not sufficient strength of mind to meet the difficulties which he had to encounter. For in A.D. 1640, when the Long Parlia-

---

[1] Wood, "Athen. Oxon.," *u. s.*, vol i., col. 511, 12.
[2] *Supra*, p. 97.
[3] Br. Willis, *u. s.*, vol. iii., p. 433; Wood, "Athen. Oxon.," vol. i., col. 634.
[4] Wood, "Hist. of the Univ.," *u. s.*, vol. ii., p. 412.

ment had shown an intention of opposing the bishops, and had made an attack upon their legislative and judicial functions, he was a victim to his own fears, as he had always been an enemy of the Puritans, and died with little or no apparent disease at his lodgings in Westminster in the February of the following year.[1]

In the early part of his episcopate, there occurred an incident in connexion with one of the churches in Oxford, which, of however little moment in itself, became of some public importance, as forming the substance of one of the charges which were brought against Archbishop Laud at his trial. As chancellor of the University, Laud had been able to do some kindness to his friend and chaplain, Morgan Owen, for whom he procured the degree of Doctor of Divinity. Soon after this, in A.D. 1637, Owen built a wall on the south side of the churchyard of the parish of St. Mary the Virgin, and erected a porch on the same side of the church, over the doorway of which he placed a statue of the Virgin and Child, as it may still be seen. Great offence was taken by the Puritan party, and it was alleged against Laud that it had been done with his connivance.[2] On the twelfth day of the trial the formal defence was made to the charge, in which it was maintained that no proof whatever had been adduced of any connexion of the archbishop with the act of Bishop Owen; for such he had now become by his preferment to the see of Llandaff.

The successor of Bishop Bancroft was Dr. Robert

[1] Wood, *u. s.*
[2] "History of the Troubles and Trial of Abp. Laud," ch. xxxiv. Lond., 1695.

Skinner, who was translated from the see of Bristol. At the time of his appointment to the diocese of Oxford, in A.D. 1641, the Long Parliament had already entered upon its course, which was to form so critical an epoch in the varied history of English liberty. Whatever may have been the fierceness of the struggle through which the Church and kingdom had to pass, it is possible to look back upon it now with a calmness of judgment which was impossible to the actors in the scene itself. Nor need we shrink from a thankful acknowledgment that the quietness which has so long endured, with so little interruption of the course of English history, is to be attributed to the fact that the great contest for freedom, with all its revolutionary incidents, occurred at so early a period in the national life. Bishop Skinner was among the earliest who experienced in their own persons the trials to which the Church was exposed. In the year which followed his accession to the see of Oxford, after the remonstrance of the House of Commons, the question of ecclesiastical reforms became the most pressing one, and the complete abolition of the episcopacy was proposed. As Bishop of Bristol, Robert Skinner was one of the thirteen bishops who were impeached at the bar of the House of Lords by order of the House of Commons for promulgating the constitution of the Convocation of A.D. 1640; but whose impeachment had been suffered to drop, in consequence, most probably, of the plea which was advanced in their behalf, that they were not liable to the penalties of a sentence of *præmunire* for anything that was then done.

Soon after this, when a bill for the exclusion of the bishops from Parliament had passed the House of Commons, but had not been favourably entertained by the Lords, much dissatisfaction was felt; and on one occasion the bishops met with violent usage on their way to take their seats, and with difficulty escaped more serious injury on preparing to leave the house after the sitting. In this emergency seven bishops, of whom the Bishop of Oxford was one, were induced, by Archbishop Williams of York, to adopt the unwise course of joining with him in a formal protest on behalf of all the bishops against the validity of any proceedings in Parliament from the 27th December, and for the future, so long as their constrained and involuntary absence should continue. Having been read by the House of Lords, the protest was favourably received by the king, to whom it offered a ready expedient for defeating any measures which he might dislike. It was also communicated to the House of Commons, as a matter in which both Houses were concerned. It was deemed to be an assumption of legislative authority, and the twelve prelates were impeached on a charge of high treason before the bar of the House of Lords. Their imprisonment followed, and "on January 30, in all the extremity of frost, at eight o'clock on a dark evening, they were voted to the Tower," as one of their number pathetically describes the circumstances of their committal.[1] After a time they obtained a temporary permission to "fly out of their cage," but

---

[1] Bp. Hall's "Account of Himself," in his "Contemplations; with Account prefixed," p. 35. Lond., 1824.

were subsequently recommitted until they were released with a bond for their reappearance, if it should be required.

On the termination of his imprisonment, which lasted for eighteen weeks, Bishop Skinner retired to the palace at Cuddesdon, where he remained up to 1643, after which he joined the garrison at Oxford, which was then held for the king, where his wife died in the June of A.D. 1644.[1] The village of Launton, the rectory of which he held with the see, having been appointed to it before he became Bishop of Bristol, became his home at a later period. And here he is reported to have lived in quiet submission to the necessities of the times.[2] But, in the midst of all his privations, he was not unmindful of the duties of his office, which he sought to fulfil at any risk, as he himself states in a letter which he addressed to the Bishop of London after the Restoration, in vindication of his conduct from the imputation of negligence during the usurpation to which he was subjected.[3]

The privations to which Bishop Skinner was exposed are to be traced to the ordinance of both Houses of Parliament in A.D. 1646, by which it was directed that from the 5th of September in that year, "the name, title, and dignity" of all the bishops in England and Wales should be "wholly abolished and taken away," while the estates of their sees were

---

[1] These dates are determined by extracts from parochial registers, for which the writer is indebted to Rev. J. C. Blomfield, R.D., Rector of Launton.

[2] Wood, "Athen. Oxon.," *u. s.*, vol. ii., col. 673.

[3] Tanner MSS., vol. xlviii., fol. 25, in the Bodleian Library.

to be vested in trustees, for the expenses of the war, into which, as was alleged, the kingdom had been mainly led by their adherents.[1] Bishop Skinner was eminently a sufferer from this invasion of his rights and property, for not only had he to suffer the immediate loss of his income in common with the rest, but he had the further embarrassment which was entailed by the debts which he had contracted at an earlier period. The punctual fulfilment of his official duties, to which allusion has been made, has rendered the name of Bishop Skinner memorable even above the rest of the bishops, at least in one respect. He was the principal, if not the only, bishop to whom the faithful in the several dioceses were accustomed to have recourse for a continual supply of clergy, when so great risk attended their ordination. But whether he continued to be the only bishop who conferred holy orders, as has been supposed,[2] or not, it is at least certain, from his own statement, that so many as three or four hundred priests received ordination from him during the time of prohibition, and not without the usual subscription to the articles and oath of allegiance, in any single instance. And for so doing he was prepared to incur the loss of "his books and his bed, having little else left." The benefit derived to the Church at large by his faithfulness in this respect was so great, that he was able to state that "Cornwall and York and all foreign counties, as well as the nearer, would bear witness for

---

[1] Scobell, "Collection of Acts and Ordinances," pt. 1, pp. 99, *sqq*. Lond., 1658.

[2] Wood, "Athen. Oxon.," *u. s.*, vol. ii., col. 673.

him" when he was accused. One of the clergy who was ordained by him, and that under some remarkable circumstances, was the celebrated Bishop Bull. In his early life he was a student of theology, and was led to desire ordination from " an unexceptionable hand;"[1] for which purpose he applied to Bishop Skinner in or about the year 1655, and was ordained by him both deacon and priest in one day, at the age of twenty-one. It was doubtless considered that the " present distress " would justify the departure from the provisions of the canon law in favour of one who was so well prepared for the office in the Church which he sought. Nor was Bishop Skinner less careful in administering the rite of Confirmation, while, as regards his constancy in preaching, it is added, that "he never failed one Sunday for fifteen years together." There could not have been a higher example of faithfulness than such a statement suggests. But it must be confessed, that there was another point as to which he was habitually guilty of what too much resembles a pious fraud, for "he took such care for all scriptures that were commanded to be read in churches, that constantly every clause that tended to the dishonour of the king or Church was branded with black lead; and this by his direction many did whom he dared to trust." In the perversion of men's minds there was thus shown a greater zeal for the Thirty-nine Articles and the oath of allegiance in their integrity than there was for the Bible itself.

An incident of the civil war must have filled the

[1] G. Nelson, " Life of Bp. Bull.," s. vi., pp. 25,*sqq*. Lond., 1714.

heart of Bishop Skinner with dismay. The diocese of Oxford, which had so long been without a palace for the bishop, and which had so recently been provided with one by the care of Bishop Bancroft,[1] was once more reduced to its former condition. The newly-erected palace of Cuddesdon, was burned down by Colonel Legge, the commander of the royal garrison in Oxford, for strategic reasons, that it might not be occupied by the forces of the Parliament, and made use of to his own disadvantage.[2] This occurred in the latter end of the year 1644. In the following year Sir Thomas Fairfax sat down before Oxford for fifteen days in the months of May and June, but was unable to force the lines which had been drawn round the city. In the following year preparation was made for a second siege; and, although Oxford might have been retained for some time longer, it was evident that it could not ultimately be preserved for the king. In the succeeding year, upon the escape of the king from Oxford on May the 5th, after he had expressed his willingness to make large concessions, but not to abandon the English Church, the articles of capitulation having been previously arranged, the city was surrendered by the garrison upon honourable terms on the 24th of June, in A.D. 1646. This naturally changed the whole aspect of things, and although a detailed account of the fortunes of the University, or of the city, is not within the limits of the present history, as this is the central town of the diocese, and is the seat of the deanery

[1] *Supra*, p. 122.
[2] Wood, "Athen. Oxon.," *n. s.*, vol. i., col. 634.

and of the cathedral, a brief mention of its condition at this time may not be out of place.

The general state of discipline in the University had declined, and greater luxury had prevailed since the royal visit in A.D. 1606. In addition to this, by the licence which attended the occupation of the city by the cavaliers, with the consequent interruption of the usual course of studies, the University had lost in a great degree its ancient and true character, as a place of religion and learning. And now a radical change was impending by which its rights of internal government were to be suspended, and its privileges controlled. The republican government would have little respect for the former grants of kings; nor would the sectarian influence spare this stronghold of the church. A parliamentary visitation was imminent.[1] After a preliminary sermon in order to prepare the way for their reception, the commissioners who were to exercise their new authority, which was to last, as it proved for eleven years, began their unwelcome office on the 24th of June in 1647. They met with a persistent opposition, nor was it always of a dignified, nor even of a courteous, character. But it was in vain; their opponents were removed on various pretences from the government of their respective colleges, and others more favourable to their interests

---

[1] The Register of the Visitors, A.D. 1647-58, is preserved in the Bodleian Library. It has been recently edited for the Camden Society, with an introduction, by Prof. Montagu Burrows, as the publication for 1881. It now constitutes the principal authority for the history of Oxford at the period under review, and has been consulted for this notice throughout.

were substituted in their place. A long list of names might be cited to show the hardships which were endured through this process. The cathedral, under its dean Dr. Samuel Fell, who was also the vice-chancellor, did not escape. He himself was deprived of his deanery, and his wife, who would not otherwise leave her home, was removed by rude hands in her chair, and placed in the quadrangle outside, nor was this without the attendant abuse which might be expected at such a scene. The canons, also, had to experience a similar loss of their preferments, and among them appear the familiar names of Dr. Henry Hammond, Edward Pococke, Robert Saunderson, and John Fell; and one at least of the students must be mentioned Barten Holliday, the Archdeacon of Oxford, a man of note in his time for learning of various kinds, and of whose poems one is still an accepted specimen of English verse.[1] Those who were expelled were not allowed to remain within five miles of Oxford;[2] Dr. Edward Reynolds was appointed the new dean, but was replaced in A.D. 1650 by the independent, Dr. John Owen, a man of courtly manners, of undaunted courage, and of high attainments, whose works, numerous as they are, are considered worthy to be reproduced in their full extent.[3]

---

[1] It is one of the pieces in Abp. Trench's "Household Book of English Poetry," p. 99. Lond., 1868.

[2] J. Walker, "Sufferings of the Clergy," pt. i., p. 138. Lond., 1714.

[3] An edition of Owen's collected works was published in twenty-one volumes, Lond., 1826; and a more recent one, Edinb., 1856.

By degrees a greater moderation prevailed within the University. The attention of the visitors was engaged in the reform of the same scandalous abuses, the colleges were permitted for the most part to elect their own officers, and there was an increasing restoration of confidence. Owen himself was a man of generous sentiments, and was not indisposed to make some allowance to the consciences of other men. The Directory for Public Worship had been appointed to supersede the use of the Book of Common Prayer at the beginning[1] of A.D. 1645 ; and, at a later period in the same year,[2] another ordinance had been passed for the more effectual carrying into practice of the Directory under the penalties which it enacted if its provisions should be transgressed. But Dr. Owen did not hesitate to allow so large an assemblage, that it consisted of three hundred persons, to meet for divine service according to the formularies of the Church of England within the precincts of his own college. Nor did Oxford fail to exhibit another instance of the same faithful adherence to the Prayer Book in the practice of the physician, Dr. Wallis, who, in his rooms in Christ Church first, and afterwards in a house opposite to Merton College, with Fell, Dolben and Allestree, was constant in the use of it.[3] The buildings of the

---

[1] On January 3rd, Scobell's "Collection of Acts and Ordinances," *u. s.*, pt. i., p. 75.

[2] *Ibid.*, p. 97.

[3] Wood, "Hist. of the Univ.," vol. ii., pt. ii., p. 612. A copy of the picture by Sir Peter Lely, in which the three friends are represented as engaged in the use of the Prayer Book, was

several colleges suffered no wanton injury. But an ordinance had been passed in A.D. 1643[1] for taking away all monuments of superstition and idolatry, with the exception of such as were funereal; and there was a further one for the same purpose in A.D. 1644.[2] It was in accordance with these that it was observed, on a visit to Oxford, in A.D. 1654, that the painted windows of the cathedral had been "much abused."[3] The college chapels, however, were so far uninjured, that it was found at New College "that the chapel was in its ancient garb, notwithstanding the scrupulosity of the times," and at Magdalene that "the chapel was likewise in pontifical order."[4]

It appeared at the same time that there was but little interference with the ancient customs of the University. The proctor "opened the act at St. Mary's, and the prevaricators their drollery." The two sermons were preached at the same church; and there was the creation of doctors by the ancient ceremonies of "cap, ring, kiss, and the rest." The Latin sermon was also preached. But, if the popular description is not overdrawn,[5] there was certainly in the religious sentiments which were prevalent at this time sufficient to make a young man shrink from exposing himself to the preliminary examination for

---

presented to Christ Church by one of the Dolben family, in A.D. 1804; and now is over the fireplace in the hall.

[1] On Aug. 28th, Scobell, *u. s.*, p. 533.
[2] On May 9th, *ibid.*, p. 69.
[3] Evelyn's "Diary," *u. s.*, vol. i., p. 292.
[4] *Ibid.*, vol. i., pp. 290–3.
[5] See "The Spectator," No. 494.

admission. For all this, however, the names of the eminent men who then made Oxford famous in every department of learning may be cited, to prove that there was no failure on the part of the University in performing its proper duties. In one respect there was a narrow escape from what would have been an irreparable loss. For no other reason than because the sum offered was insufficient, the negotiations between Cromwell and the Jews for the sale to them of the Bodleian Library, that it might be converted into a synagogue, were broken off.[1]

The general condition of the various parishes in the diocese may be estimated from the accounts which have been preserved of the sufferings which the parochial clergy in so many instances experienced.[2] There was, indeed, no confiscation of their estates, but they became personally involved in the penalties which were imposed for delinquency. An ordinance was passed in A.D. 1643 for sequestering the estates of notorious delinquents,[3] in which the clergy had a common share; while in their case there was a further provision for the receiving of evidence against any ministers who were "scandalous in doctrine," or who "deserted their cures." In the following year[4] the committee was appointed in like manner for carrying into execution the ordinance just mentioned, with all

---

[1] London News-letter of April 2, 1648, in T. Carte's "Collection of Letters," vol. i., pp. 275, 6. Lond., 1739.

[2] See in Walker's "Sufferings of the Clergy," *u. s.*

[3] On April 1st, Husbands' "Collection of Orders, &c.," p. 13. Lond., 1646.

[4] On June 27th, *ibid.*, p. 511.

other ordinances of the parliament in Buckinghamshire, Oxfordshire, and Berkshire. One of the committee for Oxfordshire was the Speaker, William Lenthall, the owner of an estate at Burford.[1] The number of the clergy who were expelled from their parochial cures or ecclesiastical preferment under this and other ordinances affecting them, appears to have comprised twenty-eight in Oxfordshire, exclusive of those who were sufferers in the University; twenty-three in Berkshire, with the addition of twenty-two who were members of the collegiate church of Windsor, and not also parochial clergy; and fifteen in Buckinghamshire, with the addition of the provost and two of the fellows of Eton College, the "ever memorable" John Hales and one other, both of whom were connected with Windsor, as well as with Eton, and are enumerated in the number for Berkshire.

It is needless to recount the various instances of the injuries inflicted upon the clergy in detail. But, as examples of the sufferings experienced in Oxfordshire, there may be mentioned these three. Dr. William O'Diss, the Vicar of Adderbury, became a marked man for his loyalty, and, finding it unsafe to remain in his parish, retired to Banbury, which

[1] W. Lenthall died at his house at Burford in A.D. 1662; having previously made a formal confession of "his own baseness and cowardice" in complying with the murderers of the king to Dr. Ralph Brideoak, the Rector of Witney, of whom he sought absolution. See Wood, "Athen. Oxon.," *n. s.*, vol. ii., col. 205. Dr. Brideoak's account is contained in a letter, which, with an explanation of the circumstances of its publication, is printed in the "Complete History of England," vol. iii., pp. 240, 1. Lond., 1706.

was held for the king. On a certain occasion, when he desired to return home, information of the intended visit having been obtained, he was watched and followed by some soldiers, and, being overtaken, was killed by a pistol shot.[1] Thomas Cole, the Rector of Lower Heyford, was "an honest, sober, blameless, good man,"[2] but his living was sequestered, and the subsequent history of it may serve to show the litle care which was taken in appointing others, to fill the vacancies which were made. His immediate successor, who had been an army preacher, was a man of a most abandoned life, and at last died a victim to his own profligacy. He was succeeded by one of the fellows of Corpus Christi College, to which the patronage belonged, but he had been created a fellow in contravention of the statutes of the college, and was himself disliked by the parishioners as being a contentious person. The remaining instance proves how little consideration would be shown to a scholar or a divine if he were opposed to the prevailing state of feeling. Thomas Lydiat, the Rector of Alkerton, was eminently such; but he was four times pillaged by the soldiers of the Parliament, and received severe personal injury. And this was for no other reason than that "he had denied them money, and had defended his books and papers, and afterwards, while a prisoner in Warwick Castle, had spoken much for the king and bishops."[3]

---

[1] Walker, *u. s.*, pt. ii., p. 323.    [2] *Ibid.*, p. 224.
[3] Wood, "Athen. Oxon.," *u. s.*, vol. ii., col. 45-7, where there is also a list of his works.

Marriage had become during the Commonwealth as a civil ceremony, and some of the parochial registers are found to contain entries of its performance according to the provisions of the act of A.D. 1656. But this was naturally distasteful to many persons, and it appears from the corresponding entries of the marriage of one Alexander Hautyn and Mary Prentice in the registers of Woodstock and of Deddington,[1] in the year A.D. 1657, that it was possible, under the protectorate, to escape from the semblance of such a marriage. It was a not uncommon practice to procure the presence of a minister at the time of the marriage, although he could contribute nothing to the actual performance of the marriage ceremony, which depended for its validity upon the simple declaration made by the parties before the Justice of the Peace.

Some extracts from the Act Books of the the archdeacon's and the bishop's courts, at the close of the sixteenth and in the seventeenth centuries, will illustrate their action and mode of procedure in respect of the cases which were brought under their cognisance.

An attendance at divine service in the parish church was a legal obligation,[2] and, strange as it may appear now, it was enforced by the ecclesiastical

---

[1] See E. Marshall's "Hist. of Woodstock," p. 217. Ox., 1875.

[2] See 5 & 6 Ed. VI., c. 3; and 1 Eliz., c. 2. A penalty of one shilling was imposed for non-attendance at the parish church, s. 14; and all persons having ecclesiastical jurisdiction were empowered to punish offenders by censures, ss. 15, 16.

courts. Accordingly, in A.D. 1596–7, Mrs. Lewes, of Iffley, was cited before the Bishops' Court as a popish recusant, and on the 12th of March, Mr. Brisburn, an officer of the court, appeared, and said:—

"That he had dealt with the said Mrs. Lewes concerning her recusancy, who now is contented to repair unto the church, but as yet not thoroughly satisfied in her conscience to receive the communion."

The next extract from the Act Book of the Consistory Court, of June 30, in A.D. 1666, shows a different reason for non-attendance, for it is a Quaker who is put upon his defence, Henry Alder, of Bladon. He is represented by his wife, who pleads his inability to attend the court from some extraordinary pressure of business, and comes to answer for him; which the judge allowing, she says:—

"That he goes under the name of a Quaker, and it is true he hath not gone to his parish church for the space of half-a-year last past; but she says that he will hereafter be more conformable to the laws of the Church of England."

The injunction is, that he "endeavour to be better informed touching the same, and go to his parish church to hear divine service therein between this and Michaelmas next."

It was a great impediment to agricultural work that there should be so many holidays as well as the Sundays, upon which it became unlawful to carry on such labour. It appears from the two following instances that the court was disposed to act with leniency, and admit with readiness the plea of necessity. Nicholas Redhead, of Iffley, is cited on this ground to appear in the Bishops' Court on the 13th of October in A.D. 1630, and denies :—

> "'That he or any of his servants did work upon Bartholomew Day;' but he confesseth, 'that he did steep an hay-rick on Sunday morning.' His confession is accepted; but "in regard that it was a case of necessity to preserve his hay,' he is dismissed with a monition."

In like manner Thomas Deeley, of Woodstock, is cited for the 21st of October in A.D. 1665, as appears from the Act Book of the Consistory Court :—

> "Charged, 'that he did work, or cause men to work on Michaelmas Day last;' when he answers, 'that in regard his house was down that day, he employed those men on work only for the preservation of his goods which lay exposed to the danger of the night and other casualties, but promiseth to do so no more.' He is 'dismissed.'"

It was not an unlikely occurrence that a man should resent the excommunication of his wife; and this happened, as appears from the Act Book of the Archdeacon's Court, in A.D. 1584, for on the 20th of October, Thomas Abbot, of Woodstock :—

> "Cited for brawling in the church, answers, 'that he disturbed the minister in the time of service, because there was an excommunication denounced against his wife.'"

There was not a more fertile subject of dispute, while the practice of collecting the tithes in substance prevailed, than the question whether any form of produce was in itself tithable, or whether any exemption could be established by an existing custom, which implied a presumption that there was an ancient composition overruling, in that instance, the common law. And no greater amount of minute and otherwise useless learning has fallen into desuetude, than that which was required for an argument upon such points; although, even in modern cases, some such questions may arise.[1] An important tithe case came before the Bishop's Court in A.D. 1630, the suit of Holliday, Archdeacon, *v.* Styles. The depositions were very numerous, and in the cumbrous form in which they were presented to the ecclesiastical court were made from time to time from the month of October to the following February, the question at issue being, whether the composition of a halfpenny each for sheep depastured in the parish of Iffley, and removed before shearing-time, could be maintained, or whether in such a case there should be an actual tithe of wool. The first witness deposed:—

> "That forty years since, of this deponent's certain knowledge, and long before that time, as he hath heard reported, there was in Iffley a custom, that such persons as have had and kept sheep within the parish, and have sold them away before they were clipped, should pay no tithe-wool to the parson of Iffley, or to his farmer-deputy; but in lieu thereof they have

[1] The liability of a railway station to pay tithe came before the Queen's Bench Division of the High Court of Justice for decision on December 12th, 1881.

always used to pay one halfpenny a-piece for every such sheep."

Another witness, however, who had been in the habit of collecting the tithes deposed, on the contrary :—

> "That he never heard that any stranger dwelling in Iffley, having sheep going and feeding in the parish, had any benefit of any custom of paying a halfpenny a sheep for sheep fed and driven from thence with the wool on their backs, and clipped in any other parish."

Such suits must have proved most detrimental to the peace of any parish, and in this instance, as several of the depositions were signed with a mark, there must have been an excitement throughout every class in it to the very lowest.

The Consistory Court also exercised its power in regulating the morals of the people. Accordingly on the 30th June in A.D. 1666, the office of the judge is promoted against William Locton, of Woodstock, who :—

> "Appears, charged 'that he is presented by the churchwardens of the said parish for keeping rude and disorderly company in his house upon a Sabbath-day, at night, being the tenth of May last past;' and answers and confesses, 'that it was so, and never before nor since, and promiseth for the future to be more careful that there be no such thing committed in his house.' He is 'dismissed with a monition.'"

On the same occasion Richard Faulkner, of Bladon, and Maria, his wife, are :—

"Cited: charged that he with his wife kept their child unbaptized near upon three weeks, and that it died unbaptized; answers and says, 'It is true, and that the only reason of his not procuring the child to be baptized was in expectation of one who had promised to be one of the godfathers to it; but he is sorry for this his offence.'"

The familiar excuse that a sponsor could not be procured was not allowed to prevail; and it was enjoined that he should do public penance in the parish church.

In A.D. 1633, another question respecting the time of harvest was brought before the Archdeacon's Court, which shows the infrequency of sermons in a country village. For Martin Royse, the Curate of Bladon, being cited, states :—

"That Dr. Prideaux, rector of Bladon, unto whom he is curate, doth preach himself constantly once in a quarter; and that there are sermons preached by the respondent for the most part every third week; but he confesseth that in harvest time there was not a sermon preached in harvest time, as is presented."

On another occasion, in A.D. 1670, Mr. Humphris, the Curate, is cited before a court held by the bishop at Combe, when he confesses :—

"That he doth not read prayers on Wednesdays and Fridays, nor wear the hood in time of officiating." He is admonished "that he do for the future read prayers on Wednesdays and Fridays, and wear the hood, and certify of it under the hands of the churchwardens on the eighth day of April next."

In A.D. 1662, after the death of the Archdeacon Barten Holliday, an application on the part of his son, who was a minor, and could not administer to his father's estate, nor act on his own behalf, was made to the Court of the archdeacon, and his half-brother on his mother's side was thereupon appointed his guardian. This case, however common and trivial in itself, may serve to recall the fact that matrimonial and testamentary causes were once adjudicated in the spiritual courts. It was just, it was even necessary, considering the amount of property which was involved in these suits, that the jurisdiction should be abolished, and the causes transferred to the civil courts, with their greater guarantees for judicial decisions. But from an historic point of view this tranference has another aspect. It presents a step in the series of legislative enactments by which the intimate union between Church and State has been gradually submitted to a process of disintegration.[1]

---

[1] The extracts cited above were supplied by the late Mr. W. H. Turner, the author of a paper on the "Ecclesiastical Court Books of the Dio. of Oxf.," in "Proceedings of the Oxf. Arch. and Hist. Soc.," *n. s.*, vol. iii., pp. 130-8, 1873-74.

## CHAPTER VI.

HISTORY OF THE DIOCESE. A.D. 1660-A.D. 1715.

The Restoration—Bishop Skinner—Act of Uniformity and its results—Bishop Fell—Magdalen College—Bishop Parker—Bishop Hall—Nonjurors—Bishop Talbot.

BISHOP SKINNER continued to reside at Launton up to the close of the usurpation. Upon the restoration of Charles II., on the 29th of May, in A.D. 1660, he resumed possession of his see. He was also appointed one of the royal commissioners for visiting the University and reinstating it in its former condition.[1] He appears to have taken an active part in supplying what must have been one of the most pressing wants of the Church, for, " after his Majesty's return, one hundred and three did at once take holy orders from him in the abbey church at Westminster."[2] The large number ordained by him at this time, together with those whom he ordained before and afterwards, was such as to give occasion to the remark which was made at his death, " that he had sent more labourers into the vineyard than all the brethren he had left behind him had done."[3]

A natural consequence of the king's resumption of his prerogative, which included the nomination to

---

[1] Wood, "Ath. Oxon.," *u. s.*, vol. ii., col. 673.
[2] *Ibid.*     [3] *Ibid.*

vacant sees, was an expectation on the part of the bishops, who had remained faithful to the royal cause, that they would be translated to higher, or at least to more valuable, bishoprics. Not unlike the rest of his brethren in this respect, Bishop Skinner desired translation to a richer see than Oxford, the revenues of which were not large. A prejudice, however, existed to his disfavour, which arose from the action of "a great and fatal enemy at Court, who maligned him because of his submission in part to usurpers."[1] Amid the circumstances of the time, this was not an unreasonable charge, considering the peace and quiet which the bishop had enjoyed in his retirement. Bishop Skinner, however, was not disposed to submit to it, and addressed Gilbert Sheldon, who was then Bishop of London, in the letter to which allusion has been made.[2] And he certainly was able to vindicate himself at once from the accusation of unfaithfulness in the ordination of clergy. But there was another charge of an entirely different character. His subscription in aid of the king's necessities was considered to have been insufficient, and in defence he urges this plea: "I was not able to present as others did, because I had not wherewithal. For I was deep in debt before I was settled at Bristol, and came thence, near three hundred pounds in debt; yet the king had what I could give him—my horses and thirty pounds, which was all the money I received till the king's return." The republican exactions were not the only causes of distress to which the bishops were

---

[1] Wood, "Ath. Oxon.," *n. s.*, vol. ii., col. 673.
[2] *Supra*, p. 126. The letter is dated June 26th, 1662.

exposed. There were moral, if not legal, claims which they could not afford to disallow. The plea was doubtless accepted as a valid one, for in the following year, very probably through his friend, who had now become Archbishop of Canterbury,[1] Bishop Skinner was translated to the see of Worcester.

During the time of Bishop Skinner's occupation of the see of Oxford, an important event had taken place, affecting the interests of the clergy of several of the diocese who had become incumbents during the Commonwealth.

The Act of Uniformity [2] was passed in A.D. 1662, and it was appointed to take effect from the Feast of St. Bartholomew, in the same year. Its provisions are naturally subject to a comparison with the terms of the king's declaration from the Court at Breda " to all his loving subjects," [3] which contained an assurance that there should be " a liberty to tender consciences, and that no man should be disquieted or called in question for differences of opinion in matters of religion, which do not disturb the peace of the kingdom ; " and the assurance was repeated in the declaration from Whitehall.[4] It was to be expected that the nice and difficult questions respecting the resettlement of the parochial clergy in their cures would be determined with a desire to give relief to "tender consciences," and to impose no unnecessary conditions. The greatest difficulty would arise

---

[1] Bp. Sheldon was translated from London to Canterbury on July 14, 1663 ; and Bp. Skinner from Oxford to Worcester on October 12th, in the same year.   [2] 13 & 14 Car. II.

[3] On April 14th, 1660.   [4] On October 25th, 1660.

from the fact that many of the intruding ministers had not received episcopal ordination.[1] But independently of this there were provisions inserted which cannot be considered essential to the well-being of the Church, for some of them have been repealed as inconsistent with the principles of toleration which have subsequently prevailed.[2] And the actual result was that more than two thousand ministers, most of whom, it must be said, were non-episcopally ordained, were ejected from their cures. In the three counties which form the present diocese of Oxford, in addition to those who were expelled from the University, there were in Oxfordshire twenty-four, in Berkshire twenty-three, and in Buckinghamshire twenty-four.[3] No provision was made for their support, as had previously been for those who suffered under the Parliament by the reservation of a fifth part of the income of their respective benefices to their use; although, for insufficient reasons, this proved to be too frequently withheld. In Oxford, the learned Theophilus Gale and the learned and excellent John Conant were among the sufferers. Some were found to reconsider

---

[1] The question, whether such ordinations were to be considered imperfect or invalid in extreme cases, was discussed by the royal commission on the revision of the Book of Common Prayer. See "Copy of the alterations in C. P. prepared in A.D. 1689, pp. 102-6, printed by order of the House of Commons, 1854."

[2] For a list of the repealing statutes see note by Dr. I. Brunel, "The Prayer Book Interleaved," p. xxvii. Camb., 1873.

[3] For these numbers see Calamy, "Life of Baxter," vol. ii., pp. 95, 504, 540. Lond., 1713.

their position; and four in Oxfordshire, seven in Berkshire, and one in Buckinghamshire, were subsequently found to conform to the statute, and are not therefore included in the numbers mentioned above. Dr. John Owen, the intruding dean of Christ Church, who, on the appointment of Richard Cromwell as chancellor, had been removed from the vice-chancellorship [1] through the opposition of the Presbyterians, and subsequently also from his deanery, became the minister of a large congregation in London.[2] The Act of Uniformity was followed by the Conventicle Act [3] and the Five Mile Act,[4] and by the effect of these statutes a more severe religious persecution was in reality carried on than had been in the time of the Commonwealth.[5]

In the June of A.D. 1663, a few months before Bishop Skinner left the diocese, a funeral of great magnificence took place in Oxford. It was the expressed wish of Archbishop Juxon, who had held the rectory of Somerton, in Oxfordshire, and had been president of St. John College, that he should be buried in the college chapel, but without unnecessary pomp and ceremonial. The former part of his will was complied with, but there was a studied neglect of the latter part, for his body was laid in state in the convocation house. Dr. Robert South, the public orator, made an oration in his praise; and there

---

[1] Wood, "Ath. Oxon.," *u. s.*, vol. ii., col. 557.
[2] Calamy, *u. s.*, p. 54.  [3] 16 Car. II., c. 4.
[4] 17 Car. II., c. 2.
[5] For this statement and the proof see T. P. Taswell-Langmead, "English Constitutional History," p. 638. Lond., 1880.

was a long procession attended with so much of the heralds' ceremony as was not prevented by the violent storm which was raging at the time. A similar wish had been mentioned by Archbishop Laud, who also had been president of the same college, and his remains were brought from the church of All Hallows, Barking, where they were interred, and buried near the grave of the founder of the college, in the same month.[1]

Upon the translation of Bishop Skinner to the see of Worcester, Dr. William Paul, the Dean of Lichfield, who had been one of the chaplains of King Charles I., and had suffered in his cause, was made bishop.[2] He was possessed of private means, and was at the same time a man of practical skill; and, accordingly, Archbishop Sheldon interested himself in his appointment, in order that the restoration of the palace at Cuddesdon, which had been destroyed by Colonel Legge,[3] might be secured. He was therefore allowed to retain the rectory of Brightwell, and hold it with the bishopric. Sensible of the obligation thus imposed upon him, the bishop at once provided timber for the work; but he died before it could be further carried on, in A.D. 1665.

The three succeeding bishops are not remarkable for any events occurring in connexion with their episcopate, but the last two have gained a place in history from other causes Nathanael Crewe, as Bishop of Durham, and Henry Compton, as Bishop

---

[1] See Wood, "Coll. and Halls," *u. s.*, p. 545, notes.
[2] Wood, "Athen. Oxon.," *u. s.*, col. 666.
[3] *Supra*, p. 129.

of London. These were followed by Dr. John Fell, the dean of Christ Church upon the Restoration. His improvement of the discipline of his college, and restoration and enlargement of its buildings, as well as his learning and piety, entitle him to be esteemed one of the most illustrious deans. During his tenure of the office, however, he was not superior to the temptation of yielding to the influence of the Court; for, at the instance of the king, he deprived John Locke of his studentship, and severed his connexion with Oxford in A.D. 1682. But he did not, with all his efforts for the good of the college, which have just been mentioned, obtain the favour of his contemporaries, and the cause of his "well-known unpopularity has remained a mystery"[1] to the present time. The energy of Fell was not less conspicuous in effecting a reformation of the habits of University life while he held the office of vice-chancellor.

Upon Dean Fell's accession to the bishopric of Oxford in A.D. 1676, the rebuilding of Cuddesdon palace, which had been interrupted, was again taken in hand, and it was after no long interval rendered available for the residence of the bishop. Bishop Fell was no less desirous of promoting the interests of his diocese than he had been to improve the state of the University and of his own college. His contribution of a large sum for the repairs of the old church at Banbury, destroyed in less propitious times, is an evidence of this; and so, too, is the endowment for performance of the daily morning and evening service

[1] Locke's "Thoughts on Education," edited by R. H. Quick, pref., p. 35. Camb., 1880.

which he attached to St. Martin's Church in Oxford, but which has in recent times been transferred to St. Mary Magdalene Church. The altered state of observance in this respect is not inaptly illustrated by a reference to this provision. It would seem almost incredible at the present time that a town of the size and importance of Oxford could require a special benefaction to secure the opportunity of daily worship in one of its parishes. The administration of the diocese by Bishop Fell was described by one of his clergy in these terms: "He was an excellent judge of men and merits, an exemplary supervisor of the clergy, a diligent assertor of the rights of the Church;" while another spoke with equal commendation of a different phase of his character, observing that "he was so eminent in the most lovely and especial duty of Christianity that he became an almoner for the charity of others, and had frequently considerable sums put into his hands, to be disposed of by him as he thought fit."[1] His fidelity to the king was evinced by the care which he took in raising a troop while he was vice-chancellor, and his faithfulness to the Church of England by his constant use of the Book of Common Prayer during its suppression, which was noticed before.[2] Nor, indeed, was Bishop Fell less distinguished in literature. Besides his well-known "Life of Hammond," he published or edited several works,[3] the

[1] See Br. Willis, "Survey of Cathedrals," *u. s.*, vol. iii., p. 435.     [2] *Supra*, p. 132, 3.
[3] A list is given by Wood, "Athen. Oxon.," *u. s.*, col. 603, 4.

most important of which was an edition of the Greek Testament,[1] which prepared the way for the larger and more complete edition of John Mill,[2] which indeed was undertaken at his advice, and was printed in part at his expense. This supplied the text in common use for a long course of years, and was uniformly adopted at the University press, until its traditions were interrupted by the publication of the text of the revisers in A.D. 1881. Bishop Fell died in the July of A.D. 1686, and was buried in the cathedral. The diocese which he administered with such care and ability could scarcely have possessed greater advantages than it enjoyed under the episcopate of such a man as John Fell.

A darker period in the history of the diocese, but relieved by the noble conduct of one of the colleges in the University, succeeds the episcopate of Bishop Fell. It was the purpose of King James II. to make use of the royal supremacy, which he inherited, in such a manner as to defeat the very object with which it had been originally assumed, and to reinstate the authority of the pope. And Oxford was destined to be the scene of a determined attack upon religious liberty. A combination of circumstances appeared to favour the attempt. Soon after the king's accession, Obadiah Walker, the Master of University College, declared himself a Romanist, and caused an oratory to be constructed in his college, in which a resident Jesuit priest

---

[1] Oxon., 1675.
[2] Oxon., 1707, reprinted at Leipsic, with additions by Lud. Kuster, in 1709 and 1723.

officiated as chaplain, according to the Roman Catholic rite; and for this an authoritative permission was obtained, so that he could not be deprived. Thomas Massey, who was neither of sufficient age, nor weight, nor learning, obtained an offer of the deanery of Christ Church, which was vacant by the death of Bishop Fell, who was also dean, through the instrumentality of Walker; and did not hesitate to renounce his Churchmanship on bended knees before the king, and to pronounce himself a Romanist; upon which he received the letters patent from the king, and was installed in the cathedral on the 19th December in A.D. 1686. He also prepared a chapel in his own college for the performance of the Romish services.[1] The bishopric of Oxford was given to Samuel Parker, a parasite of the king, who was distinguished during his residence in Oxford in early life by his strictness of demeanour as a presbyterian; who afterwards became in all appearance a true son of the Church of England;[2] who still called himself a Protestant, when his religious sympathies evidently inclined towards Rome, but who certainly was not a Romanist from the circumstances attending his death.[3] The presidentship of Magdalen College was also vacant in consequence of the death of Dr. Henry Clark,

---

[1] Wood, "Fasti Oxon.," *u. s.*, vol. ii., col. 870.

[2] Wood, "Athen. Oxon.," vol. ii., col. 616-8.

[3] See Bp. Burnet's "History of the Reign of James II.;" edited with illustrative notes by Dr. Routh, p. 261 note, c. Oxf, 1852. This edition forms a principal authority for the history of Magdalen College at this time.

which occurred in March, A.D. 1687. And this determined the method of the attack, which in its result has added so much to the fame of the college, and has made illustrious for the defence of his rights and privileges the president, who at a later time became the bishop of the diocese, John Hough.

The two Universities at this time occupied a position of the highest esteem and influence. The king had already failed in an attempt to obtain a degree in arts at Cambridge for a Benedictine monk, and had not received with favour the proposal that he should found a college of his own at Oxford; and he now sought to promote his designs by securing the nomination of one of his partisans as the new president of Magdalen College. The statutes provided that the election should be made by the fellows of the college in the manner specified; but a mandamus was sent in order that the office might be conferred upon Anthony Farmer, who possessed no statutable qualification, and was a man of infamous life. The mandamus was in itself illegal, and there was not accordingly the mere question of fitness. The fellows upon this, remembering their oath to obey the statutes of their college, proceeded to the election of their president in the usual manner on the 15th of April, and made choice of one of their number, John Hough, who in addition to his other qualifications was esteemed a man of great firmness and constancy, —a character which his subsequent conduct did not falsify. The election was confirmed by the visitor, and the matter was so far settled. The office was no longer vacant, and the college was justified in assuming an attitude of resolute opposition to the invasion of its rights. But the question was not to rest here.

In the end of the summer the king made a more lengthened progress than was customary with him, and in the course of it arrived at Bath. Leaving the queen here he proceeded to Oxford with the Quaker William Penn, passing over the scene of the battle of Edge Hill on the way, however inattentive to the lessons of the past which its memories might have taught, and resting at the royal seat of Woodstock Park. During his short stay in it he exercised, as he had at Bath,[1] the privilege of the royal touch; and copies of the certificates which were given to ensure compliance with the condition that no person should be presented a second time, are still in existence. Two are subjoined.

"September the 2d 1687.

Granted then by the Minister and Churwardens a certificate testifying, that Sarah the daughter of Robert Pullin had not to the best of their knowledge been touch'd at any time before by His Majesty for the disease commonly called ye Kings evill.

Granted at the same time two other certificates testifying that Mary the daughter of John Lowick alias Oliver, and that Margaret the daughter of Joan Galy widow had not to the best of their knowledge been touch'd at any

---

[1] Life of Bp. Ken., by a Layman [J. L. Anderdon], pt. i., pp. 377, 382. Lond., 1853.

time before by His Majesty for the disease commonly called the Kings evill."[1]

The king reached Oxford early in the month of September, and took up his abode at the deanery, where there was a chapel which he could attend for his own form of service. The fellows of Magdalen were summoned to attend the king. They were treated with insolence, but remained unshaken, and he was compelled to return to Bath, oppressed by the sense of his defeat. The Quaker Penn was employed to tempt Hough with the prospect of succeeding to the bishopric on the death of Parker, who was in ill health, but equally without success; such a proposal had no inducement for those whose only demand was justice. As a last resource a special commission was directed to the Lord Chief Justice of the King's Bench and other commissioners, that they might exercise their power as visitors, for which purpose they came to Oxford, and held their session in the hall of Magdalen College on the 21st of October. A dispute ensued, but the college remained unmoved. The president made a dignified protest, and appealed to "the King in the Courts of Justice." Hough, however, was literally hissed at; and, because he would not deliver the keys of his house, the doors were broken open, and Parker was put in possession. Parker, be it observed, was the bishop of the diocese,

---

[1] From the parish book of St. Mary's, Woodstock. There are certificates also for an earlier visit in June of the same year; but there are no others after this date. This extract is by favour of the Rev. A. Majendie, Rector of Bladon-with-Woodstock.

whose religious interests he sacrificed to the will of the king. These proceedings concerned the nation no less than the college and the University, and, indeed, were the cause that "the Church party and the clergy sent over a very pressing remonstrance to the Prince of Orange, that he would interpose and espouse the concerns of the Church;"[1] so closely are the civil and religious liberties of the kingdom connected with each other.

After this the fellows and demies, who were still recalcitrant, were ejected, but Parker's tenure of his office was very brief, for he died in his lodgings within the college on the 20th of March in the following year.[2] His successor was Timothy Hall, who was one of the four clergy who, in the numerous parishes of London, alone permitted the declaration of indulgence to be read in their churches. The see of Oxford was the reward for his mean compliance with the king's injunction. He was consecrated on the 7th of October; but, when he came to take possession of the bishopric and to visit the palace, he was received with marked disrespect, for the dean and canons refused to perform the ceremony of installation, the vice-chancellor and heads of colleges took no notice, and the graduates of the University declined to receive holy orders from him.[3]

The office of president became vacant in Magdalen

---

[1] Bp. Burnet, *u. s.*, p. 181.
[2] Bp. Parker was the author of several works, which are enumerated by Wood, "Athen. Oxon.," *u. s.*, col. 616-21.
[3] Wood, "Athen. Oxon.," *u. s.*, col. 686.

College by the death of Parker, and in respect of this appointment also the king showed a similar disregard of the feelings of others. A most uncongenial successor was forced upon the college; for Bonaventure Giffard, a doctor of the Sorbonne, and Bishop of Madaura, in Africa, who had been one of the four papal vicars in England, was nominated as president[1] in contravention of the statutes which provided for the election. The natural result of this was, that the use of the English Prayer Book was discontinued in the chapel, and the Roman form of service instituted in its place. This, however, was not to continue long; and even before the actual termination of the king's reign the state of the previous settlement of the affairs of the college was changed. Among the concessions which were made by the king upon the eve of the revolution, was the dissolution of the Court of High Commission, through the action of which the president and fellows of Magdalen College had been ejected. And this was followed by a reference of the case of the college to the Bishop of Winchester, who was the visitor, and the readmission of the members who had been expelled to their former place. The day of their restoration was observed to be the anniversary of their expulsion.

The diocese must have been placed in a difficult position, in regard to the supply of clergy, by the refusal on the part of the graduates of the University to be ordained by Bishop Hall, as well as by his own departure from the diocese upon the abdication of

---

[1] Bp. Burnet, *u. s.*, p. 262.

the king. In this emergency recourse was had to a bishop who was in Oxford at the time of Whitsuntide in A.D. 1689. And Baptist Levinz, the Bishop of the Isle of Man, ordained on that occasion as many as eighty-four persons in Magdalen College chapel on the 29th of May.[1] Bishop Hall did not long survive. He died in great poverty at Hackney, in the spring of A.D. 1690.

But not only had the bishopric lost its head—the deanery had also become vacant by the departure of its occupant from a similar cause. For Thomas Massey, the popish dean, had retired to London, and had then gone to Paris, through apprehension of popular violence in consequence of his being a Roman Catholic.[2] His successor was the celebrated Henry Aldrich, who was appointed in A.D. 1689, and who is stated in the letters patent to have succeeded upon the death of Bishop Fell,[3] as if no notice were to be taken of the intruder, whose appointment would be null and void of itself. Like his predecessor Fell, Dean Aldrich was a man of high cultivation,[4] an excellent governor of his college, and a man of architectural taste and skill. The buildings of his college were indebted to him for much im-

---

[1] Wood, "Athen. Oxon.," *u. s.*
[2] Wood, "Fasti Oxon.," *u. s.*, vol. ii., p. 870.
[3] Wood, "Coll. and Halls," *u. s.*, p. 441, n. 116.
[4] His "Artis Logicae Compendium" was long in use, but has been superseded as a text book. His round "Hark! The bonny Christ Church bells" is a popular one still. The correct version is given in "Notes and Queries," 2nd Ser., vol. i., p. 260, with an explanation at 3rd Ser., vol. x., p. 271.

provement, and the church of All Saints in Oxford was built from his designs.[1] With the Regius Professor of divinity in Oxford, the "double-faced Janus," and the Margaret Professor, Dr. John Hall, he was a member of the Royal Commission for the Revision of the Book of Common Prayer in A.D. 1689. Two of these, however, Dean Aldrich and Dr. Jane, discontinued their attendance after the third session.[2] The alterations which were proposed were extensive, and Convocation disapproved of the scheme of revision; the Prayer Book, therefore, remained unchanged.[3]

Before the episcopate of Bishop Hall closed, the question of the lawfulness of taking the oath of allegiance to William and Mary became an urgent one, and was discussed with much force of argument on either side. The 1st of August in A.D. 1689 was fixed by Act of Parliament as the day upon which every clergyman possessed of a benefice, and every one holding office in the Universities should take the oath under the penalty of immediate suspension. But this was to be followed by deprivation on the 1st February in the following year, if the refusal remained at that time. When the day arrived, it was found in many instances that it was so, and most of the clergy who thus became subject to the penalty resigned their livings quietly. This could not but

---

[1] In A.D. 1708. Ingram, "Memorials of Oxf.," vol. iii. Parish of All Saints, p. 11.

[2] It is so stated in the Diary of the proceedings of the Commissioners, "Report," *u. s.*, p. 108.

[3] See *supra*, p. 147.

entail, in some cases, a loss of home and of support, which closely resembled that which had twice occurred in the earlier part of the same century. Eight bishops and an approximate number of four hundred of the clergy followed the example of the Primate Sancroft. In a list of nonjurors, which has been preserved,[1] the names of three clergymen in the archdeaconry of Oxford, of five—with two schoolmasters in Berkshire, and of four in Buckinghamshire, are enumerated. Thirty-one names occur of clerical and lay nonjurors in the University, accompanied by the statement that there were several others. Among these may be noticed the name of Henry Dodwell, the Camden professor of ancient history, who is also known for his speculations on conditional immortality;[2] and who retired to Cookham, and subsequently to Shottesbrook, at which last he died, after having promoted the reunion of the dissentients with the rest of the English Church upon the death of Lloyd, the last of the non-juring bishops who insisted upon his rights. To one of the names in Berkshire, and to one in Oxfordshire, the description of a "penitent" is attached, which implies an accession to the society of the nonjurors after a previous compliance with the principles of the existing government, this being

---

[1] See "A list of several of the clergy and others in the Universities of Oxford and Cambridge who were thought not to qualify themselves after the Revolution." Appendix vi., Kettlewell's "Works with Life," vol. ii. Lond., 1719.

[2] See "An Epistolary discourse, proving from the Scriptures, and first Fathers, that the Soul is a principle naturally mortal;" by Hen. Dodwell. Lond., 1706.

esteemed a sinful compliance. There was a solemn form of reconciliation and admission to meet such a condition in which the penitent is described as uniting himself to "the faithful remnant of the Britannic churches."[1] One of the steps which led to final reconciliation of the two bodies took place in a village within the present diocese, but in the county of Berkshire, when Dodwell resorted to his parish church at Shottesbrook, upon the occasion mentioned above,[2] and joined in a correspondence with Robert Nelson upon his conduct. Trifling an act as this may appear to be in itself, it was considered to advance the cause of reunion. There was, indeed, an attempt to perpetuate the disagreement by effecting a union with the Greek Church; but it completely failed, and the separation gradually died away, although individual instances of adherence to the principles of the nonjurors were to be met with for a lengthened period.

From the first Oxford had been a favourite place of resort to the nonjurors, from the opportunities of study which were offered in the various libraries which it possessed. These were rendered the more necessary by the loss of books which so many had sustained in common with their other privations. The nonjurors who came to Oxford with such an

---

[1] See Kettlewell's "Works," *u. s.*, Appendix xiii.

[2] *Supra*, p. 161; T. Hearne's "Diary," at A.D. 1710, vol. i., pp. 186, 7. Lond., 1869. Lord Macaulay terms Hen. Dodwell "the most learned man" of the Jacobite party ("Hist. of Engl.," ch. xii., vol. iv., p. 226), but points out his strange theories (ch. xiv., vol. v., pp. 87, 8. Lond., 1858).

object would be in the best position for maintaining a high character and a freedom from dependence on others for their support. They would not be liable to the imputations to which many others were subjected on account of their servile adherence to the patrons to whom they were indebted for the means of life, and in whose households they were but too content to occupy an unworthy, if not a menial, place. John Wesley, indeed, in reference to the great resort of the nonjurors to Oxford, was led upon one occasion to remark, that it "was paved with the skulls of Jacobites,"[1] so many remained to find their last home within its walls. Among the residents with such higher principles may be mentioned Samuel Parker, the son of the former bishop of that name, who was a writer on ecclesiastical subjects,[2] and whose son, as a bookseller, established the firm in the Turl Street, Oxford, which is still represented by members of his family, who have inherited the same love of letters, as well as the same name. Nor must Richard Rawlinson, the antiquary and benefactor to the Bodleian Library, be omitted, who was consecrated a bishop for the nonjurors, but studiously avoided an appearance of being other than a layman in his dress and manner;[3] to whom must be added a man of congenial spirit—Thomas Hearne, who, in his respect for the value of ancient documents

---

[1] T. Lathbury, "History of the Nonjurors," p. 375. Lond., 1847.

[2] Information verified by favour of James Parker, Esq.

[3] R. Rawlinson was consecrated in A.D. 1728. W. D. Macray, "Annals of the Bodleian Lib.," p. 168. Oxf., 1868.

as the authorities for history, was the precursor of the best school of English historians.

Upon the death of Bishop Hall, at the time when so many of the English sees were receiving new bishops, the prelate selected for the diocese of Oxford was Dr. Hough, the ejected and reinstated president of Magdalen College; and he was consecrated upon the 11th of May in A.D. 1600, being allowed at the same time to retain the presidentship.[1] This appointment was a suitable reward for his fidelity and constancy in the trying circumstances in which he had been placed. And, indeed, it was the subject of remark that, in the choice of bishops for the various sees, "men of moderate principles and calm tempers were sought for;"[2] and that the course adopted had the effect of "removing the jealousies that some other steps the king had made were beginning to raise." After remaining in the see of Oxford for nine years, Bishop Hough was translated to the diocese of Lichfield, and was succeeded at Oxford by John Talbot, the Dean of Worcester.

Bishop Talbot was not a man of eminence, either in the Church or in the State, but he had his opinion upon public questions. He supported the Union with Scotland in his place in Parliament in A.D. 1707, this being a subject which was not discussed without reference to the supposed interests of the Church, for it was alleged that it "was a real danger the Church ran into, when so many votes of

---

[1] Wood, "Fasti Oxon.," *u. s.*, col. 890.
[2] Bp. Burnet, "History of his own Time," vol. iv., p. 132. Ox., 1823.

persons tied to Presbytery were admitted to a share in the legislature."[1] And, again, upon the impeachment of Sacheverel for his sermon on the 5th of November, when his case was brought up to the House of Lords, he was one of the four bishops who spoke against him.[2] Nor did he escape religious controversy; for one of his charges was attacked by Laurence, the persistent opponent of the validity of lay, or heretical, or schismatical baptism.[3] He was translated to the bishopric of Salisbury.

Francis Atterbury, who occupies so prominent a place in the history of the English Church at this period, was dean of Christ Church for a short time before his appointment to the bishopric of Rochester; but it was at this later time that he was distinguished by the part which he took in public life.

[1] Bp. Burnet, "History of his own Time," vol. v., p. 285. Ox., 1823.
[2] *Ibid.*, p. 435.
[3] "The Bishop of Oxford's Charge Considered;" by R. Laurence. Lond., 1712.

## CHAPTER VII.

HISTORY OF THE DIOCESE. A.D. 1715-A.D. 1882.

Bishop Potter — Bangorian Controversy — John Wesley and Methodism in Oxford — Succeeding Bishops — Bishop Lloyd — Bishop Bagot — Addition of Berks — Bishop Wilberforce — Addition of Bucks — Wilberforce College — Bishop Mackarness.

A PERIOD of fresh religious controversy was approaching at the time when Dr. John Potter succeeded to the bishopric of Oxford, in A.D. 1715. He was one of the queen's chaplains, and was supported by the influence of the Duke of Marlborough; but his varied and extensive learning was a better recommendation. An early work on Grecian Antiquities continued for more than a century to be a standard authority. His "Discourse on Church Government" long retained a high place, as containing an able exposition of the constitution, rights, and government, of the early Church, and a vindication of the principles of the Church of England in respect of this as in accordance with those of the first three centuries, and of the age succeeding to these. The edition of the works of Clement of Alexandria, which was published at Oxford in the same year in which he became bishop, is still the best and most complete. The danger which imperilled the soundness of doctrine within the Church at this time arose from the opinions which Dr. Hoadly, the Bishop of Bangor, had promulgated, and out of which the Bangorian controversy sprang. Bishop Hoadly published a work, entitled "A Preservative against the Principles and Practices of the Nonjurors," and preached his celebrated sermon before the king on the 31st of March in A.D. 1717, on "the Nature of the Kingdom of the Church of Christ." [1] In these he exhibits the type of a latitudinarian prelate. And in common with other opponents Bishop Potter engaged in controversy with him. He warned his clergy against the errors of Hoadly in his charge, and the bishop in reply defended himself. This required of Bishop Potter a vindication on his part, in which he also took occasion to point out, that he was not liable to the imputation of favouring popery to which he had been subjected, when he drew attention to the faith and doctrine of the early Church, as the most effectual means after the study of Scripture of preventing any injury to the truth.

Many important principles were involved in the sentiments of which Hoadly was the advocate, which involved the questions of Church authority and the exercise of private judgment, and which would have proved on their acceptance subversive of legitimate government. It was a fit occasion for the Convocation to interpose, and the duty was not avoided. A committee was appointed to examine the obnoxious sermon, and a representation of its true character was presented on the 10th of May, which was not, however, formally adopted, although it was approved. In consequence of this, a censure upon the bishop was

---

[1] See for this sermon "Hoadly's Works," vol. ii., p. 403. Lond., 1783.

prepared. But the government interfered, Convocation was prorogued, and the opportunity of deliberation was taken away; nor was this regained, until the efforts of the greatest of Oxford's bishops were successful, and the suspended right was restored in A.D. 1854, after a debate had been achieved in 1852.

At this period in the 18th century, a great change in the efficiency and spiritual influence of the Church had supervened. The school of Caroline theology had died out, the voice of the Church had been rendered silent, the habits of clerical life had deteriorated, and a taste for general literature in disparagement of the ancient study of patristic literature had been introduced. There was, moreover, an increasing population in the great centres of industry, but which had not yet been met by a corresponding increase of spiritual zeal and ecclesiastical organisation, in order to cope with the emergencies of the times. On the contrary, there was an absolute want of provision for the less wealthy parishioners in many of the churches, who were excluded from their rightful place by the appropriation of the seats. And the general state of education throughout the diocese may be inferred from the fact that in the whole county of Oxford only fourteen towns or villages were enumerated as having "charity schools" corresponding with the present parochial schools, and distinguished from the endowed "Free" or "Grammar schools," in which number no more than five hundred and three scholars received any education.[1] There

[1] The list is given by R. Cox, in the "Magna Britannia," Oxon., p. 497. Lond., 1720.

was, too, a general declension of faith, and an increasing prevalence of infidelity and irreligion in the higher classes of society. It was in such a spiritual dulness, that another question of the first importance claimed the attention of the Bishop of Oxford, as arising in the first instance within his diocese. For Oxford was the early home of Methodism, the place in which was first nurtured the great religious movement, which was to awaken the spiritual emotions of so many within the English Church, whom no want of sympathy nor failure of recognition should have caused in the end to quit her pale.[1] And this was the diocese in which had to be determined first of all the problem how the new spirit of zeal and energy was to be directed, while nothing that was unsound in doctrine or unsafe in practice was allowed to be introduced. As it is, the revival which should have been a source of new strength and vitality to the Church in its progress and development has entailed a grievous loss. The sequel of the history will show that the Bishop of Oxford, whose attention was so soon directed to this new revival, was prepared to exercise a wise and sound discretion in regard to the altered state of feeling prevailing within the Church.

John Wesley was at first a member of Christ Church. He was admitted to deacon's orders by Bishop Potter in A.D. 1725, and preached his first sermon within the diocese, in the village of South

---

[1] The authorities relied upon for the early history of Methodism in connexion with Oxford are given in L. Tyerman's "Life of John Wesley," Lond., 1876; "Life of Whitefield," Lond., 1876; "The Oxford Methodists," Lond., 1873.

Leigh. Nor did the occasion of his doing so ever pass from his mind. It was fresh in his recollection on a subsequent visit to the same parish after an interval of forty years.[1] Nor did he forget the generous treatment which he received from Bishop Potter to the day of his death. He spoke of him as "a great and good man," and in one of his latest sermons [2] he recurred to the advice which the bishop had given to him half a century before, and for which he often thanked the Almighty; this advice being that "if he wished to be extremely useful he must not spend his time in contending for or against things of a disputable nature, but in testifying against notorious vice, and in promoting real essential holiness."[3] In the following year John Wesley was elected a fellow of Lincoln College, and after a short absence, during which he acted as his father's curate, returned to Oxford in A.D. 1726. Soon after this, in a sense of the increasing danger of unbelief, the vice-chancellor thought fit to issue a formal notice, in order to warn the University against those who professed themselves the advocates of human reason in disparagement of divine revelation, which, however, Dr. Bradshaw, the dean of Christ Church, refused to have posted in the hall of his college. In such a state of the public mind, Wesley was ordained a priest in A.D. 1728.

---

[1] Wesley's "Works," p. 420, cited in Tyerman's "Life," *u. s.*, vol. i., p. 44.

[2] The sermon was written in A.D. 1787. "Works," *u. s.*, vol. vii., p. 176, *ibid.*, p. 43.

[3] "Works," *u. s.*, viii., 334; Tyerman's "Oxford Methodist," *u. s.*, p. 1.

And then, in the November of the next year, with his brother Charles, a student of Christ Church, William Morgan a commoner of the same college, and Robert Kirkham, of Merton College, he began to hold meetings on some evenings in each week for religious conference, and especially for the study of the Greek Testament. These are to be accounted the first Oxford Methodists, this title replacing that of the Holy Club, by which the small society was first known, their methodical way of life suggesting an allusion to the ancient school of physicians who were so styled.[1] As the appellation itself implies, this practice of devotional study was accompanied by a corresponding strictness of life, by abstinence in their daily habits, by visiting the poor, especially the prisoners, and by the observance of weekly communion.

It is pleasing, again, to be able to refer to the sympathy which this religious movement received from Bishop Potter. His chaplain, on reference being made to him, commended the design of visiting the prisoners in Bocardo, and of preaching a sermon there once every month; and he said at the same time, that he would answer for the bishop's approbation, who, as it proved, described himself as being greatly pleased with their work.[2] And this approbation was more fully expressed in another statement, which he made in answer to some objections which were raised against them. "These men,"

---

[1] Southey's "Life of Wesley," vol. i., ch. ii., p. 29. Lond., 1858.

[2] Tyerman's "Oxford Methodists," *u. s.*, p. 7.

the bishop observed, " are irregular, but they have done good, and I pray God to bless them."

George Whitefield, who was a servitor at Pembroke College, and whose personal character and force of popular eloquence were to have so large an influence upon the rise and progress of Methodism, obtained an interview with the two Wesleys by a charitable interest in behalf of a prisoner who attempted suicide, and was led to cast in his lot with them in A.D. 1735. In the same year the father of the two brothers died, and John Wesley was induced to undertake a mission to the colony of Georgia. In consequence of this the band of Oxford Methodists became separated; and to trace the subsequent course of the movement originated by them becomes a subject of general importance, and passes the range of diocesan interests.

Bishop Potter was translated to the see of Canterbury in A.D. 1737, when his successor at Oxford was Thomas Secker, the son of Dissenting parents, who had been induced to conform to the English Church by the influence of the celebrated author of the "Analogy." Bishop Secker was a man of high respectability rather than of eminent talent, and, after continuing in the bishopric of Oxford for a few years longer than his predecessor, was, like him in this respect, preferred to the see of Canterbury. Of the seven immediate successors in the bishopric of Oxford, William Lowth, the first in the line, was the author of a well-known " Introduction to English

---

[1] Tyerman's " Life of John Wesley," *u. s.*, p. 43.

Grammar," which was for many years accepted as a sufficient guide. His " Lectures on the Sacred Poetry of the Hebrews " supplied in a similar manner such information as was required upon the subject of which he wrote; and the same remark is applicable to his latest publication, the " Translation of the Prophet Isaiah." The other bishops in the series have less claim to particular reference ; but John Butler was a political writer of some note, for the "Letters of Junius" were at one time ascribed to him; while Bishop Moss is remembered as a munificent benefactor to the school at Wheatley, a parish adjoining Cuddesdon, and in the patronage of the bishop, for the maintenance of which he contributed a no less sum than three thousand pounds.

In succession to these there follows a bishop who was of a very different and of a far higher degree of excellence. Bishop Lloyd was a man of theological learning, who, although he was not without his share in the questions of political life, had yet in his own personal attainments and character the highest claim to occupy the position to which he was advanced. As Regius Professor of Divinity at Oxford, he had brought to the chair a greater discrimination than that of the popular controversialist, who can see no distinction between the formal decrees of Trent and the practical Romish system. And, accordingly, he may be considered to have been the first to recall to notice the right method of treating such questions. This afterwards attained to great prominence among the questions of the day. In such teaching Bishop Lloyd was "the revered master" to whom Dr. Pusey and Dr. Newman confessed that they owed so much,[1] the Bishop of Oxford whom the latter avowed that he "held in affection and veneration."[2] And there is other testimony to a similar effect. Bishop Lloyd was described by Mr. Gladstone, who was a contemporary with him at Christ Church, as being "a man of powerful talents, and of a character both winning and decided, who, had his life been spared, might have acted powerfully for good on the fortunes of the Church of England, by guiding the energetic influence which his teaching had done so much to form."[3] Although a man of such intellectual power, Bishop Lloyd was not known as an author. It was stated at the time of his death[4] that he acknowledged no writing as of his authorship except a single article on the view of the Roman Catholic doctrine, which had appeared in a Review.[5]

Bishop Lloyd's connexion with political affairs arose out of the following circumstances.[6] The question which deeply agitated the public mind was the expediency of the proposed relief of the Roman Catholics from the disabilities by which they were oppressed. Upon a vacancy occurring in the representation of the University from the removal of

[1] "Tract XC., with an historical Preface," by E. P. Pusey, Prof., p. 28. Ox., 1870. [2] *Ibid.*
[3] "A Chapter on Autobiography," by W. E. Gladstone, p. 53. Lond., 1868.
[4] "Annual Register," vol. lxxi., p. 232.
[5] "The British Critic," Oct., 1825.
[6] The authority for the statement in the text is "The Diary and Correspondence of Charles Abbot, Lord Colchester," vol. iii. Lond., 1861.

Charles Abbott to the Upper House as Lord Colchester in 1817, it was proposed by the authorities at Christ Church to nominate Canning as a candidate. This was defeated by the resolute opposition of Lloyd, who was one of the Censors, and the name of Peel was substituted instead; upon which he was deputed to be the bearer of a letter conveying the intelligence, as his former tutor and his constant friend. Peel's success was assured; and Lloyd himself became Bishop of Oxford in A.D. 1827.

In the mean time the course of public opinion in reference to the Roman Catholic claims had greatly changed, and notably in the instance of Bishop Lloyd. And, accordingly, when the Duke of Wellington proposed the Catholic Relief Bill in the House of Lords on the 2nd of April, A.D. 1829, and was opposed by the Archbishop of Canterbury and the Primate of Ireland, who spoke after him, the Bishop of Oxford, as the fourth speaker in the debate, professed himself an advocate of the measure, and gave his support to the Bill. It became law in the same session of parliament. But the change of sentiment was not shared by George IV., and there remained a feeling in his mind that he had been unfairly deserted by his friends, and that violence had been done to his kingly conscience, in respect of which he was extremely sensitive. Under this sense of wrong, he showed no sympathy towards those who had become political converts, as he himself had become from the necessity of the case; and he was so far unmindful of his high position on a public occasion as to offer a personal slight to Bishop Lloyd. The injury was deeply felt by the bishop, and was supposed to have had a prejudicial effect upon his health. But, whether it were so or not, the immediate cause of his illness and death was a dinner at Somerset House, on his returning from which he complained of a chill from sitting in a draught of air. This passed into a fatal attack of inflammation of the lungs, and the bishop died shortly afterwards, at the early age of forty-four.

The time during which Bishop Lloyd occupied the see was not sufficient to allow of any marked effect taking place in the administration of the diocese. But his wish to cultivate the friendship of his clergy, and to find opportunities of intercourse with them in other than a formal and official manner, was shown by his practice of holding public days at which they might be present with the ladies of their families without an invitation from himself. The custom ceased under his successor, who did not reside at Cuddesdon, and has not been renewed.

The next bishop was Richard Bagot, a member of a noble family, who was also at the time of his appointment Dean of Canterbury, and Rector of Blithfield in Staffordshire, a parish of which the patronage belonged to his family, and in which it was his custom to reside. This absence of the bishop from the seat of the bishopric implies a state of opinion within the Church which has passed away. It is one of the results of the adjustment of the episcopal revenues by the ecclesiastical commissioners that the only excuse for such a practice has been removed. It was one of the abuses of the power of granting leases for fines, that a large portion of the annual revenues of the see might be anticipated by the bishop who granted the lease, by which means the revenue of his successor might be proportionately reduced. Under such a state of things the annual receipts of the Bishop of Oxford had become greatly diminished, and it came to be pleaded in this as in other dioceses, that the impoverished resources of the bishop were an excuse for holding other preferment, and justified an habitual disuse of residence within the borders of the see. And it is not impossible that in this instance the wrong done to the claims of the diocese was reduced within its narrowest limit. Bishop Bagot himself was a man of the highest personal character, of much practical wisdom and forethought, and eminently discreet in the choice of his subordinates. No bishop indeed who has ever occupied the see has perhaps received a more sympathetic tribute of esteem and gratitude than is contained in the following recognition by Cardinal Newman of the tenderness with which he was treated in his passage through so great anxieties by Bishop Bagot. After speaking of the point of honour which he made to obey his bishop, Dr. Newman observes:—"I was rewarded by having all my time for ecclesiastical superior a man, whom, had I had a choice, I should have preferred out and out to any other bishop on the bench, and for whose memory I have a special affection, Dr. Bagot, a man of noble mind, and as kind-hearted as he was noble. He ever sympathised with me in my trials which followed. May his name ever be blessed."[1]

[1] Dr. Newman's "Apologia pro Vita Sua," ch. ii., p. 51. Lond., 1875.

In arranging the territorial distribution of the diocese, the ecclesiastical commissioners were induced to make a great change in the extent of the diocese of Oxford. The whole county of Berks, with the parts of Wiltshire which were enclosed in it, was annexed by virtue of an order of Council of the 5th of October, A.D. 1836, which took effect from the publication of it in the "London Gazette" on October the 7th, as Bishop Bagot was disposed to accept this addition to his previous see, though for various reasons he altogether disapproved of the commission itself.[1] The whole county of Buckingham, with a parish isolated in Oxfordshire, was also annexed to the see by an order of council of the 19th of July, A.D. 1837. This further addition, however, Bishop Bagot declined to accept, as rendering the diocese too large for his supervision. The actual annexation accordingly was deferred, and this latter part of the scheme had no immediate effect, but was carried out on the first subsequent avoidance of the bishopric in A.D. 1845.

As a part of the arrangements attendant upon the annexation of the county of Berkshire to the see of Oxford, an important accession of dignity accrued to Bishop Bagot and his successors by the transference of the Chancellorship of the Order of the Garter from the Bishops of Salisbury to the Bishops of Oxford. The order was originally founded by the letters patent of King Edward III.,[2] which provided for the constitution of the officers for the service

[1] "Charge at the third Visitation," pp. 7, 8. Ox., 1838.
[2] Dated on St. George's Day, April 23rd, 23 Ed. A.D. 1349.

of the knights; and it was appointed that the Bishop of Winchester and his successors for ever should be the prelates of the order. It further appears, from the memorial of Bishop Seth Ward, the Bishop of Salisbury, whose energetic interference caused the restoration of the office of Chancellor to himself and his successors, that the office of Chancellor of the Order of the Garter was erected by letters patent of King Edward IV.; who then also ordained, by his charter granted to Richard Beauchamp, the Bishop of Salisbury, that he and his successors for ever should enjoy and execute the office, in consideration that the chapel of St. George was within the diocese of Salisbury, and for other considerations mentioned in the charter.[1] In accordance with this, it is stated in the preamble that out of love to the order the bishop had given himself daily to the superintendence of the building of the chapel; and it was, therefore, for his unremitting diligence as master and surveyor of the works at Windsor that he obtained this honour. After it had been held by him and his successors for a series of years, the appointment became alienated from the see and passed into the hands of laymen. Bishop Seth Ward presented his petition to King Charles II. in behalf of the ancient claim of his see; a chapter of the order decided in his favour, and he regained the office for himself and his successors, and was himself ap-

---

[1] See in S. H. Cassan's "Lives of the Bishops of Sherborne and Salisbury," pt. iii., pp. 158–61. Salisb., 1824.
[2] 3 Pat. 15 Ed. IV., m. 18; Cassan, *u. s.*, pt. i., p. 258.

pointed chancellor by letters patent[1] of the same king upon the death of the last lay-chancellor in A.D. 1671. When the archdeaconry of Berks became separated from the diocese of Salisbury and incorporated in the diocese of Oxford, it was provided that the chancellorship should be transferred with it, inasmuch as the chapel of St. George, at Windsor, which contained the stalls and banners of the knights of the order, and was their proper church, had by the recent changes become a part of the see of Oxford; and there was, accordingly, no sufficient reason for the chancellorship to be held by an independent bishop. Bishop Bagot accordingly became the Chancellor of the Order of the Garter, while the Bishop of Winchester, in respect of whose diocese no similar change had occurred, retained the high position of the prelate of that order.

When the proposed reconstruction of the diocese had been thus far completed by Bishop Bagot's consent to the former part of the scheme for its rearrangement, he "put the rural deaneries of Berkshire upon the same footing with those in Oxfordshire."[2] He had already restored the office of the rural dean in the archdeaconry of Oxford, and those whom he appointed to it were able, upon his resignation of the see and the accession of Bishop Wilberforce, to render him important service in a diocese with which he could but imperfectly be acquainted.[3] In some other ways, and specially by

[1] Dated November 23, in 23 Charles II., A.D. 1671.
[2] "Charge," *u. s.*, p. 12.
[3] Information from the late Rev. Charles Barter, Rural Dean.

his efforts to promote the observance of Ascension Day, a festival which "had fallen into neglect and desuetude," and also of Lent, Passion Week, and Ember Days, and divers others of the seasons set apart by the Church for an especial measure of devotion,"[1] he began to revive that better form of attention to the requirements of the Church which now prevails. So again, by establishing the diocesan board of education, by instituting a training college for schoolmasters, and by appointing the deanery inspectors of schools, he was commencing, on however small a scale, the system of diocesan organisation, which, in its subsequent development, has been to other dioceses the pattern and example.

The influence of John Henry Newman, now at length raised to the cardinalate, came from Oxford as its natural home, and the early associations of his life belong to its history. It is remembered, as one of the associations of a village church in Oxfordshire, that his first sermon was preached at Over Worton, the home of various members of the family of the Wilsons, so well known for their religious character, with whom his sympathies would then be found. And it has been remarked, that the word "development," upon which so much of his after life turned, was made use of in the sermon.[2] Another church, the church of St. Clement, which is now destroyed, but the burial-ground of which remains at the entrance to

---

[1] "Charge," *u. s.*, p. 12.

[2] Information by favour of Rev. William Best, Vicar of Dunstew, formerly Curate to Dr. Wilson, the Rector of Over-Worton.

Oxford on the London road, was one in which he for some time was accustomed to officiate. The church of St. Mary the Virgin, in Oxford, was the church in which so many of his sermons, of such untold influence, were preached. But it is the public life which rose upon this which placed him in that relation with the bishop of the diocese, to which allusion has been made.

At an earlier period in the episcopate of Bishop Bagot, the new religious movement which was to exercise so large an influence on the English Church, like other revivals of which the mention has occurred, began at Oxford; and, without any attempt to enter fully into its history, some of the facts in connexion with the action of the bishop, as head of the diocese, may be noticed. Upon the return of Mr. Newman, after an absence from England, in A.D. 1833, he found that a movement had already commenced in opposition to the specific danger which was threatening the religion of the nation and the Church.[1] He joined in this step the friends of his own college, and those who were associated with them, in order to combat the growing spirit of liberalism; that is, "the anti-dogmatic principle and its developments,"[2] which had then become prevalent. In the same year, on the 14th of July, John Keble, the author of the "Christian Year," and to whom the movement itself in its earlier stage was mainly due, preached the assize sermon in the University pulpit, which was published under the title of "National Apostasy,"

---

[1] "Apologia," *u. s.*, ch. ii., p. 36.
[2] *Ibid*, p. 48.

and which Dr. Newman always considered "as the start of the religious movement of 1833."[1] Later in the same year, Dr. Newman himself[2] began the series of the "Tracts for the Times," the first number of which has the date of September the 9th. His object in this series, was to contribute something towards the practical revival of doctrines which, although held by the great divines of the English Church, had become obsolete with the majority of her members, or withdrawn from public view by the more learned and orthodox who adhered to them.[3]

The series of "Tracts" was continued until there appeared the ninetieth number, bearing the date of January 24, 1841, which Dr. Newman published "to meet a wish earnestly set before him by parties whom he revered,"[4] to vindicate the catholicity of the English Church, and to rescue from a conceived misinterpretation the Thirty-nine Articles themselves. A memorial was presented by the "Four Tutors." The book was condemned by the Hebdomadal Council, but any action on the part of the University was stopped by the veto of the proctors. The bishop expressed his opinion that the Tract was objectionable, and might tend to disturb the peace of the Church, and gave his advice that the series should be discontinued. And Dr. Newman addressed a letter to the bishop in explanation of the position which he assumed. With a view to save the Tract itself

---

[1] "Apologia," *u. s.*, ch. ii., p. 35.   [2] *Ibid.*, p. 40.
[3] Advertisement prefixed to vol. i., 1833-4, pp. iii, iv.
[4] "Tract XC.; with Historical Preface by Dr. Pusey," Pref., p. viii.

from condemnation, the series was discontinued, but only with the supposed understanding that, although some of the bishops might mention it in their charges, it would not be censured by them as a body. The result proved that there was a miscalculation in this respect; Bishop Bagot even, in despite of what he had said the year before, severely condemned the method of interpretation in his charge as "making the Articles mean anything or nothing."[1] And accordingly, although other reasons conduced to the same result, "the ostensible, direct, and sufficient reason"[2] for Dr. Newman's resignation of the parish of St. Mary's, in Oxford, with the then hamlet of Littlemore, "was the persevering attacks of the bishops on Tract Ninety." The resignation was completed on the 18th of September in 1843,[3] and with this the connexion of events with the present history ceases; although Dr. Newman, in his private capacity, retired to Littlemore, the village for which as Vicar of St. Mary's he had done so much, and continued to reside upon the property which he possessed there, until he was formally admitted into the communion of the Roman obedience, to the grief and loss of the English Church, on October the 8th, A.D. 1845.

At the close of the year 1845 Bishop Bagot accepted the offer of translation, and was removed to the see of Bath and Wells. By this step the completion of the scheme of the Ecclesiastical Commissioners, to which allusion was made, was rendered

---

[1] "Apologia," *u. s.*, ch. iv. p. 220.
[2] *Ibid.*, p. 207.   [3] *Ibid.*, p. 215.

practicable. The appointment of Bishop Wilberforce, as his successor, was introductory to the extension of the diocese to its present limits, within which it comprises the three counties of Oxfordshire, Berkshire, and Buckinghamshire. In the state of the arrangements for the future diocese, there was presented to the bishop on his accession the problem of uniting the different parts of the diocese under one uniform system, and of bringing into harmonious action those who had no previous co-operation, and whose traditions were not identical. It was with this question to be solved that his great designs were to be carried into effect; and, from the occasion upon which Bishop Wilberforce met his clergy at his first visitation, it was manifest to them that in the organisation of the diocese the highest principles would be brought into action, and the highest degree of efficiency prepared for. Nor did the subsequent course of events fall below the expectations which were then conceived. The improved condition of the fabric of the churches themselves, the rearrangement of the interior for the better accommodation of the poor, the more frequent ministrations of every kind, the frequent calls to newness of life, became everywhere familiar subjects. And coincident with this was the successive institution of the several societies, by which the united efforts of the diocese at large were made effectual for the promotion of its spiritual interests, or the completion of the necessary framework for such an end. If an opposition arose from any smaller section of the diocese, it was disarmed by the prudent management of the bishop himself, or was rendered ineffectual by the more abundant sympathy of the larger part; or it even passed away in the mutual co-operation of the less extreme of his opponents with those who were his steadier friends. The bishop's force of will, combined with his sympathetic feeling towards those who were still dissentient, prevailed to carry on without serious diminution his great diocesan work.

It must, however, be allowed that there were questions of a higher range, in which there was not found the same successful result, within the diocese itself. In the instance of Dr. Hampden and of Dr. Pusey, in respect of whom the deeper questions of theological interest were involved, the course which was adopted by the bishop will not approve itself to the calmer judgment with which such questions can be considered at the interval of time which has elapsed.

But these are subjects which, although they are intimately connected with the progress of religious interests within the diocese, it is not desirable to pursue in the present sketch. And this becomes a less noticeable omission, if, indeed, it is considered an omission at all, as the correspondence of the bishop and the history of his life, which can alone supply the materials for a full and complete inquiry, are still in the course of publication.

In consideration of the results which have followed a similar practice in so many instances since, it may be allowed to mention, among the incidents in the history of the diocese at this time, that the church of St. Thomas the Martyr in Oxford is probably the one in which the use of the ecclesiastical vestments was first resumed. In a letter from the present vicar, the

Rev. Thomas Chamberlain, who has held the incumbency from the year A.D. 1842, it is observed:—
"There is no doubt, I think, that we were the first to restore the chasuble. The date, I believe, was 1851, but I am not quite sure. It is curious that I never have had the least opposition, or complaint of the vestments. But I need not say we have always been careful and practical in our way of proceeding."[1]

That Bishop Wilberforce at a later period of his episcopate, which had continued for a longer time than that of any one of his predecessors in the see, should have been content to exchange the diocese of Oxford for that of Winchester,—a diocese, indeed, of higher dignity, but not of higher culture; and that he should have been willing to remove from the scene of his earlier episcopal labours, in which so many difficulties had been encountered, and so many victories won, in which, too, he had received, under every variety of circumstance, the most perfect sympathy, must have been attended on his part with a loss of associations which no new diocese could supply; as it was certainly accompanied, on the part of the clergy and laity to whom his presence had become so familiar, by a sense of regret which could not be transient. But a similar acceptance of promotion has not been deemed unworthy by the greatest bishops of past ages in the English Church. Just before the close of his episcopate Bishop Wilberforce instituted an inquiry into the "expenditure in the several parishes of the

[1] From a letter to the writer in 1881, in answer to an inquiry as to the use of the vestments.

diocese upon the churches, church endowments, schools, houses of mercy, and parsonage houses from A.D. 1845 to A.D. 1869"; and from the returns thus obtained he gave this tabulated summary:[1]—

|  | £. | s. | d. |
|---|---|---|---|
| "In the Archdeaconry of Oxford | 720,164 | 13 | 1 |
| In the Archdeaconry of Berks | 828,310 | 13 | 11 |
| In the Archdeaconry of Buckingham | 555,157 | 5 | 0 |
|  | 2,103,632 | 12 | 0 |
| Add | 16,919 | 15 | 3 [2] |
| Aggregate total expenditure within the Diocese | 2,120,552 | 7 | 3" |

After the death of the bishop, by which he was so suddenly called away in the midst of strength and usefulness, a memorial was sought, by which his name might be perpetuated in the older diocese. And this was found in the enlargement of the college at Cuddesdon—the institution of which he had commemorated with so much affection each year—by the addition of a new chapel and lecture-room, accompanied by a change of name in the college itself, which became the Wilberforce College for the time to come. Succeeding generations of clergy will thus have a constant recollection of its earliest patron and friend. The cathedral of Christ Church has also a memorial of its own in the bishop's throne, the cost of which was raised by subscription, that it might be connected with the remembrance of his episcopate.

[1] "Charge at the eighth Visitation, Nov. 11, 1869," p. 13, and Appendix III., pp. 46, 7. Ox., 1869. [2] Unexplained.

The successor of Bishop Wilberforce in the see of Oxford is the present head of the diocese, and it is not within the proper purpose of this history to describe the position of the diocese under his presidency. But two points of essential importance must not be passed over, for the gain which they have been the means to procure. A conference has been established for the diocese, consisting of clerical and lay members, which has held its sessions from the year 1873. A previous synod of the whole of the clergy of the diocese, including the curates who had licences, was held at Oxford, in order to determine the question of its formation. And it may be observed that a marked feature in its constitution is the small number of official members, in comparison with the elected members, both of the clergy and the laity, which it contains. A signal benefit has also been conferred upon the Church at large, and not upon the diocese alone, in the vindication of the authority of the bishop and his perfect liberty of instituting, or of not instituting, a suit, when it is desired to promote the office of the judge under the provisions of the Clergy Discipline Act.[1] The earliest stage is now placed under his control beyond dispute; and a prosecution cannot be entered upon without his consent, obtained in the first instance. This was established in a cause arising within the diocese, in which the Bishop of Oxford was appellant from the decision of the Queen's Bench Division of the High Court of Justice, in the suit between

---

[1] 3 & 4 Vict., c. 86.

Dr. Frederick Julius and the Reverend Thomas Thelluson Carter, respecting the ritual observances which had been practised in the parish of Clewer.

The ancient endowments of the bishopric of Oxford came into the possession of the ecclesiastical commissioners upon the avoidance of the see by Bishop Wilberforce, and were commuted for an annual payment of five thousand pounds, which was fixed as the amount of the future endowment up to the year A.D. 1877. But in this year there was an order of the Queen in Council which sanctioned a new scheme of the commissioners, by which lands in the parishes of Aylesbury, Burford, Cropredy, and Cuddesdon, and the rent-charge arising in the parishes of Wokingham, Great Marlow, Blewbury, and South Leigh, of an estimated equivalent value, were granted to the see.

The patronage vested in the bishop, in addition to the appointment of the three archdeacons, consists of one hundred benefices, of which in the year A.D. 1877 forty were of the annual value of three hundred pounds, or above that sum, twelve of these reaching the value of five hundred pounds.[1]

The archdeaconry of Oxford is a valuable preferment, for, in addition to the fees attached to the office by an order in council, gazetted the twentieth of March, in A.D. 1846, a canonry of Christ Church was annexed to the archdeaconry, charged, however, with the annual payment of three hundred pounds in favour of the archdeaconry of Buckingham.[2]

---

[1] See "Ox. Dio. Calendar," 1877, pp. 129, 130.

[2] Information by favour of George Pringle, Esq., Secretary to the Ecclesiastical Commission.

PRESENT ENDOWMENT AND PATRONAGE. 191

The total number of the incumbencies in the diocese amounts to six hundred and forty-seven, which are comprised in thirty-one deaneries; and the state of the clergy is thus described in a return made to the House of Commons "with regard to the curates of the Church of England for the year 1879."

| Number of Incumbents resident. | Number of Incumbents non-resident. | Number of Curates in sole charge. | Number of Assistant Curates. |
|---|---|---|---|
| 519 | 57 | 11 | 148 |

This return presents a favourable contrast in respect of the number of non-resident incumbents in comparison with the returns from some other dioceses. It does not, however, commend itself as a return, which, as a whole, is to be considered absolutely complete.

## CHAPTER VIII.

UNION OF BERKS AND OXON, WITH HISTORY OF ARCH-
DEACONRY OF BERKS. A.D. 705–A.D. 1856.

Union of Berks and Bucks with the diocese of Oxford—Early History of the Archdeaconry of Berks—Historical Events—Councils of Windsor and Reading—Coverdale at Newbury—Sufferers for Religion—Bishop Jewel—Dr. Twisse—Nonjurors—Wantage and Clewer—Endowment.

THE annexation of Berkshire and Buckinghamshire, of the diocese of Oxford, by the orders of Privy Council in A.D. 1836 and 1837, which in the former instance took effect during the episcopate of Bishop Bagot and in the latter during the episcopate of Bishop Wilberforce, has already formed the subject of remark in the course of this history.[1] The addition of the two counties, or of the two archdeaconries, as they are to be considered from an ecclesiastical point of view, at so late a period as this, leaves the greater part of their respective histories to be described in the volumes of the present series which are concerned with the history of the dioceses of which they previously formed a part. And, accordingly, the account of the successive bishops by whom the two archdeaconries were administered, and their own corresponding position in ecclesiastical history, are subjects provided for

[1] *Supra*, pp. 178, 185.

elsewhere. But it remains to describe in this place their separate associations, and trace their several lines of descent, which will be found to be united in either case, although at different periods, with the larger and as yet undivided see of Wessex; from which, indeed, the archdeaconry of Oxford itself, representing the diocese in its limited extent, was an offshoot like themselves. The three archdeaconries accordingly belong to the same parent stock.

The description of the archdeaconry of Berkshire, which comprises the county of Berkshire and certain isolated places in the county of Wiltshire, is to be taken up at the time when the first division of the see of Wessex was made,[1] upon the formation of the two dioceses of Sherborne and Winchester in A.D., 705. It was stated in the former account of this division, upon the authority which was then adduced,[2] that the county of Berks was assigned to the bishopric of Sherborne, and became part of the see of which the first bishop was the saintly Aldhelm; whose successors in the bishop's stool of that see are connected with the history of the diocese of Salisbury, of which they were the early representatives; for an account of whom, therefore, a reference must be made to the volume in which that bishopric is described.

In its subsequent history, the archdeaconry of Berkshire was united with the diocese of Sherborne during the lives of the successive bishops, but after the death of Asser, who was the last in the series, the

[1] *Supra*, p. 12.
[2] Haddan and Stubbs, after William of Malmesbury and the "Saxon Chronicle," *supra*, p. 13.

friend and biographer of King Alfred, the diocese of Sherborne in its turn also became subdivided. Asser died in A.D., 909, and the king, Edward the Elder, in conjunction with the bishops, determined that every province of the West Saxons should have its own bishop, and that the district should have five sees for the future instead of the two which it possessed before. Upon the first arrangement, when Werstan was appointed to the diocese of Sherborne, in the year which has just been mentioned, there were left to him at that time " the three counties of Dorsetshire, Berkshire, and Wiltshire. But soon afterwards, in the lifetime of the same king, the see of Ramsbury, in Wiltshire, was created,"[1] with which Berkshire appears to have been united. These two counties, accordingly, formed the new see of Ramsbury, while Dorsetshire by itself was allowed to constitute the reconstructed and diminished see of Sherborne. This distribution of the three counties in the two bishoprics continued to exist for nearly a century and a half; but upon the expiration of this term a reunion of the three counties was effected by Bishop Herman, who was appointed to the see of Ramsbury in A.D., 1045, and obtained the see of Sherborne at the later date of A.D. 1058. Soon after this, being in possession of the two sees, he prevailed upon the king, Edward the Confessor, to accede to his proposal for their reunion. This proceeding on the part of Herman has been described in these terms : " He united the bishopric of Sherborne, which he had obtained from King Edward, with his

[1] Will. of Malmes., " De Gestis Pontificum Angl.," *u. s.*, lib. ii., sect. 80, p. 178.

original see, and fixed the episcopal seat of both dioceses at Sherborne; but during the reign of William I., by the authority of a synod and the king's munificence, he transferred his see to Salisbury."[1] The place to which it was thus removed was properly the town of Old Sarum.

There has been occasion in the earlier part of this history[2] to notice the decree of the council by which, as in a former instance, the newly-formed see of Sherborne had the bishop's chair removed to the more important site of Old Sarum, after an interval of seventeen years. This council was the synod of London in A.D., 1075, which wisely determined that the sees which had been placed in villages should be removed to towns, in order that by this means the spiritual wants of the population, as it gathered around the more important centres of industry, might not remain unsatisfied. The removal of the bishop's chair to Old Sarum, then a place of more importance than Sherborne, determined its position for a longer time. This continued to be the seat of the bishop until its place was transferred to Salisbury by Richard Poore, the then bishop, in A.D. 1217. And it consequently determined the relative position of the archdeaconry of Berkshire, until it became annexed to the see of which it now forms part. And it may be observed that the Church could more readily meet the necessities of the times than could the state; for the political privileges of the borough of Old Sarum were allowed to exist, depopulated as it had

[1] Flor. of Worc., *u. s.*, p. 176; "List of Bishops," *ib.*, p. 420.
[2] *Supra*, p. 23.

become with the loss of its civil importance, until these also were swept away by the Reform Act.

Connected with the early history of this archdeaconry there arises the further question, whether it ever had within its limits the seat of a bishopric? In favour of the supposition, it may indeed be alleged that the line of bishops, in succession from Bishop Æthelstan, in A.D. 909, to Bishop Roger, in A.D. 1107, has been designated by the title of "Bishops of the church of Sunning."[1] But the true explanation is probably to be found in the suggestion which was offered long since, when it was stated that this title appeared to "derive its origin from the palace of the Bishops of Salisbury at Sunning, near Reading,"[2] Sunning, or Sonning, being one of the country seats belonging to the see. "The Bishops of Sunning" accordingly may have gained their title as such, in a popular sense, from their occupation of the palace, which they possessed in that place, and in which they occasionally made their residence. And again, when there is mention of a "Bishop of Berkshire and of Cornwall," as there is of other "occasional shire-bishops,"[3] it may legitimately be supposed that these were of a temporary character, without distinct sees, holding an analogous position with that of suffragan bishops in later times, deriving their titles from some part of the see on which they were dependent.

[1] Florence of Worcester, "List of Bishops," *supra*, p. 195.
[2] J. Leland, "De Reb. Britann. Collectanea," vol. i., p. 316, Oxon., 1715.
[3] See Haddan and Stubbs, *u. s.*, vol. iii., p. 596 note *a*.

The county of Berkshire is stated to have contained, at the time of the Domesday Survey, six thousand three hundred and twenty-four inhabitants.[1] It appears by the "Taxation of Pope Nicholas IV., c. A.D. 1291,"[2] that there were four deaneries in the archdeaconry of Berks which derive their names from the four principal towns, of Abingdon, Wallingford, Newbury, and Reading; and that there were one hundred and thirteen parochial churches, some of which had dependent chapelries; and that four chapelries were separately assessed; while, of the towns which gave their names to the deaneries, Abingdon had two churches, Reading three, and Wallingford five. In the next ecclesiastical survey in A.D. 1340, there are found to be one hundred and eighteen parish churches.[3] In this Wallingford is described with the two churches of All Saints' and St. Lucian; but as it is elsewhere stated that "by the patents and donations of Edmund, Earl of Cornwall, and lord of the manor of Wallingford, there were fourteen churches in Wallingford,"[4] and as the earl himself died in A.D. 1300, it seems that in this instance there once was a large number of dependent churches or chapels besides the mother churches, which were afterwards reduced in number to three.[5] The name of Wallingford itself, the Welshmen's or the strangers' ford, has historical reminiscences of its

---

[1] Sir H. Ellis, "Introduction to Domesday Book," *u. s.*, vol. ii., p. 423.   [2] Pp. 186-190.
[3] "Nonarum Inquisitiones," pp. 1-10, *u. s., supra*, p. 36.
[4] J. Leland, "Itin.," vol. ii., p. 39. Oxon., 1769.
[5] *Ibid.*

own. It was crossed perhaps by Aulus Plautius in his expedition,[1] as it was by the West Saxons, in their invasion of Oxfordshire and Buckinghamshire, and subsequently by the Norman Conqueror, in his advance. Again, in the "Valor Ecclesiasticus of King Henry VIII.,"[2] the parish churches in the archdeaconry are found to have increased in number to one hundred and fifty-two, with a still larger increase in the number of the chapels annexed to them.

From various causes the county of Berkshire has been the scene of events in ecclesiastical history which, from their local associations, may be detached from the general account of the ancient diocese of which it formed part. They may properly be considered to belong to the separate history of the archdeaconry which finds its place in the present volume. Under the same description may be classified the foundation of the religious institutions of a monastic or collegiate character, with which the archdeaconry is so closely identified, as well as certain incidents in their subsequent history—care being taken to avoid the merely predial disputes which are in themselves of no general interest.

In the reign of Henry III. an opportunity was afforded for independent action on the part of the clergy of Berkshire, which may serve to illustrate the condition of the Church from one point of view, and to exhibit the firmness with which they opposed themselves to an existing evil. England at this time

---

[1] E. Guest, on the campaign of Aulus Plautius, in "Archæol. Journal," Sept., 1866, vol. xxiii., p. 159.

[2] *Supra*, p. 83.

was in a state of undue submission to the see of Rome. The papal legate had a real, but undefined authority. The king was considered as, in a certain sense, a dependent son of the Church of Rome. And England was also an important source of the papal revenue, which was levied in various ways, and caused a constant drain of the national wealth. One, but not by any means the only, method of obtaining money was the taxation of the clergy, who were required to constitute a twentieth, or a fifteenth, or a tenth part, as might be claimed, on the pretence of a subsidy for the Holy Land. This was not paid without great reluctance, which was aggravated by the circumstance that this was not exclusively applied to the purpose for which it was alleged to be raised. The tax was imposed upon all the property of the Church, the clergy, and the monasteries; and England was considered to place abundant resources at the command of the pope. At this time there was an implacable hostility between the Pope Gregory IX. and the Emperor Frederick II. The war, which had originally begun upon the failure of the emperor to keep faith in respect of the proposed crusade in A.D. 1227, and which had led to his excommunication, had indeed been brought to a close. But it was renewed in A.D. 1239, a few years after the marriage of the emperor with the king's sister, Isabella. In consequence of this renewal of hostilities the pope demanded a subsidy from the English clergy. The bishops, in a synod held in London, at the close of July,[1] protested in this behalf,

---

[1] Mat. Par., *u. s.*, *ad* A.D. 1239, p. 498.

that "the importunity of Rome had so often exhausted the goods of the Church that it could no longer be endured," and refused to comply with the request.

In the following year, the pope sent into England Peter de Rubeis, who endeavoured by every form of chicanery to induce the heads of religious houses, to whom he made application, to allow the claim. But it was in vain. They appealed in person to the king, who, however, with Otho, the papal legate, at his side, was found to treat them with great harshness for their refusal, and to offer one of his safest castles for their imprisonment. The legate, after this, summoned the bishops to meet him at Northampton; who excused themselves at once from any further action on their part, on the ground that their archdeacons were much better acquainted with the means of the clergy than themselves, and that application should be made to them. The expedient next adopted was to call together the clergy[1] of Berkshire, with some others, in the hope that they would not refuse to accede to the demand which the legate was present to make. But he was equally unable to prevail upon them to do so. They adhered to the former determination of their brethren, and were so far from giving way, that they even strengthened their refusal by some additional reasons which they offered for themselves. The tenor of their answer was to this effect :—The subsidy was intended to aid the pope in his contest with the emperor, against whom it was not lawful to proceed

---

[1] Mat. Paris calls them " Rectores Ecclesiarum de Bercshyre et quosdam alios," *u. s.*, *ad* A.D. 1240, p. 534.

as against a heretic, because, although he had been excommunicated, he had never been formally convicted of heresy. His invasion even of the Roman patrimony was not a sufficient reason for the war, as the Church was not dependent for its protection on the arm of flesh. Moreover, while the see of Rome had its own patrimony, so also had other churches, which should be free in respect of it, and not subject to any tax for its defence. It would be an evil precedent to submit in the present instance. And, besides this, the emperor was not only an ally of their king, but was connected with him by marriage. The country, too, was already impoverished and had need of its own resources for its own service. These weighty reasons had the desired effect of convincing the legate that the resolution of the assembly was not to be shaken; and he was therefore compelled to resort to the expedient of creating dissension among his opponents, and went himself to the king in the hope of attaching him to this cause, and obtaining his assistance.

Such was the part which the clergy of the archdeaconry were forward in taking upon a question of great public importance, which, in the end, attained to much larger proportions, but was finally settled by a compromise, through which the clergy "were reduced to compound with the pontiff for eleven thousand marks."[1] But yet this action of the clergy, though not immediately successful, was a step in the furtherance of a cause, which was ultimately to prevail—the cause of national

---

[1] Lingard, "Hist. of Engl.," vol. ii., ch. vi., *u. s.*, p. 207.

freedom, and its complete independence in respect of the see of Rome.

In A.D. 1240, the county of Berkshire was again the scene of an opposition to the papal claim: in this instance of so large a demand as of a fifth. All the archbishops, bishops, and chief abbots, with certain of the nobles, assembled at Reading; and after the legate, as before, had declared the reasons for which the pope was induced to make war against the emperor, and the instant need of a subsidy, they made answer through the bishops, " that they could by no means consent to so intolerable a burden, which touched the whole Church, without a longer deliberation."[1] Upon this, the further consideration of the question was deferred to a later day. The Archbishop of Canterbury, however, St. Edmund, himself a man of the county, and born at Abingdon, was found to consent shortly afterwards to the imposition of the tax. But he had for his own part a grievance of a different kind. The king, through his bad economy, was continually in want of money, and adopted the practice of keeping the bishoprics, abbacies, and other benefices vacant, in order to obtain their revenues to supply his necessities. St. Edmund, who could not accept this abuse of the royal prerogative, procured a bull from Pope Gregory IX., empowering him to fill such vacant benefices after the lapse of six months; but the concession was revoked upon the king's remonstrance. Dissatisfied with the evils of the times, which he could not prevent, and feeling deeply the conduct of

---

[1] Mat. Par., *u. s.*, p. 526.

the legate towards himself, he left his see, and, after a visit to the French Court at Paris, retired to the Abbey of Pontigny, which had already afforded a refuge to his predecessors, Langton and Beket. He was canonised by Innocent IV. at the short interval of six years after his death.

A few years after the incidents which have been mentioned, there was another cause of grievance within the archdeaconry, through which the Abbot of Abingdon found himself placed in great strait.[1] Among the forms of papal oppression, which were peculiarly offensive, and against which the nobility of England had in vain reclaimed, was the practice which was adopted by the popes of preventing the bishops from collating to any benefice without their consent. In this condition of things the abbot was charged by the pope, Innocent IV., to make provision for a foreigner, a Roman, by presenting him to a benefice. The nominee was not disposed to accept any but a valuable one, but kept his intention concealed. In the mean time the church of St. Helen at Abingdon became vacant, in A.D. 1248, and the man fixed upon it. The very day, however, upon which the vacancy occurred, the abbot received a peremptory command from the king to present Ethelmar de Valence, who was his half-brother, being the son of his mother, Isabella, by her second marriage with the Earl of March. He was already possessed of several benefices, although totally undeserving of advancement in the Church.[2] The abbot was perplexed at this, "as if

[1] Mat. Par., *u. s., ad* A.D. 1248, p. 754.
[2] Ethelmar was appointed Bishop of Winchester in A.D.

he had been placed between two revolving millstones," and consulted his convent and his friends. Upon deliberation it was considered the safest way to comply with the king's demand, who, on his part, promised him protection, which promise, as the event proved, he failed to make good. Ethelmar was presented, and, as might be expected, the other claimant was greatly annoyed and applied to the pope. The abbot was immediately summoned to Rome. As he was old and infirm, the journey itself was a burden to him; but besides this he was put to great expense; nor did he regain his liberty except upon an annual payment of a fine of fifty marks, to the great detriment of his house.

The king, Henry III., was at Reading in A.D. 1259, and the circumstances attending his visit have an interest of their own from their connexion with the social and religious history of the times. The Jews had recently been adjudged to be guilty of the murder of the boy named Hugh at Lincoln,[1] whom they were alleged to have stolen and kept for some days, at the expiration of which he was crucified in solemn mockery of our Lord. His body had been discovered in a well by his mother, upon which the legal investigation had ensued. A severe infliction of punishment naturally followed. Ninety of the Jews in Lincoln were sent prisoners to London. The whole of the people was declared to be implicated in the matter, and further vengeance was threatened.

1249, a step which led to much contention, from his delay in obtaining consecration.

[1] Mat. Par., *u. s.*, A.D. 1255, p. 912.

In this state of things, the Dominicans, whose mission to the Jews in Oxford has been already mentioned,[1] ventured to intercede in their behalf, and undertook the office of saving them from the impending injury.[2] Their efforts were ineffectual, and they had to experience in consequence so great a loss of popular favour, that, when they begged for alms in London, they could find no one to give them relief.

In this emergency the Jews found another protector. Richard, the Earl of Cornwall, and the king's brother, interposed and received the Jews in pledge from the king, on the payment of a large sum of money, which had to be supplied to him for this purpose by the Jews themselves. It was after Easter, during the visit which the king made to Reading, that this suit was thus effectual, and the king's promulgation of his pardon took place. But pending this result the persecution had not ceased, for the king's disposition was not shown until eighteen of the principal Jews had been executed, who were hanged in London near the close of the preceding year.

The councils which were held in Berkshire are of sufficient importance to claim a separate place. So early as in A.D. 1070, on the Whitsunday of that year, the 23rd of May, the king presented Thomas, a canon of Bayeux, whom there has been already occasion to mention,[3] to the archbishopric of York, and his chaplain, Walkeline, to the bishopric of Winchester. In this the Conqueror exercised the ancient

---

[1] *Supra*, p. 41.
[2] Annales de Burton, in "Ann. Monastici," *u. s.*, vol. i., pp. 240-248.     [3] *Supra*, p. 22.

prerogative of the English kings, by disposing of the highest benefices of the church.[1] But he intimated at the same time the mode of treatment which the English Church was to expect by the promotion of foreign ecclesiastics, with whom, however excellent a choice might be made, it could have no national sympathies.

On the following day, at the command of the king, the papal legate, Ermenfrid, who was left in England alone, held a synod at the same place. Here Ethelric,[2] or Heca,[3] the Bishop of Sussex, the throne of whose see was placed at Selsey, and who had been confessor to King Edward, was uncanonically deposed; and at the same time several abbots were deprived of their office. The bishopric of East Anglia, which comprised the united see of Elmham and Dunwich, was given by the king to Arfast, or Herefast, and the bishopric of Sussex, just mentioned, to Stigand, both of whom were his chaplains. He also promoted several foreign ecclesiastics to the vacant abbacies. As the two archbishoprics were vacant at this time, one by deposition and the other by death, Walkeline was consecrated bishop by Ermenfrid, the legate, who was the titular Bishop of Sion, on the octave of Whitsunday.

In A.D. 1072, the contest which had existed between Lanfranc and Thomas, the Archbishop of York, respecting the jurisdiction of the Archbishop of Canterbury, was settled before the king at

---

[1] See E. A. Freeman; *supr.*, p. 18.
[2] Flor. of Worc., *u. s.*, p. 175.
[3] "Anglo-Saxon Chron.," *ad an.*

Windsor.[1] This has been already noticed, and its connexion with the present state of the diocese pointed out.[2]

Again, in A.D. 1114, there was another council at Windsor[3] on Sunday, the 26th of April, at which Ralph, the Bishop of Rochester,[4] who had been previously Abbot of Say in Normandy, was chosen for the archbishopric of Canterbury. It is not unimportant, that he received investiture from the king by the ring and pastoral staff, as in this Henry resumed the right of investiture of bishops, which for a time, "to gratify Anselm," he had waived in violation of the ancient customs of the realm.[5] It was between Ralph and Thurstan, who was elected Archbishop of York a few months later, that the great controversy arose, on Thurstan refusing the customary submission that was often "ventilated"[6] before the king and the pope, before any settlement of it could be obtained.

There are two councils of a later date, which are noticed in "Collections of Councils," as having been held at Reading, besides some others which, as being of a less formal or a less prominent character, are not so commonly mentioned.[7] The former of these two took

[1] Wilkins, "Conc.," *u. s.*, vol. i., p. 381.
[2] *Supra*, p. 22.
[3] Flor. of Worc., *u. s.*, p. 225.
[4] Mat. Par., *u. s.*, p. 65; see note in *var. lect. ad loc.*
[5] Abp. Bramhall, "Vindication of the Ch. of Engl.," pt. i., disc. ii. "Works," vol. i., p. 263, A.C.L. Oxf., 1842.
[6] Mat. Par., *u. s.*, p. 65, l. 57.
[7] For these see Wilkins, "Conc.," *u. s.*, vol. i., pp. 546, 678; vol. ii., p. 24.

place in A.D. 1206, but does not appear to have had any important results. In that year John of Ferento, the papal legate, had traversed the whole of England, and had collected a large sum of money. He then, with the desire to perform some act of ecclesiastical authority before his departure, held a council at Reading on the morrow of St. Luke's Day.[1] He next placed all his goods and his treasure in safe keeping, and made his way with all speed for the coast, from which he set sail, and bade farewell to English ground. In this procedure there is to be recognised the manner in which the realm was subjected to the exactions of the papal court through the influence of the legate's presence.

The other council, which was held in A.D. 1279, was of greater importance, and the canons which were enacted formed an integral part of the English ecclesiastical law. A vacancy had occurred in the see of Canterbury from the resignation of Robert Kilwarby, who had been made a cardinal, and had left England, and gone to reside in Rome. The monks of Canterbury proceeded to the election of his successor, and unanimously chose Robert Burnell, who was the Bishop of Bath, to fill his place. But the election was annulled by the Pope Nicholas III., who appointed John Peckham, a Franciscan of eminent learning, in his stead. This was a form of encroachment upon the liberties of the English Church to which the Parliament is found at a later time to oppose its firm resistance. Peckham was consecrated

[1] Mat. Par., *u. s.*, p. 214; Flor. of Worc., *u. s.*, p. 312; Hard., "Conc.," *u. s.*, tom. vi., p. 2, col. 1,974.

at Rome during Lent, and soon afterwards came to
England. Nor was it long before he summoned a
council of the bishops to attend him at Reading, in
which he promulgated his constitutions, which were in a
great measure the same with the decree of the council
of London,[1] and of other councils. By these it was
provided, with much benefit to the discipline of the
clergy, that all incumbents of parishes with the cure
of souls should be content with one benefice; and
that all who obtained preferment should be admitted
to holy orders within a year. There were also various
provisions for the due administration of the Sacraments, and other matters of ecclesiastical order.[2] Some
of the enactments, however, appeared to contradict
the king's prerogative, and these he was subsequently
compelled to retract; and to agree generally "that
the great charter should not be affixed to the doors
of the churches; and that he would grant and allow
that neither to the king, nor to his heirs, nor to his
realm, should any prejudice arise in the future by
reason of any of the articles contained in the council
of Reading."[3]

The habits of life which a Berkshire clergyman
might be thought capable of adopting at the beginning of the sixteenth century, may be learned from
the foundation charter of the almshouses at Childrey
in A.D. 1526; for it is provided that the priest of

[1] *Supra*, pp. 23, 195.
[2] The canons occupy in Harduin's "Conc.," *u. s.*, tom. vii., coll. 779-90.
[3] Extract from the Close Rolls, 7 Ed. I., m. 1., dors., in Wilkins, "Conc.," *u. s.*, vol. ii., p. 40.

the chantry within the church, who was also to be the chaplain, should not be "otherwise beneficed; and that if he should be guilty of immorality, or keep hounds, or be a common hunter, or a stirrer-up of contention in the town of Childrey, or parts adjacent, he should be removed."[1]

The town of Newbury, in the early part of the year A.D. 1540, was visited by Miles Coverdale, who had a commission to inquire into the existence of popish books and other abuses, as they were deemed, connected with religion.[2] Two years previously, the name of Thomas Beket had been erased from the calendar, and his office removed from the breviary by the king.[3] The curate of Newbury was directed "to call for all such books, as were either incorrect, or against the king's most lawful act concerning Thomas à Beket, or the Bishop of Rome." And the subject of Beket was one upon which especially he was intent, and he gave audience to two inhabitants of Henley-upon-Thames, who came to him "reporting that in a glass window of our Lady Chapel, in the church of the said Henley, the image of Thomas à Beket, with the whole feigned story of his death, is suffered to stand still." He wrote to give notice of this to Cromwell in due course, charging the offence upon "the great and notable

---

[1] "Proceedings of Oxf. Architect. and Hist. Soc.," New Ser., No. xx., p. 62. Ox., 1872.

[2] Coverdale, "Remains," Letters ix., x., xi., pp. 498-502. Camb., 1846. Park. Soc.

[3] Burnet, "Hist. of the Ref.," *n. s.*, vol. i., p. 394; Lingard, "Hist. of Engl.," *n. s.*, vol. v., p. 54.

negligence of the Bishop of Lincoln,"[1] who did not weed out such faults."

This was not the first time that a Beket window had caused excitement within the limits of the present diocese. In A.D. 1537, while "the priests and paradoxers were expatiating with an obvious application upon the glories of the martyr, the Church's victory, and the humiliation of the king,"[2] to the listening crowd in the chapel of New Woodstock, a groom from the Court was lounging about among the people, who interrupted the speakers disdainfully by observing that "he saw no more reason why Beket was a saint than Robin Hood." Nothing was said of this to the king, but "a priest carried the story to Gardiner and Sir William Paulet; the man was hurried off on charge of heresy to the Tower, and, appealing to Cromwell, there followed a storm at the council table."

The purpose of Coverdale thus exhibited in the attention paid to the report from Henley, is an intimation of the future spoliation which awaited the painted glass of church windows at a later time; when historic representations, if the scenes were offensive to the prevailing sentiments of the time, were not spared.

Those who suffered the penalty of death for their religious opinions in the sixteenth century may claim a brief account. The first group to be mentioned

[1] The Bishop of Lincoln was John Longland.
[2] Froude, "Hist. of Engl.," ch. xiv., vol. iii., p. 51. Lond., 1870; from a letter of William Umpton to Cromwell, "MSS. State Paper Office," 2nd Ser., vol. xlvi.

consists of those who suffered at Windsor in A.D. 1543. The Act of the Six Articles[1] had become law on the 28th of June, in A.D. 1539, and the penalties which it enforced were most severe. All who disputed against the accepted sacramental doctrine were condemned to the stake, while those who opposed the remaining five were to die a felon's death. It was under the former of these enactments that the three men of Windsor, Anthony Peerson, Robert Testwood, and Henry Filmer, were burnt, two others narrowly escaping the same punishment with them, Robert Bennet and the celebrated musician, John Marbeck.[2] In order to establish a case against Peerson Dr. London,[3] the warden of New College, who was one of those who sat upon his trial, placed within the church in which he officiated some chantry priests, a class of the priesthood which never ranked high, as spies to observe the reverence which was paid to the Holy Sacrament, and to note his words. In the case of Testwood, there were other charges also of a lighter character. Marbeck was subjected to five separate examinations ; one of the things alleged against him being the simple fact that he had begun to make a concordance to the Bible in English, having been induced to attempt this in preference to copying out the whole of Matthew's Bible, which he had com-

---

[1] 38 Henry VIII., c. 14, entitled, "An Act for abolishing diversity of opinions in certain articles concerning Christian religion." It was qualified in some respects by a later statute, 35 Hen. VIII., c. 5.

[2] Foxe, "Acts and Mon.," *u. s.*, vol. v., p. 466, *seq.*

[3] See *supra*, pp. 85, 86.

menced, through want of means to purchase it. He was in the end condemned with the others, but was pardoned through the good offices of Bishop Gardiner. The other three endured their sufferings with much constancy.

A remarkable circumstance attending the death of these gospellers was the entire change which took place in the king's mind. Having casually asked the high sheriff, while hunting, respecting the execution of the law at Windsor, he received answer that the execution of these men had proved a great trial of conscience, as a conspiracy had been formed against them. The king turned away his horse's head, exclaiming, "Alas, poor innocents." But the matter did not end here. He caused London and two lawyers, Simon and Ockham, who were the chief conspirators, to be examined upon oath; and then, as they were found guilty of perjury, there was passed upon them the severe, but well-merited sentence, that they should ride through Windsor, Reading, and Newbury, with papers on their heads stating their offence, and with their faces turned to the wall, and also to stand in the pillory in each of these towns, for their false accusation of the gospellers, and for perjury.[1]

Another execution took place in the same year,[2] and possibly at Windsor, in which a canon of the church was the sufferer, and for a very different cause. James Mallet, who had also been master of the Hospital of St. Giles, at High Wycombe, which he had resigned, was then Canon of Windsor. He was

[1] Foxe, "Acts and Mon.," *u. s.*, vol. v., p. 496.
[2] Ashmole, "History of Berks," vol. iii., p. 256. Lond., 1719.

a man of a great age, and had held his canonry since A.D. 1516. Among the guests whom he invited to his table was a man who spoke to him, while he was at dinner, of the disturbances which had occurred upon the dissolution of the monasteries, and which formed a common topic of conversation at the time as having recently taken place. The canon, on hearing what was told him, remarked, in what is described as an English adage, "Then has the king brought his hogs to a fair market." For this he was delated by his treacherous guest, and at the interval, as it would appear, of some years, was put to death by the king, with a tyrannical exercise of power which nothing could surpass.

Newbury was the scene, on more than one occasion, of suffering in the cause of religion. In A.D. 1518, Christopher Shoemaker, who was an inhabitant of another parish in the diocese, Great Missenden, came from time to time to Newbury, and endeavoured to promulgate the opinions which he had embraced, concerning the Holy Sacrament and the worshipping of saints, and pilgrimages, and for this was burned.[1]

In A.D. 1556, in the Sandpits at Newbury, there took place the execution of three others, the details of whose sufferings are better known, Julius Palmer, John Gwin, and Thomas Askin, for their steadfast adherence to the teaching of the Reformers, which they had embraced. Julius Palmer was the most eminent in this group of sufferers. He had been a fellow

---

[1] Foxe, *u. s.*, vol. iv., p. 217.

of Magdalen College, in Oxford, and master of the grammar school at Reading. In the previous reign he had been expelled from his college for his consistent maintenance of the old faith; but he had been restored upon the accession of Queen Mary. A witness of the constancy with which Ridley and Latimer had suffered, he was deeply impressed by their firmness, as he had been by what he had heard of the deaths of others, and became gradually convinced that their cause was the cause of truth. While undergoing this change of sentiment, he was unable to join heartily in the service of his college chapel, and, from the suspicions which were excited by this, felt it necessary to retire from it. It was then that he became master of the school at Reading, where he was again exposed to persecution, and not least from his own mother. On returning to Reading to receive the stipend which was due to him, he made his lodging at an inn, known as the Cardinal's Hat. Here he was betrayed to those who sought to take him while he was in bed. After a previous examination he was sent to Newbury, at which place Dr. Jeffrey, the chancellor of the diocese, was to hold his visitation on July the 16th. There, in the parish church, four or five seats were prepared within the choir for the chancellor and the other visitors by whom the three were to be tried. He was strictly examined as to some Latin verses which he had published, entitled the "Epicedion," which, as being written in disparagement of the Bishop of Winchester, had given great offence; and also as to his opinions on the Holy Sacrament. Money was not wanting to induce him to recant. Sir Richard Abridges, the Sheriff, offered him a yearly stipend and maintenance; and the chancellor was stated to have promised him a living. But he set his hand to his articles; the next morning, the sentence of his condemnation was read; he was delivered to the secular power, and was burnt with his two companions in the afternoon of the same day. An additional instance of cruelty at his execution was the act of a servant of one of the bailiffs of the town, who threw a fagot at his head, which caused the blood to gush out; upon which the sheriff, with a just retribution, struck the man who had done this upon the head with his own walking-staff, so that he was made to suffer in the same way himself.[1]

Bishop Jewel in early life, while he was still residing in Corpus Christi College, was "a preacher and catechiser at Sunningwell, near Abingdon";[2] and it has been considered that the parish may still retain an interesting memorial of his connexion with it. Annexed to the church is a singular building, or porch, as it may be termed, of an hexagonal form, with projecting Ionic columns at the angles supporting an entablature. On four sides of it are windows of debased Gothic, consisting of one light within a square head. The doorway in its details is of mixed Roman and Gothic features. This is supposed to have been erected by Jewel, the character of it corresponding with the date at which Jewel held the curacy, the middle of the six-

---

[1] Foxe, "Acts and Mon.," *u. s.*, vol. viii., p. 218.
[2] Wood, "Athen. Oxon.," *u. s.*, vol. i., col. 132.

teenth century.[1] It has even been supposed that the church itself was built by him, for the same reason.[2]

The position which was occupied by an incumbent of Berkshire, Dr. William Twisse, of Newbury, will illustrate the course of proceedings in the early part of the civil war, from a religious point of view. After addresses had been made to them in favour of such a scheme, the Lords and Commons determined by an ordinance of the 12th of June, in A.D. 1643, that an assembly of learned divines should be called to meet in Henry VII.'s chapel at Westminster on the 1st of July in the same year, to consult with the Parliament "for settling the government and liturgy of the Church of England, and for vindicating its doctrine." On the 22nd of June the king issued his proclamation forbidding their meeting under the severest penalties. The list of members was completed by direction of Parliament,[3] and Dr. Twisse was appointed prolocutor; and, to supply the place of those who might refuse to attend the meetings, there were appointed the "superadded divines." On the 1st of July, the day of the opening of their proceedings, Dr. Twisse preached the sermon, which was a preliminary part of the ceremonial. He was a man of venerable age, and was a laborious and painstaking divine, and of exemplary life, but less celebrated as

---

[1] M. H. Bloxham, "Principles of Gothic Arch.," p. 308. Lond., 1845.

[2] J. H. Parker, "Architect. Topography," Berks, No. 64 Ox., 1850.

[3] See the list in Neal's "History of the Puritans," vol. iii., p. 51. Lond., 1795.

a preacher than as a disputant and controversialist. He exhorted the members "to discharge faithfully their high calling to the glory of God and the honour of His Church. And he much bemoaned the one thing which "in his judgment" was wanting, "the royal assent."[1] The assembly after this determined upon the course to be adopted, which in the end led to important results. The "Directory for public worship" was authorised;[2] the solemn league and covenant was settled, and received a formal recognition in solemn form on the 25th of September in St. Margaret's Church at Westminster; the shorter, and the longer Catechisms were agreed upon, both of which were also approved by the general assembly of the Kirk of Scotland in A.D. 1648, and still constitute the authorised forms of instruction; the trial of the competence of ministers was instituted.

Dr. Twisse, however, did not continue to hold the office of prolocutor for a longer time than one year, at the expiration of which he became weary of the duties of it, and retired to his parish in Newbury. It was in his power to accept preferment; but he declined to leave his parish without being able to secure a successor whom he could approve of, which he was not permitted to do. He was, indeed, himself so well fitted for his position there, that upon conference with the Bishop of Salisbury the king was unwilling that he should leave Newbury.[3] This

---

[1] Fuller, "Church Hist.," *u. s.*, cent. xvii., ch. xi., p. 199.
[2] *Supra*, p. 132.
[3] Wood, "Athen. Oxon.," *u. s.*, vol. ii., col. 41.

favour, however, did not prevent him from sustaining severe losses in his retirement, "being forced thence, as his brethren said, by the royal party;" in compensation for which he was appointed one of the lecturers at St. Andrew's Church, in Holborn. He died in the month of July, A.D. 1646, and was buried in Westminster Abbey, the whole assembly of divines attending his funeral. But his remains were not suffered to rest in peace, for after the restoration they were exhumed[1] and removed from the Abbey,—a mode of treatment to which the body of Admiral Blake was subjected, and so far as the intention of the royalists was concerned, Cromwell's body too, although it may possibly have been saved from the actual indignity. The reinterment of the remains of Dr. Twisse took place in St. Margaret's churchyard, which was close at hand.[2]

The clergy who were exposed to ill treatment in their parishes during the civil war have been enumerated with the clergy of Oxfordshire at the same period;[3] and also those who were ejected from their cures after the Restoration.[4] Some mention has also been made of the nonjurors in Berkshire, and the influence which one of their number was enabled to exercise.[5] The notice of the several periods need not be repeated here.

Near the close of the same century, in A.D. 1692,

[1] Benj. Brooks, "Lives of the Puritans," vol. ii., p. 16.
[2] Kennet's "Register," p. 534, in A. P. Stanley, "Memorials of Westminster Abbey," ch. iv., p. 225. Lond., 1868.
[3] *Supra*, p. 134.
[4] *Ibid.*, p. 147.     [5] *Ibid.*, pp. 161, 162.

there was born at Wantage, of Presbyterian parents, one who in future years, as the author of the "Analogy," Joseph Butler, the Bishop of Durham, has exercised the most powerful influence upon minds of the highest cultivation. Nor is this the only birth from which the town has become famous. For, in A.D. 849, King Alfred "was born in the royal vill, which is called Wanadirg."[1]

At a more recent date there has arisen another and a very great reason for notice, in connexion with the progress of the Church within the diocese. In A.D. 1856, there was opened, as previously at Clewer in the same archdeaconry, in A.D. 1849, a house of mercy for the reception of penitents: which, with the kindred institutions in either place, has shown the capacity of development possessed by the English communion. The sisterhoods which were formed, and by which the ministrations of the various works of charity were carried on, were brought in an especial manner under the knowledge of the bishop of the diocese; and he was therefore able to state emphatically:—"High Christian genius, firm faith,ardent love, and undaunted courage, alone could have founded them; patience, sobriety, and judgment, alone could have maintained them."[2]

At the present time the deaneries in the archdeaconry, which have been subdivided, are nine in number; while the parishes are as many as one hundred and ninety-two. The present endowment of the archdeaconry of Berkshire, as compared with

[1] Asser, "Ann. Res. Gest. Aelfr. M.," p. 1. Oxon., 1872.
[2] Bp. Wilberforce, "Charge," *u. s.*, p. 19. Ox., 1869.

its condition in this respect at an earlier time, may be thus stated.[1] The archdeaconry, down to the year A.D. 1855, was endowed with the appropriate rectory of North Moreton in Berkshire,[2] and by an order in council, gazetted the 28th of September in that year, that rectory, with the consent of the bishop and the then Archdeacon Randall, was disannexed from the archdeaconry, and was vested in the ecclesiastical commissions, the same order securing to the archdeaconry on their part an annual payment of one hundred and fifty-eight pounds; which sum, together with an estimated annual receipt of forty-two pounds for fees, makes up the statutory endowment of two hundred pounds yearly. The archdeacon retains the patronage of the vicarage of North Moreton, which is the only benefice in his presentation. The impropriation had been made at an early date, for the church is retained as annexed to the archdeaconry in the report of the survey of Henry VIII., at which time the office was held by Robert Awdeley.[3]

[1] This information is by the favour of George Pringle, Esq., Secretary to the Ecclesiastical Commission.

[2] In the passage referred to, *supra*, p. 220, n. 1, Asser also states that the county of Berks derived its name from the wood "Berroc," where the box grew plentifully, which is an accepted derivation.

[3] "Val. Eccl. Hen. VIII.," *u. s.*, vol. ii., p. 74.

## CHAPTER IX.

MONASTIC AND COLLEGIATE HISTORY OF BERKS,
FROM A.D. 675.

Benedictine Order—Abingdon—Reading—Windsor.

THE archdeaconry of Berkshire was richly endowed with monastic and collegiate institutions. The Benedectine order of monks, the Black Monks, as they were named from the colour of their habit, obtained a greater influence in England than any other order, from the number and importance of the foundations which owed obedience to the rule of St. Benedict, who was the great legislator for the monasticism of the West. A monastery of this order had been founded at Rome by Gregory the Great, which he had himself entered, before he succeeded to the papacy; and St. Augustine, who came into England at his bidding, was sent from this house with his fellow-monks on his mission into England. It is, therefore, to the arrival of St. Augustine that the preponderating influence of the order in this country may be traced. At a later period a large proportion of the religious institutions was subject to its rule; nor did the diocese of Oxford, as comprising the three counties, form any exception to this. There are in Oxfordshire itself the well-known names of St. Frideswide's Monastery,[1] Eynsham Abbey,[2] the Nunneries of God-

---

[1] Founded A.D. 727; *supra*, p. 73-75.   [2] Before A.D. 1105.

stow,[1] and of Littlemore,[2] Gloucester College or Priory,[3] and of Durham College.[4] The order was represented by numerous but less eminent foundations in Buckinghamshire, as Bradwell Priory[5] and Missendon Abbey,[6] and the Nunneries of Ivinghoe,[7] Little Marlow,[8] and Burnham.[9] But in no one of the counties within the present diocese were there establishments of this order of so great wealth and importance, and of so high distinction as in Berkshire. Not to notice the less prominent foundations as at Hurley[10] or at Wallingford,[11] there were two abbeys which attained to the greatest constitutional privilege, which could be recognised within the realm; and were centres of the highest civilisation and culture, as well as of the deepest religious influence, of which the adjoining country, through long years, derived the benefit, at Abingdon and at Reading.

The town of Abingdon, at an early period of its history, possessed a Benedictine abbey, of which the mitred abbot was summoned with the barons to parliament.[12] This foundation has had a long and eventful course, for the first dedication of the site to a religious use was made in the seventh century. An

---

[1] A.D. 1138.
[2] Probably A.D. 1177.
[3] A.D. 1283; *supra*, p. 91-7.
[4] A.D. 1280; *supra*, p. 41.
[5] A.D. 1155.
[6] A.D. 1293.
[7] c. A.D. 1160.
[8] Before A.D. 1189.
[9] A.D. 1266.
[10] Before A.D. 1087.
[11] Before A.D. 1093.
[12] The authority relied upon for the various particulars in the history of the abbey is the "Chronicon Monasterii de Abingdon." Edited by Joseph Stevenson, in 2 vols., 1858. Rolls' Ser.

account of the situation, which is found in the chronicle of the abbey, describes it as being on table land surmounting a rising ground of a delightful aspect, in a retired spot, enclosed within two most pleasant streams, equally grateful to the eye of the spectator and convenient for the use of the inhabitants.[1] The original name which the site bore was Sevekesham. It was a royal seat; and it is stated that some crosses and images, the relics of an earlier British Christianity, were discovered in the ground. Such a statement, however, must be received with caution, as it has an obvious tendency to enhance the dignity of the monastery from earlier associations. It is also opposed to the more authentic history, for, when Birinus came into Wessex in A.D. 634, he found the people most completely pagan.[2] The earlier traces of their conversion, if such had ever taken place, must have entirely disappeared before his arrival. It is a safer statement which represents the present name of Abingdon, which has replaced the former one, as a patronymic, connoting the settlement of the descendants of Abba, one of the early colonists of Berkshire.[3]

In the course of the forty years which followed the first preaching of Birinus a great change had been produced. At one of the missions which were sent out from Selsey, Hean, the nephew of one of the under kings of Centwin, Cissa, whose rule extended over Wiltshire and a large part of Berkshire, was

[1] "Chron. Mon. de Abingd.," *u. s.*, vol. i., p. 3.
[2] Beda ("Hist. Eccl.," iii. 7), describes them as "paganissimi."
[3] "Chron. Mon. de Abingd.," *u. s.*, vol. ii., pref., p. v., n. 1.

present. He was moved by the zeal of the preacher, and determined to lead a life of religious purity, in which resolution he was joined by his sister Cilla. They then obtained from their uncle a grant of land, about A.D. 675, to which they added their own patrimony. Cilla, who was endued with the greater energy, at once built a nunnery, which she dedicated in honour of St. Helena, on a spot which was in consequence named Helenstow, the site of the present church of St. Helen.[1] This was subsequently removed to Wytham. Hean, on the other hand, was deficient in zeal and deferred the execution of his project; culpably so, as the grant had been on the condition that a monastery should be erected on the land, of which Abingdon was the central point. Cissa has thus been reputed the original founder of the abbey.[2] After the death of Cissa and his successor, Ceadwalla, who had made a further donation, Ini found on his accession, after an interval of thirteen years, that the engagement of Hean was still unfulfilled. He, as a first step, suspended any further action; and when upon the settlement of the affairs of his kingdom he was able to attend to the spiritual welfare of his subjects, he altogether withdrew the grants which had been made to Hean. The character of Ini and his conduct, both as a benefactor to the Church and as a lawgiver, forbid the supposition that it was from

---

[1] See Tanner, "Notitia Monastica," Berks, xi. Lond., 1787; and Leland, "Itin.," *u. s.*, vols. ii., p. 43; vii., pt. ii., p. 75.

[2] Will. of Malmes., "De Gest. Pontif." *u. s.*, lib. ii., sect. 88, p. 191. "Chron. Mon. de Ab.," *u. s.*, vol. i., p. 1., n. ii., pp. 268-270.

any want on his part of an interest in religion that he did this; and it must be attributed to the offence which was caused by Hean's inexcusable delay.¹

In the division which Ini made of the see of Wessex,² the bishopric of Sherborne received the county of Berkshire, and it came within the jurisdiction of St. Aldhelm, the first bishop of the new see. The influence of Aldhelm was exerted in favour of the foundation of the abbey of Abingdon, which, for various reasons, it would be desirable to establish in so remote a corner of Wessex. There, accordingly, it was placed, and the Benedictine rule of constant labour, for those who were subject to it, would be a source of general improvement in the vicinity, as well as a centre of religious culture. And in the course of years, by fresh grants and the gradual development of its resources, it attained a high place. In the border contests it must have suffered much anxiety, lest it should become a prey to the invader. But the great scene of disaster was at a later time. When the Danes overran the county, spreading desolation everywhere, c. A.D. 866–871, the monasteries were an attractive spoil from the wealth of every kind, which they not only possessed of their own, but received for safe keeping from the owners. And so "they came at last," as the chronicle pathetically remarks,³ "to the sacred and venerable home at Abingdon, which so many holy kings and true men had endowed, with such lionlike ferocity, and such

---

[1] "Chron. Mon. de Abingd.," u. s., vol. ii., pref., pp. 11, 12.
[2] *Supra*, p. 13.
[3] "Chron. Mon. de Abingd.," u. s., vol. i., p. 47.

hateful greed, that the monks were scattered and the monastery destroyed, with only the bare walls left. Thus strangers, and pagans, too, came into the place of those who were beloved of God."

When the success of King Alfred had at length rolled back the tide of events, the abbey was rebuilt. The king made a grant of land at Appleford to a faithful dependant, Deormodus, with power to leave it to his sons. And he made choice of the abbey to succeed to the inheritance, devoting it, after the usual form of such donations, "to God and the blessed Mary and the church of Abingdon;" and after his death the king further ratified and confirmed the bequest.[1]

Near the close of the second century after the abbey had been thus rebuilt and reinstated, a third reconstruction took place, c. A.D. 946–55. It was seen that the abbey had once more become neglected and impoverished, consisting of but a few small buildings, and with a large proportion of the estates repossessed by the king.[2] At this conjunction of affairs another patron was found. St. Ethelwold was in great favour with King Eadred. He was born of a good parentage at Winchester, was largely endowed with every grace of mind and body, and had been brought up at Glastonbury under the care of Dunstan. The king's mother, Edgiva, induced her son to give him the ancient site of the monastery at Abingdon, to which, accordingly, he went, with an attendant band of clergy; and, having succeeded in collecting a numerous body of monks, was made their abbot by

---

[1] "Chron. Mon. de Abingd.," *u. s.*, vol. i., pp. 49–51.
[2] *Ibid.*, p. 124.

the king's command. In this capacity he received from the king a grant of the royal lands at Abingdon, with a grant of money from the Treasury, to which a further sum was added by Edgiva. He continued to govern the abbey with prudence and success until, after a term of fifteen years, he was appointed to the bishopric of Winchester, for which see he was consecrated by his friend, Archbishop Dunstan. Having been canonised after his death, he is one of the saints whose names are connected with the history of the diocese.

One of the early possessions of the abbey may claim notice from its connexion with the present site of the bishop's palace. In A.D. 956, by a charter, of the genuine character of which there is no suspicion,[1] King Edwy granted the vill of Cuthenesdune to Earl Elfer, who, with the king's permission, immediately conveyed it "in pure and perpetual alms to God and the blessed Mary, and the House of Abingdon, and the monks therein serving God." The boundaries show that the land of the vill extended then, as it does now, from the high ground to the River Thame. And the charter is also interesting as pointing out the origin of the name, which signifies the hill of Cuthen, or Cuthwin,[2] an early settler, whose memory is obscured in the present designation of Cuddesdon. After a lapse of four centuries, the mill which is mentioned in the original grant, and was the old mill

---

[1] "Chron. Mon. de Abingd.," *u. s.*, vol. i., pp. 200–203; ii., p. 513.

[2] See "List of Early Settlers," *ibid.*, vol. ii., p. 89; and Glossary, s.v. "dune," p. 480.

of the lord, became the scene of a fierce conflict. The see of Lincoln was vacant in A.D. 1066, by the death of Wulfwy, and had not yet been reconstructed by Remigius;[1] but the estates were in the process of settlement, for which Peter, the king's chaplain, who was afterwards Bishop of Lichfield, and removed the chair of the bishop to Chester, was the acting commissioner. He desired that a sluice at Cuddesdon Mill, where his property and that of the abbot joined, should be destroyed, while the Abbot Aldred was equally desirous that it should be maintained. The two leaders appeared with a large body of retainers on either side; but the abbot brought with him the relics of the Martyr St. Vincent, and made oath upon them that his claim was just. A miraculous storm and earthquake is said to have established his right. The existence of the sluice, however, was too great a grievance to be quietly endured; and the bishop's men, on a subsequent occasion, broke it down; but he repaired it at his own cost.[2] The mill itself was lost during the incursion of the Danes, but was recovered to the convent by the Abbot Faritius.[3]

The church of Cuddesdon is mentioned as then existing in a bull of Pope Eugenius III. for the confirmation of the privileges and estates of the abbey,[4] which bears the date of April the 7th, A.D. 1152.

It is not required to trace the successive grants of the abbey, nor to describe further the disputes which arose in the course of its history; but there

---

[1] *Supra*, pp. 20, 23, 24.
[2] "Chron. Mon. de Abingd.," *u. s.*, vol. ii., p. 118.
[3] *Ibid.*, p. 288.  [4] *Ibid.*, pp. 195 199.

are some other points of interest which occurred at the time of the Conquest, and which may well be mentioned. After the arrival in England of William the Norman in A.D. 1066, Abbot Aldred, who was a man of prudence, thought it best to follow the example of the nobles, and take the oath of allegiance to the new sovereign.[1] But this availed to save neither the abbey nor himself from harm. The Queen Matilda conceived a wish to obtain the most valuable ornaments which the church of the convent possessed, and sent to the abbot for them; upon which he took counsel with the monks, and despatched some to her, which, however precious, were still not the best which they possessed. She refused to accept them, and demanded others which should be more beautiful and costly than these. The abbot upon this, having a present dread of the foreigners, sent those which had been kept back, which consisted of a chasuble of cloth of gold, the best cope, a vestment, and a copy of the gospels, both of which were enriched with gold and jewels.[2]

At first the abbey was used by the king as a state prison, and among the prisoners confined in it was Egelwine, the Bishop of Durham, who died during the time of his imprisonment. After this the abbot himself appears to have incurred the king's displeasure, upon which he in his turn was committed to the custody of the Bishop of Winchester for the rest of his life,[3] and Ethelhelm, a Norman, was

---

[1] "Chron. Mon. de Abingd.," *u. s.*, vol. i., p. 484.
[2] *Ibid.*, pp. 485–493.
[3] *Ibid.*, pp. 485, 486, 493.

substituted in his place. The new abbot did not fail to make use of his office for his own private advantage. He sent for his relations from Normandy, and put them in possession of many of the estates of the abbey; to such an extent, indeed, was this done, that he disposed in this way of as many as seventy estates in a single year. He also prohibited the commemoration in divine service of St. Ethelwold and St. Edward, as being merely rustic Englishmen. He came to his end by a miserable death.[1] After the king had thus provided for the occupation of the abbacy by one of his Norman dependants, he issued his mandate to the sheriff of the county, and to Archbishop Lanfranc and others, requiring them to maintain the rights and privileges of the abbey and of the abbot Ethelhelm; and his example in this respect was followed by his successor,[2] in A.D. 1087.[3]

A general chapter of the Benedictine order was held at Abingdon in A.D. 1291, which had an intimate connexion with the interests of the foundations, subject to this rule in Oxford; the necessity for which arose in the following way. In consequence of a decree of Pope Innocent III. at the Council of Lateran in A.D. 1215, the Benedictine monasteries in England had been formed into united congregations for the two provinces of Canterbury and York. Later on, in the same century, John Giffard, the baron of Brimesfield, purchased certain land and

[1] "Chron. Mon. de Abingd.," *u. s.*, vol. i., p. 284.
[2] *Ibid.*, vol. ii., p. 1.
[3] *Ibid.*, p. 17.

tenements in Oxford from the Knights Hospitallers, and obtained a licence in mortmain,[1] in A.D. 1291, to assign this acquisition to the Benedictine college in Oxford, and to the whole community of the order in the province.[2] The chapter was held at Abingdon in the same year for the pupose of imposing an equal tax upon the greater abbeys of this rule, in order that lodgings might be built at this college, which was known as Gloucester College or Gloucester Hall, for the use of the novices belonging to this order, who should come to Oxford as students for the advantages of the academical life.

The chronicle to which reference has so frequently been made for the history of the Abbey of Abingdon, contains also a large amount of information respecting the internal arrangements of the convent during the earlier period of its existence, and the offices of the different functionaries by whom its affairs were administered, from the high position of the abbot and prior to the menial service of the hayward, the woodward, and the like. There are various minute details which are to be observed upon the appointment of the abbot,[3] as the pulling off his shoes when he goes to meet the brethren, and the formal resumption of them, and the office in the church, and finally, the feast in the refectory, after which his admission was complete. The occasions are related upon which he is to celebrate mass, and perform divine offices, the immediate attendance which he is to give to any

---

[1] Dated March 12th.
[2] Ingram, *u. s.*, vol. ii., Worcester Coll., pp. 1, 199.
[3] "Chron. Mon. de Abingd.," vol. ii., app. iv., pp. 340, *sqq.*

brother in dangerous sickness, and the constant care that no sacred rite shall be omitted. Provision is made for his journeys beyond the precincts of the abbey, as well as for the attention which he is to receive within it; where everything is ordered with reference to the claims of his precedency, as when he is not required to go to the common lavatory before refection, but is to have water, in the Homeric fashion, poured over his hands; or when the refectioner is instructed to take his spoon with the right hand while he collects the rest with the left; and so again when he wishes, after the manner of the times, to be let blood, his chaplain is to inform the prior. But withal it is contemplated that his scholarship might possibly fail, and so it is enjoined that "if the abbot shall make a mistake in the chapel in the pronounciation of an anthem or a hymn he shall be condoned."[1]

Minute directions are given for the election of the prior. No official qualifications, however, are presented in reference to the abbot, the prior, or the sub-prior, possibly on account of their greater dignity. But, in respect of the lower officers, there are to be found some sketches of the character which they usually possess, in which a knowledge of human nature will not fail to be discerned. So, while the precentor is required to be "mature in his habits, erudite in wisdom and learning, and versed above all else in ecclesiastical customs," the cook is to be "lowly in heart, benignant in mind, sparing of him-

---

[1] "Chron. Mon. de Abingd.," vol. ii., app. iv., p. 346.

self, profuse to others, a comfort to the sorrowful, a refuge to the weary, sober-minded and respectful, a shield to the needy, to all in the community a father and patron." The keeper of the infirmary, again, is to be "cheerful in his exhortation, humble in reproving, assiduous in consolation, endowed with religion and honesty, honey and milk under his tongue, a support to the weak, to all in the community a defence and shield."

Some miscellaneous observations may also be suggested by the further directions which are comprised in this ordinance; not only is there to be an especial care of all who are sick, but in the event of death there is to be an honourable burial, with the insertion of the name in the martyrology, as carefully as in the modern register. An officer is appointed to attend to the guests—for they were jealous of their reputation for hospitality—who is required to be a man of large mind and good accomplishments, able to converse, and withal, discreet in repeating what he hears. A weekly, and even a daily distribution of alms, a maundy it is called, is to be made, nor is a casual applicant to be denied relief. The greater and typical maundy in the holy week is to be observed with its due solemnity. As was seen in the case of the abbot, so, when others are bled, it is not to be done without care, nor without the preparation of a proper diet; and for this even the official who is to supply the light required for the cupping vessel, is named. And, for the general customs of the land, the condition of the English bondman is intimated when there is mention of his release from slavery by will.[1] It is illustrative also of the high position of the abbot in the kingdom, and the great privilege of conferring knighthood which he possessed, when it is said, that "if any new soldier is girt with the sword by the abbot himself or by any other, within the precincts of the abbey, he shall offer his sword upon the altar, and shall redeem it, as he shall be able, from the sacrist."[2] It was a congenial work to the Benedictine to take care for the library; and this was placed under the precentor, whose fitness for the office of librarian was secured by his special qualifications. But, alas, so bright a picture of a religious and peaceful community has a darker side. There is need of corrective discipline; and so the refectioner is admonished that he must provide bread and water for the monks under sentence, and the master of the infirmary that he must keep the keys of the prison cell.

Such was the ideal of the conventual life which the Benedictine rule, as exemplified in so large a foundation as that of Abingdon, presented in the earlier stage of its existence; which was also, it cannot be doubted, preserved within the house for a long period of time. But at a later date, and from whatever causes the decline of good discipline may have begun, there was found in the end to have been in the condition of this monastery as signal and lamentable an instance of failure in preserving the soundness of moral life, as the worst enemies and adversaries of the system could have shown; if, at least, and there

---

[1] See the will of Abp. Ælfric, A.D. 1006, "Chron." *u. s.*, v. i., pp. 417–419. Compare with this the manumission "per testamentum." Justin., "Inst.," i. v. 1. [2] *Ibid.*, vol. ii., p. 380.

seems no reason to question in this instance its general correctness, the report, which was produced by the visitation of this house, contains a true account of its actual condition.

When the blow fell, which was to annihilate at once not this abbey alone, but the entire system of which it formed part, the abbot, Thomas Rowland,[1] was equally ready with his predecessor, at the time of the Conquest, to meet the impending danger by a timely submission. The monastery of Abingdon was surrendered to the king by the abbot and twenty-five monks under the common seal of the convent, on the 29th of May, in A.D. 1537. The value of the yearly revenue had been returned as of £1876. 10s. 9d. By this act he was able to secure the favour of the king with much advantage to himself. The inmates of the abbey had been notoriously guilty of shameless immorality, nor had the abbot himself been less guilty than the rest; but he obtained the large annual pension of £200, and was allowed to retain the manor of Cumnor,[3] in which he might find a place of residence for himself. This was one of the earlier possessions of the abbey, for Cumnor is found to have a place in the grant of Ceadwalla.[4]

---

[1] He is described by Wood on the occasion of his becoming a bachelor of divinity in A.D. 1514, as "Thomas Rowland, sometimes written and called Rowland Penticost." Fasti Oxon., *u. s.*, vol. i., col. 655.

[2] List of surrenders, in Burnet's "Hist. of the Reformation," documents, vol. iv., p. 80. Ed. Nares.

[3] Dugd., "Mon.," vol. i., p. 510.

[4] "Chron. Monast. de Abingd.," *u. s.*, vol. i., pp. 8, n. 1, 126. Cf. *supra*, p. 225.

Another foundation at Abingdon is not without interest. There formerly existed the guild or brotherhood of the Holy Cross,[1] which was possessed of certain lands so early as the twelfth year of King Richard II., and which had the charge of a cross of much splendour, which was erected in St. Helen's Church, and of maintaining the services of the charity which belonged to the fraternity. In addition to other works of piety and charity the guild undertook the construction of the two bridges at Burford and Culhamford, and the forming of the causeway between Abingdon and Dorchester, under the authority of a licence from King Henry V., in A.D. 1415. The guild was authorised to exist as a corporation by Henry VI., in A.D. 1441, for the purpose above mentioned, and for the maintenance of thirteen poor people. It was founded anew by King Richard III. in A.D. 1483. This fraternity was dissolved under the Act of the first year of King Edward VI., but at the instance of Sir John Mason, who was a native of Abingdon, and a fellow of All Souls' College, Oxford, and had great influence at court in consequence of his public services, it was reconstituted as the Hospital of Christ of Abingdon, by letters patent, of May the 18th, A.D. 1553; which were confirmed by a subsequent charter on the 26th of June, after signing which the king used these words "Lord, God! I yield Thee most hearty thanks that Thou hast given me life thus

---

[1] The authority for the statements in the text is the "Account of the Brotherhood of the Holy Cross, and of the Hospital of Christ in Abingdon," written by Francis Little in 1627, and published by C. D. Cobham. Ox., 1873.

long to finish this work to the glory of Thy name." The succession of the masters is still kept up. The hall of the hospital contains an ancient monument [1] respecting the building of the bridges, the maintenance of which was so eminently the charitable office of the fraternity, in the necessities of old time.

At Reading there was a Benedictine abbey, the abbot of which, like the Abbot of Abingdon, was summoned as one of the barons to parliament. This foundation derives an additional interest from its association with the history of Henry I. There had previously existed on its site a nunnery, which was built by Elfrida, the wife of King Edgar, so well known for her part in the murder of her stepson, Edward the Martyr. The foundation of this nunnery was a few years later than the crime, and the thought of atoning for the past may well have been present to her mind. This building, however, had long since disappeared, and the abbey, of which the remains may still be seen, was begun by King Henry in A.D. 1121, and completed in A.D. 1125. The charter of the foundation recites, that "the Abbeys of Reading, Cholsey, and Leominster having been destroyed for their sins, and their possessions forfeited;" these were now transferred to the new monastery which the king had built in performance of an act of penitence which had been enjoined upon him.[2] The situation of Reading, as a centre of communication, was a desir-

---

[1] "Account of the Brotherhood of the Holy Cross, and of the Hospital of Christ, in Abingdon," app. A., *u.s.*, pp. 121-4.

[2] "Pro indicta sibi poenitentia." Will. of Malmes., "De Gest. Pontif," lib. ii., sect. 89, *u. s.*, p. 193.

able one for an institution, a principal object of which was the entertainment of strangers who might pass through it. And so it is recorded that the king built this monastery between the River Kennet and the River Thames, in a spot which was well suited for the reception of persons having occasion to travel to the more populous cities of England; and that, in after-time, the special object of the foundation was so well maintained, that it was observable that guests arriving every hour consumed more than the inmates themselves. The monks were of the Cluniac branch of the Benedictine order.[1]

The king also granted to the abbey at its foundation the privilege of a mint,[2] and he preserved his connexion with it to the end of his life. On one occasion, when he was abroad, he obtained the hand of St. James, which he bestowed as a precious relic upon the abbey.[3] And at last, when he was overtaken by his sudden malady during his visit to Normandy in A.D. 1135, Hugh, the priest of Rouen, whom he had appointed abbot, and who was also there, was summoned to his bedside,[4] and passed "three melancholy days" in attendance on him, receiving his confession, conferring absolution, administering the Holy Sacrament, and affording such consolation as he was able. The king died at St. Denis on the 1st December.

---

[1] William of Malmesbury, "Chron.," *u. s.*, bk. v., p. 447.
[2] Dugd., "Mon.," *u. s.*, iv., 33.
[3] Mat. Par., *u. s., ad* A.D. 1113, p. 72.
[4] The abbot wrote a letter to the pope, giving an account of the king's death, which is given at length in Will. of Malmesb., "Chron.," "Modern Hist.," bk. i., *u. s.*, p. 489.

The body was embalmed at Rouen, and a portion of it was buried in the church of a monastery near. It was then removed to Caen, from which place, on the cessation of the storm which prevented the crossing of the channel, it was brought to England. And then, "after the festival of Christmas was ended, the King Stephen went to meet it, attended by a large body of nobles, and, for the love he bore to his uncle, supported the bier on his shoulders, assisted by his nobles, and thus brought the corpse to Reading."[1] There a magnificent funeral awaited it, and the body "was deposited with the highest honours in a tomb, constructed, according to custom, before the high altar in the principal church, dedicated to the Most Blessed Virgin, which the king himself had endowed with lands and enriched with many ornaments." It appears to have been on this occasion that Henry de Blois, the Bishop of Winchester, found opportunity to abstract the hand of St. James.[2]

In the following year, on the anniversary of the king's death, his widow, Adelicia of Louvaine, attended by her brother and the officers of her household, made a visit to the abbey church, where she was received by the Bishop of Salisbury, the abbot, and a large number of ecclesiastics. In testimony of her regard for the memory of her husband, she placed a rich pall on the altar with her own hands, and gave, by a royal charter, "to God and to the church of St. Mary at Reading for ever the manor of Eastone, in Hertfordshire, which formed part of her dower," "for

---

[1] Florence of Worcester, "Chron.," ad A.D. 1135, pp. 249, 250. Lond., 1854.   [2] Mat. Par., *u. s.*, p. 75.

the health and redemption of the soul of her lord
the most noble King Henry, and of her own," and of
the rest in whose behalf such charters commonly
ran.[1] But although the church of the monastery received these distinguished marks of royal favour, and
was used for so high solemnities, it appears not to
have been formally consecrated. The year A.D. 1164
was a year of great importance in the life of Archbishop Beket, for it was during its course that he
rejected the provision of the Constitutions of Claren-
don, by which the clergy were subjected to the jurisdiction of the temporal courts, and left England to
seek a refuge abroad. But still, in the early part of
it he found an opportunity of visiting Reading, and it
must have been a day of high importance to the
town when the archbishop proceeded to consecrate
the church in the presence of the king and of ten
bishops who took part in the ceremonial.[2] Henry II.,
who had lately succeeded to the throne, was desirous,
it would seem, to seize the first occasion of doing
honour by a royal visit to a place which was so intimately connected with the life and memory of his
grandfather; and it may be conceived that the presence
of the king was the reason for which the archbishop
came to consecrate the church, which was a function
more properly belonging to the diocesan. But, however, the privilege of being accounted the king's
rightful diocesan, wherever he might at any time be,

---

[1] A translation of the charter, from the original in the possession of Abel Smith, M.P., is contained in Strickland's
"Queens of England," *u. s.*, vol. i., p. 127, n.

[2] Mat. Par., *ad* A.D. 1164, *u. s.*, p. 102.

had been vindicated at the marriage of King Henry I. at Windsor, in A.D. 1121. Previously to the ceremony of the consecration, the hand of St. James, which had been abstracted, was restored.[1]

In the reign of Henry II., in A.D. 1185, the abbey was the scene of a remarkable incident. Heraclius, the unworthy patriarch of Jerusalem, attended by Roger Desmoulins, the master of the Hospital of St. John, came to England, to request the personal assistance of the king in the holy war, and to offer to him at the same time the keys of the Holy Sepulchre and of the Tower of David, and the royal standard, which the king received with great reverence of their sacred character. They also brought a letter from Pope Lucius III. in support of their application, urging the necessity of the king's presence to oppose Saladin. They had an audience granted them at Reading, but the king deferred his answer until he should meet them again in London. The result was a professed acceptance of the proposal, which was made the occasion for claiming a subsidy of a tenth. The king went so far as to cross the channel with the embassy on their return; but having done this he went no farther on his way than to his own possessions in Normandy.[2]

In the eventful year A.D. 1215 the Abbot Simon[3] was charged with an important duty, which plainly

---

[1] Mat. Par., *ad* A.D. 1156, *u. s.*, p. 95.

[2] Mat. Par., *ad* A.D. 1185, *u. s.*, pp. 142, 3. It was upon the occasion of this visit that Heraclius consecrated the Temple Church in London.

[3] Dugd., "Mon.," *u. s.*, vol. iv., p. 31.

shows the position which he occupied. It was the time of England's great degradation. Two years before the pope, Innocent III., had relaxed his interdict, the king had made his submission, and had resigned the kingdom into his hand, and had done homage to him before Pandulph, after which absolution had been granted to him. The Great Charter had been signed in this year, A.D. 1215, on the 15th June, but the king had been absolved from his oath by the pope in August. And, finding the opposition of the barons continue, he had applied to the pope for his aid. An excommunication, accordingly, had been pronounced against the barons generally, and against certain who were mentioned by name specially, while their lands were placed under an interdict.[1]

The next thing was the promulgation of this sentence; and the office of seeing that it was duly performed was intrusted by a papal letter to the Bishop of Winchester, the Abbot of Reading, and Pandulph. The preamble states the reason for adopting this course, and directs that the excommunication of the opponents of the king and the subjection of their lands to an interdict should be published throughout England and Wales in solemn form, with the tolling of bells and lighting of candles on Sundays and holidays except they should make satisfaction and return to their allegiance.

A "pleasant story," as it is termed by the narrator,[2]

---

[1] Mat. Par., *ad* A.D. 1215, *u. s.*, p. 271; Rymer, *u. s.*, vol. i., p. 139. Lond. 1816. Record Edition.

[2] Fuller, "Church Hist.," cent. xvi., bk. vi., *u. s.*, p. 299.

respecting a visit to the abbot which was made by King Henry VIII., after he had been hunting in Windsor Forest, shows the good understanding which prevailed between them at that time. But this was soon to be rudely interrupted among the proceedings which accompanied the dissolution of the monasteries, in the course of which no victim whose ill treatment could promote the king's design was spared by Cromwell and himself. At the time of the dissolution of the monasteries the Abbot of Reading was one of the three[1] who alone were prepared to suffer the last extremity of punishment, rather than violate their conscience and yield submission to the demands of the king. Neither bribery, nor terror, nor any other dishonourable attempts could overcome their constancy. They were, therefore, brought under the power of the king by a different method, under the pretext of law. The oath of supremacy was tendered to them; and, upon their refusal to take it, they were adjudged to be guilty of high treason.[2] And so Hugh Farringdon, the thirty-first Abbot of Reading, with two secular priests of his own abbey, John Rugge and William Onion, was hung, drawn, and quartered within sight of the old home, with all its sacred associations, on the 15th of November,[3] in the year A.D. 1539. The abbey had been returned to be of the annual value of £1,938. 14s. 3¾d. It remained in possession of the

---

[1] The others were the abbots of Colchester and Glastonbury.

[2] See 28 Hen. VIII., c. 10, the act passed in A.D. 1536 for "Extinguishing the Authority of the Bishop of Rome," s. 7.

[3] T. G. Law, "Calendar," *u. s.*

Crown, until the site was granted by Edward VI., on the 4th of June, in A.D. 1550, to his uncle, the Protector, Edward Seymour, the Duke of Somerset; who at no great distance of time experienced in his own a similar reverse of fortune with that of his predecessor, and was beheaded on Tower Hill, in A.D. 1552.

Among the possessions of the abbey at the time of the dissolution were the impropriate rectories of the two ancient churches of Reading—St. Giles's and St. Lawrence. When the connexion with the abbey was dissolved these would be placed at a disadvantage from the rectories passing into the possession of owners who would have less care for their interest than the adjacent convent may be supposed to have felt. But "the advowson of St. Lawrence was purchased by Archbishop Laud, augmented and given to his college."[1] Laud was a native of the parish of St. Lawrence, and the house in which he lived has only recently been destroyed. He desired in this way to consult for the best interests of a parish which was dear to him from early recollections, and the patronage remained with St. John's College, until it was exchanged for other preferment with Bishop Wilberforce.

One other foundation claims a separate notice from its connexion with the English sovereigns, and the order of knighthood of which mention has been made, as well as the magnificence of the building in which the religious associations of the locality are centred. Windsor itself had been a seat of the

---

[1] MS. note of Dr. Rawlinson in the Bodleian copy of Ashmole's "Hist. of Berks," *n. s.*, at vol. ii., p. 349.

English kings, but it had been granted by Edward the Confessor to the abbot and monks of Westminster,[1] to whom it belonged when the Domesday Survey was compiled. Enamoured of the beauty of its situation and convinced of its importance as a military position, the Conqueror effected an exchange by which it was reunited to the possessions of the Crown. There existed within the precincts of the castle, from early times, a free chapel, which, as being a royal foundation, was exempt from all ordinary jurisdiction, it being part of the privileges of the Crown to attach such exemption to the chapels erected within the royal demesnes. A chapel was built by King Henry I., and he was married in it to his second queen, Adelicia of Louvaine; on which occasion there ensued the contest between Ralph, the Archbishop of Canterbury, and Roger, the Bishop of Salisbury, respecting the performance of the marriage ceremony. It was claimed by the former as archbishop, and by the latter as Bishop of Salisbury, the diocese in which the fortress of Windsor was situated. The ecclesiastical referees who were consulted upon this question decided in favour of the archbishop, on these grounds, that the king and queen were specially within the ministrations of the archbishop; and, moreover, that the bishops of the whole of England only held their several dioceses[2] from and by him. The ceremony of the marriage was accordingly

---

[1] The charter ("Cod. Dipl. A.S.," vol. iv., p. 227) is noticed in Freeman's "Hist.," *u. s.*, vol. iv., p. 341.

[2] "Parochias." Eadmer, "Historia Novorum," lib. vi., p. 136. Lond., 1623.

performed by him. But the right to officiate at the coronation was a still more important cause of dispute, and Ralph, who was aged and infirm, deputed the Bishop of Winchester to take his place, rather than the Bishop of Salisbury, lest it might establish a precedent. The king, however, preferred to have the office performed by Roger, who was highly esteemed by him, and provided that it should be so done at an early ceremonial. He afterwards appeared on the throne crowned. And when Ralph saw that this had been done, he indignantly removed the crown from the king's head with his own hand.[1]

In the reign of Edward III. a great change was effected in regard to the position of the chapel and of the institutions connected with it. There had previously been no incorporation nor endowment; and the services of the chapel were maintained by an annual payment from the exchequer. But in the twenty-second year of his reign, in A.D. 1348, the king founded the college of St. George, and appointed by his letters patent[2] that there should be a custos, or warden, twelve secular canons, thirteen priests or vicars, four clerks, six choristers, twenty-four alms' knights, with such other inferior officers as were necessary, in honour of St. George and of St. Edward the Confessor. The military knights accordingly formed part of the original foundation, and were supported from its revenues. In the following year he established, in its complete form, the Order of the Garter,[3] which he dedicated to the Holy Trinity, the

[1] Eadmer, "Historia Novorum," *n. s.*, lib. iv., p. 137.
[2] Dated August 6th.  [3] *Supra*, p. 178.

Virgin Mary, St. George, and St. Edward. On the occasion of this dedication there was a splendid pageant, of which the chapel which then existed was the scene. The king walked in solemn procession with his newly-created knights, and the religious service attending their installation was performed by the prelate of the order, the Bishop of Winchester, William de Edyngdon. It is to King Edward III. that Windsor Castle owes its chief renown; and "it was by the advice and persuasion of William of Wykeham that the king was induced to pull down great part of the castle, and to rebuild it in the magnificent manner in which it now appears."[1] The rebuilding of the chapel was a part of the design which was completed under the superintendence of William of Wykeham as the architect.

The chapel, which was thus erected by Edward III., was found in the next century to have fallen into decay from the badness of the materials, and King Edward IV. resolved to take down the existing building and construct a new chapel in its place. Like his predecessor, he intrusted the work to an ecclesiastic—Richard Beauchamp, the Bishop of Salisbury, under whose superintendence it was entered upon in A.D. 1474; but, although its grandeur is greatly owing to his skill and judgment, he died before the completion of the chapel in A.D. 1481, and Sir Reginald Bray was appointed his successor. The reward which the Bishop of Salisbury received for himself and his successors in the Chancellorship of

[1] "Life of Wykeham," by R. Lowth; in Cassan's "Lives of the Bishops of Winch.," *u. s.*, vol. i., p. 198.

the Order of the Garter has been already noticed.[1] These two are buried within the church which is so greatly indebted to their care. It has been justly characterised as "one of the finest perpendicular buildings in the kingdom."[2] The royal tomb-house at the east end of St. George's Chapel is of a later date. It was built by Henry VII. for his own place of burial, but he raised for himself a still more magnificent building at Westminster: and the mausoleum originally intended for himself was granted by his successor to Cardinal Wolsey, who had made great preparations in fitting it for his own entombment before his plans were interrupted by his fall, upon which it reverted to the Crown.

The free chapel of Windsor came within the provisions of the Statute, by which all such foundations were granted to Henry VIII.;[3] but it had not actually been seized and taken into possession before the death of the king, which took place in the year which followed the passing of this Act. It, consequently, was within the general provision of the Statute of Edward VI.,[4] by which, "such free chapels as were not seized before, nor accepted, by the former Statute," were granted to him. But there was a saving clause, by which it was excepted and preserved in its former state: for it was specially ordained that the act should not, in any wise, extend to certain foundations, among which was enumerated

---

[1] *Supra*, pp. 178, 180.

[2] Rickman, "Architecture in England," p. 184. Lond., 1835.

[3] 37 Hen. VIII., c. 4.  [4] 1 Ed. VI., c. 14.

"the free chapel of St. George-the-Martyr, situate in the Castle of Windsor."[1]

The choir of St. George's Chapel has been used on different occasions as the burial-place of the sovereign from the time of the funeral of King Edward IV., who, with his queen, is buried in the tomb, marked by the ironwork of the smith and painter, Quentin Matsys. It is a tomb of great beauty, but has lost the tabard which was suspended over it,[2] which was carried off by Captain Fogg, when he also plundered the treasury of the altar-plate in A.D. 1642. The body of Henry VI. was removed to the chapel by Richard III. from its first place of interment at Chertsey. And Henry VIII. was also buried here after appointing in his will that he "should be buried and interred in the choir of his college of Windsor, midway between the stalls and the high altar." The last of the kings who was buried in the chapel itself was King Charles I.[3] When permission had been refused for his burial in Henry VII.'s chapel at Westminster, Herbert and Juxon obtained leave for the interment at Windsor, in such place as they might select. There was some difficulty in making choice of the spot; but one of the lords who were present struck the pavement, and found it return a hollow sound; upon which an examination was made, and a vault was discovered, in which were the coffins of

---

[1] Ed. VI., c. 14, *u. s.*, sec. 19.

[2] E. Ashmole, "The Institution of the Garter," p. 149. Lond., 1672.

[3] See the narrative of Sir Thomas Herbert, in Wood, "Athen. Oxon.," *u. s.*, vol. ii., col. 526-8.

Henry VIII. and Jane Seymour. The body was then brought from "the king's usual bedchamber," in which it was placed to await the result—the snow falling so thickly during the short transit upon the pall of black velvet that it was entirely covered by it. The burial was not accompanied by the ceremonial of the English offices, as the governor, Colonel Whichcote, refused his permission for the use of it, in consequence of the prohibition in the " Directory for Public Worship." [1] There was no other inscription than the one written upon a strip of lead, " King Charles, 1648." The date of the interment was February 2nd, in A.D. 1649, according to the new style. In this vault the coffin remained unidentified, "obscure the place, and uninscribed the stone," [2] until the royal tomb-house was altered in A.D. 1813. An opening was then accidentally made by one of the workmen in the wall of the vault, through which the coffins were seen. And, accordingly, in order to remove the doubt which existed as to the burial-ground of King Charles, a complete examination of the spot was instituted in the presence of the Prince-Regent, Sir Henry Halford,[3] and some others, which confirmed the accuracy of Herbert's description of the place of burial as being "over against the eleventh stall on the sovereign's side." The coffin, with the pall upon it, was discovered, and was

---

[1] *Supra*, p. 132.
[2] Pope, " Windsor Forest," l. 318.
[3] See Sir H. Halford's " Account of the opening of the Coffin of K. Charles I." Lond., 1813 ; which is repeated in his " Essays and Orations." Lond., 1831 and 1842.

opened, by which means the opportunity of further identification was gained.

From the time of the burial of the Duchess of Brunswick in A.D. 1813, and the removal to it of the body of the Princess Amelia, the vault underneath the chapel has been used for the interment of the reigning family. But Wolsey's Chapel itself has been converted, by the reverence of the Queen for the memory of the Prince Consort, into a memorial chapel, the interior of which has been fitted with the highest forms of art, so that it may be considered to have attained a magnificence which is unequalled in any building of a similar character.

The chapel of St. George has more recently been the scene of the marriage of the Prince of Wales, and of other members of the royal family.

The collegiate chapter at present consists of a dean and four canons. The dean is the Registrar of the Order of the Garter. The offices of the dean and the registrar were consolidated at a chapter of the Order in A.D. 1635, "that so it might pass to future times from example into rule."[1]

---

[1] Ashmole, "The Institution of the Garter," *u. s.*, pp. 248, 249.

## CHAPTER X.

UNION OF BUCKS WITH BERKS AND OXON, WITH HISTORY OF THE ARCHDEACONRY OF BUCKS. A.D. 1075-1846.

Union with Oxford—Early History of the Archdeaconry of Buckingham — Sufferers for Religion — Hooker — Clergy during the Commonwealth—Extracts from Parish Register—The Restoration—Endowment.

THE third archdeaconry in the diocese of Oxford, as it is now constituted, is the archdeaconry of Buckingham, which comprised the whole county of Buckingham. In this instance, as in that of the Archdeaconry of Berks, it is to be observed that the general history is to be found in the account of the see of which it so long formed part, which is comprised in the history of the see of Lincoln. It is even a later addition to the diocese of Oxford than was the archdeaconry of Berks, both in respect of the Order of Council, which authorised its union, and of the consent of the bishop who accepted it.[1] For insomuch as Bishop Bagot declined to become responsible for the administration of a see which would be so largely increased, the proposed arrangement was suspended until he resigned the bishopric, and the appointment of Bishop Wilberforce in A.D. 1845, rendered possible the transfer of the archdeaconry from the see of Lincoln.

[1] *Supra*, pp. 178, 185, 192.

As a part of the old diocese of Lincoln, it was contained within the same see as was the archdeaconry of Oxford down to the early part of the sixteenth century; and the outline of its history has therefore been given in the description of the changes which the sees of Wessex and of Mercia experienced before the seat of a bishopric was fixed at Lincoln, within a few years from the Norman Conquest. The remarks, accordingly, which are now to follow will properly be confined to the notice of some particulars which may be considered independently of the general history of the archdeaconry in connexion with the last-named see.

The time when the archdeaconry of Buckingham was formed as a separate jurisdiction is clearly defined. It was the act of Remigius who, after taking possession of the see of Lincoln in its new condition, in A.D. 1075, and devising the means of its administration, "placed archdeacons over the several counties of his diocese."[1] The county of Buckingham received as its archdeacon, under this arrangement, Alured or Alfred the Little, who was succeeded by Gilbert, a man distinguished by his courtly manners and elegant writings, both in verse and prose. Their successor was Roger, who is described as subsequently Bishop of Chester; and to him succeeded David, who was brother to Alexander, the Bishop of Lincoln. These were the first five of the archdeacons. The explanation of the title "Bishop of Chester," which is assigned to the third in succes-

---

[1] Henry of Huntingdon, Letter to Walter, "Chron.," *u. s.*, p. 305; *supra*, p. 31.

sion, is to be found in the earlier history of the diocese, for the present bishopric of Chester was established by King Henry VIII. Peter, the thirty-fourth bishop of Lichfield, removed the episcopal throne to Chester; and the thirty-sixth bishop, Robert Peckham,[1] made a second removal to Coventry. He was the immediate predecessor of Roger de Clinton, the former archdeacon of Buckingham, so that at the time of Roger's appointment to his bishopric "it had three seats: at Chester, at Lichfield, and at Coventry."[2]

The archdeaconry which was instituted in the manner described above comprised the county of Buckingham, which is computed to have contained at the time of the Domesday Survey a population of five thousand four hundred and twenty.[3] At a later survey, for the taxation of Pope Nicholas IV.,[4] about the year A.D. 1291, there is mention of one hundred and sixty-seven churches, five of which number are named chapelries, and are separately assessed, while several of the churches have also dependent chapels annexed to them. These were distributed in eight deaneries. In the subsequent record, in A.D. 1340, the separate places assessed, five of which are described as chapelries, amount in number to

---

[1] Mat. Par., *ad* A.D. 1132, *u. s.*, p. 72. But other authorities state that the removal to Chester was effected by the thirty-fifth bishop, Robert de Lindsey.
[2] Mat. Par., *ibid.*
[3] Sir H. Ellis, "Introduction," *u. s.*, vol. ii., p. 427.
[4] "Tax. Eccl. P. Nich. IV.," *u. s.*, pp. 32-34.
[5] "Nonar. Inquis.," *u. s.*, pp. 326-340.

one hundred and ninety-eight. In the "Valor Ecclesiasticus" of Henry VIII.,[1] there are two hundred and twenty-nine churches, to which an addition of ten is to be made for the chapelries which are also mentioned. The vicarage of Aylesbury and Buckingham are described as "peculiars[2] of the church of Lincoln"; there are also two parishes, with two separate chapelries, which are "peculiars of the Archbishop of Canterbury"; and four parishes constitute the "jurisdiction of St. Alban's, in the diocese of London, in the archdeaconry of St. Alban's." These four are the vicarages of Aston Abbott, Grandborough, Harwood, and Windsor, the rectories of which were impropriate to the abbey of St. Alban's. There are seven deaneries, the number being diminished by the omission of Monks Risborough, which is one of the peculiars of the archbishop.

The scanty provision which was made for the education of the people in the eighteenth century may be inferred from the circumstance that in a list[3] of the "charity schools," by which is intended the common parochial schools in Buckinghamshire, in A.D. 1720, only forty are enumerated, and some of these have very few scholars.

The notice of the sufferers for religion in the archdeaconry of Buckingham brings under review the history of the followers of Wycliffe, the Lollards, whose name has already occurred in the course of this history.[4] Upon the death of Wycliffe there was

---
[1] *Supra*, p. 83.   [2] *Supra*, pp. 33, 34.
[3] Coxe's "Magna Britannia," vol. i., *n. s.*, Bucks, p. 217.
[4] *Supra*, p. 59.

no organised party to inherit the name and influence of their teacher, but those who embraced his doctrines became known as the Lollards; but the origin of their designation has not with certainty been determined. These were not without high support, for "the good Queen Anne," the first wife of Richard II., and the widow of the Earl of Lancaster, were alike favourable to their cause. Their number was large; and in their opposition to the existing condition of the Church and clergy there was much to attract religious sympathy; but there was also in their social and political opinions a character which could not but excite suspicion as to its tendency. At the close of his reign the king opposed himself to the remonstrance which their leaders put forth, and his successor, Henry of Lancaster, in spite of his parentage, was the first king who caused a statute to be passed in England for the burning of heretics,[1] by which they were required to abjure their tenets, and, in the event of a refusal or of a lapse into heresy, judgment was to be recorded against them, and they were to be delivered to the secular power that they might be burned. Nor was this statute suffered to fall into disuse. Its powers were soon enforced in the case of William Sautree, and after other instances, in the more famous example of Sir John Oldcastle (Lord Cobham), although for a time he escaped the infliction of the sentence. In the early part of the reign of Henry V. another statute was passed to extend its powers,[2] and this became the operative statute for the

---

[1] Hen. IV., c. 15; *supra*, p. 59.
[2] 2 Hen. V., c. 7.

future. Henry VI. was in like manner disposed to take the part of the Church; but during the wars of the Roses the occasion for religious persecution was less urgent. In the reign of King Henry VII. the increase of the number and of the influence of the Lollards attracted attention, and the persecution of them for their so much suspected tenets was renewed.

In this renewal of severity the archdeaconry of Buckingham had a full share. The first to suffer was William Tylsworth, who was burned at Amersham in the Stanley close, in A.D. 1506. He was of advanced age, and in his case there was shown the additional cruelty of compelling his daughter to kindle the fire with her own hand.[1] The persecution was extended with all its force into the surrounding neighbourhood. More than sixty persons had to bear faggots for their penance, and there were thirty who were burned on the cheek as well. The cause alleged for this ill usage was of a religious character. The victims of it were opposed to the doctrine of Transubstantiation, and what they deemed to be superstition and idolatry of any kind; and they claimed to read and hear Holy Scripture for themselves.[2] Another inhabitant of Amersham who is singled out for particular notice is Thomas Chase, who was brought before the blind Bishop of Lincoln, William Smith, at the episcopal palace of Wooburn. There he was imprisoned and put in irons in the cell called "little ease," where he was cruelly taunted by the bishop's chaplain at his daily visit.[3] After a patient endurance of such treat-

[1] Foxe, "Acts and Mon.," *u. s.*, vol. iv., p. 123.
[2] *Ibid.*, p. 124.  [3] *Ibid.*, and p. 125.

ment, he was found strangled, and a report was published that he had killed himself, in consequence of which he was denied the right of interment in consecrated ground, and was buried by the "cross roads" in Norland Wood, near Wooburn. Robert Cosins, who was associated with the early reformers of Amersham, was burned at Buckingham in A.D. 1507. Another, Thomas Man, who suffered as a relapsed heretic at Smithfield in A.D. 1518, was also one of those who had taught at Amersham. He had joined in the great abjuration in Buckinghamshire in A.D. 1511, and had subsequently been imprisoned at Oxford in St. Frideswide's monastery.[2]

Upon his appointment to the see of Lincoln in A.D. 1521, John Longland, who is known as the bishop who probably suggested to Henry VIII. the expedient of the divorce, felt "no little discomfort and heaviness" from the number of heretics, as he deemed them, within his diocese. In his anxiety he applied to the king, who thereupon addressed a letter to the sheriffs and other officers, charging them to assist him "in the executing and ministering of justice unto the said heretics according to the laws of Holy Church."[3] The brief summary of their opinions gives little warrant for the severity of the proceedings which were taken by the bishop in his desire to extirpate them from his diocese. The penance which was imposed was of a uniform character for all, and was an imprisonment in some religious house, the pre-

---

[1] Foxe, "Acts and Mon.," *u.s.*, vol. iv., p. 214.
[2] *Ibid.*, pp. 208–214.
[3] The letter is given by Foxe, *ibid.*, p. 241.

cincts of which they were not to pass, while such as were able were to do some labour in return for their maintenance.[1] Among those who made submission and were sentenced to do penance, there were some who were relapsed heretics, and under the statute already mentioned, inasmuch as they had made their abjuration under Bishop Smith, were now committed to the secular power, and were condemned to be burned. John Simson accordingly, who was one of the number, suffered in this manner at Amersham; and on this occasion, as on a previous one, there was the uncalled-for aggravation of punishment in his children being compelled to set fire to their own father.

Later in the same century, a village near Aylesbury, Drayton Beauchamp, gained a reputation which still continues from its association with the name of Richard Hooker, who was appointed to the incumbency in A.D. 1584. Here he exchanged "the tranquillity of his college, that garden of piety, of pleasure, of peace,"[2] for "the thorny wilderness of a busy world," and "the corroding cares that there attend a married priest and a country parsonage," which, in his case, were so painfully exemplified. While he was living in this parish there occurred the visit of his two pupils, who had to lose "their best entertainment, which was his quiet company," but too soon, when "Richard was called to rock the cradle,"—

---

[1] The terms of their treatment are contained in a letter to the Abbot of Eynsham, which is printed, *ibid.*, p. 244.
[2] Walton's Life, prefixed to "Hooker's Works," vol. i., pp. 32-35. Ox., 1836.

an incident which drew forth a pious expression of contentment on his part, and a fitting intercession on the part of the son of Archbishop Sandys, who was one of the visitors, with his father, through whose interest Hooker was preferred to the Mastership of the Temple, which had so great an influence upon his future life.

A general account of the sufferings of the clergy during the time of the Commonwealth, or at the Restoration, as also of the nonjurors, has been already made.[1] But one instance of a treatment of exceptional severity may be noticed. Anthony Tyringham,[2] who was Rector of Tyringham, and who also held a canonry in Worcester Cathedral, had gone on one occasion to the village of Maids Morton, and on his return through Buckingham had been joined by his two nephews. As they approached Stony Stratford they were overtaken by a party of dragoons, who took away their money and their outer clothes, and sent them as prisoners to Aylesbury. On the way they were further plundered by their guard; and when Tyringham himself was unwilling to take off his cassock one of the men cut through his hat, wounding his head, and also struck his fingers. A false alarm of resistance was raised; upon which the captain in command "with a full blow struck at Mr. Tyringham, and with his sword cut his arm and cubit bones across the elbow almost asunder; and Mr. Tyringham, almost threescore years of age,

---

[1] *Supra*, pp. 135, 147, 148, 161, 162.
[2] " Mercurius Rusticus;" by Bruno Ryves. No. xiii., pp. 137-139. Lond., 1685.

except two, bore this barbarous usage with undaunted courage." His arm hung powerless from the shoulder; but he was not permitted for some time to have it bandaged.

In this condition they were sent on their way a second time; and after riding for four hours, while Tyringham was weak and fainting from loss of blood, as they approached Whitchurch, a short distance from Aylesbury, they again attacked him, and took away his boots, his jerkin, and his hat and cap. In this state, after an hour longer in the wind and rain and darkness, he reached Aylesbury; and upon examination of his arm the surgeons who were called to him pronounced that it must be removed the next morning. This accordingly was done, and he bore it with great firmness. It appears that he recovered from the immediate effects of the injury; but he died at some time previously to the Restoration.

The extracts which are subjoined from the register of a parish in Buckinghamshire will further exhibit the treatment to which the villagers were exposed during the Commonwealth, and their feelings under it; and at the same time show the power of a passive resistance which can be maintained under such conditions.

The register at Maids Moreton contains an interesting notice[1] of the treatment which that parish received under the action of the parliamentations and of the opposition, not altogether unsuccessful, with which it was met by the resolution and firmness

[1] The writer is indebted for this extract to the Rev. B. W. Johnstone, Rector of Maids Moreton.

of the rector and his parishoners, although in the instance of the former, at the expense of his own life. There is also an exemplification of the manner in which the registers were appointed to be kept under the new regulations:—

"Ann. Dom. 1642. This year the worst of parliaments, wickedly rebelling against the best of princes, King Charles I., the kingdom suffered a long while under most sad afflictions; especially churches, whilst they pretended reformation, were everywhere robbed and ruined by the rebells. In this church of Morton the windows were broken, a costly desk in the form of a spread-eagle guilt, on which we used to lay Bishop Jewell's works, was hewed to pieces as an abominable idoll, the crosse (which with its fall had like to have beate out the brains of him who did it) was cut off the steeple by the souldiers, at the command of one called Colonell Purefoy, of Warwickshire. We carried away what we could, and among other things the Register was hid, and for that cause is not absolutely perfect for divers years; though I have used my best diligence to record as many particulars as I could come by."

There is an entry at a later date, in A.D. 1653, which evidently proves that the provisions of the ordinance for registration, which then took effect, met with no favourable reception. Nor is there any hesitation in drawing the inference that the authors of it were thereby "insinuating that children ought not to be baptised, and encouraging people to withhold their infants from the sacred ordinance." But, however this may have been, it is certainly a proof of the good faith of the rector and his parishoners when it is added :—

"But there was never any that I know of that mind in Morton. And though the baptism of some be not expressed here, yet these are to certify all whom it may concern, and that on the word of a priest, that there is no person hereafter mentioned by the then register of the parish, but was duly and orderly baptised."

The rector, George Bate, appears to have been one of the unrecorded sufferers[1] of that time; for a notice, which was inserted in the register by his son under the same year, contains a statement that he died " heart-broken with the insolence of the rebells against the Church and king."

After the Restoration the position of the two parties in the state being changed, the intruding ministers were ejected, and sometimes under circumstances of great hardship. One of those who were so ejected in Buckinghamshire was a man of learning, Samuel Clark, the son of the Rector of St. Benet Fink. He had been a fellow of Pembroke College, at Cambridge, and had officiated in the parish of Grendon. Besides other publications, he was the author of an edition of the "Bible with Annotations,"[2] which was well received. It was even recommended by Bishop Cleaver to the attention of the younger clergy;[3] and it has been

---

[1] His name is not mentioned by Walker, in "The Sufferings of the Clergy," *u. s.*

[2] Fol. Lond., 1690.

[3] T. H. Horne, "Introd. to Critical Study of the Holy Scriptures," vol. v., p. 295. Lond., 1846.

described as having supplied " an excellent fund for some modern commentators, who have published a great part of it with very little alteration." [1]

The present state of the archdeaconry and of the provision for the archdeacon are thus to be described.[2] The archdeaconry of Buckingham was prospectively transferred from the diocese of Lincoln to that of Oxford by an order of the Queen in Council, gazetted on the 18th August in A.D. 1837. And by another Order in Council, gazetted the 20th March in A.D. 1846, the canonry of Christ Church, which, by the same order, was annexed to the archdeaconry of Oxford, was charged with the yearly payment of three hundred pounds in favour of the archdeaconry of Buckingham. It is not known that the archdeaconry of Buckingham had, or has, any corps of endowment other than this charge; and in a printed return made in the year A.D. 1841, which is in the possession of the ecclesiastical commissioners, the archdeacon's receipts are set down as derived from sources other than endowment; that is, from procurations, visitations, fees, and the like.

There are at the present time twelve deaneries, with two hundred and sixteen incumbencies.

[1] Chalmers, "Biogr. Dict.," vol. ix., p. 403, *ibid.*
[2] The writer is indebted for the following statement to George Pringle, Esq., the Secretary to the Ecclesiastical Commission.

## CHAPTER XI.

Monastic and Collegiate Foundations—Prebend of Aylesbury—
Bonhommes at Ashridge—Eton College—Conclusion.

THE monastic and collegiate foundations in Buckinghamshire, though more numerous than the similar institutions in Berkshire, are with the exception of Eton College, of smaller endowment and less public importance than those which have been described as existing in that archdeaconry. But these have points of interest of a different kind, and one of them will illustrate another phase of ecclesiastical life,—a remark which also applies to one, at least, of the principal parishes. And this, from its present position, may be noticed first.

The ecclesiastical history of Aylesbury derives its chief interest from the connexion which existed between this church and the cathedral of Lincoln. At an early period a bishop of that see, in compliance with a papal requisition, presented a foreigner, who was a relative of his own, to the rectory; and he appropriated it in the usual form to the deanery of Lincoln, so that it became annexed to it. But at a period subsequent to this the process was reversed. Pope Innocent IV. and Othobon, the papal legate, became convinced of the injustice which was committed in the impropriation and consequent abstraction of the revenues of the parish. Grosseteste, the Bishop of Lincoln, was also desirous of repairing the wrong by effecting a separation. And the opportunity of so doing occurred in the following manner.[1] Upon the death of Hugh Pateshull, the Bishop of Coventry,[2] in A.D. 1240, when the first of the bishops designate had died before consecration, and the second had resigned the appointment into the hands of the pope on finding that his nomination was distasteful to the king, Roger de Weseham, the Dean of Lincoln, a man of irreproachable character and of considerable learning, through the intervention of Grosseteste, was appointed the new bishop. This was done without any previous consultation with the king, in order that he might not in his accustomed manner place an impediment in the way. By this method of proceeding, Bishop Grosseteste was able to effect the purpose, which he had long desired, in his wish to promote the interests of the parish. The possession of the rectory of Aylesbury conferred a great additional influence upon the dean. And there is found to have been a recurrence of the rivalry which so often takes place between the bishop and the dean; and Grosseteste is stated to have had a further reason for the step which he took. He was actuated by the consideration that it was through so rich an endowment that the dean "was able to lift up the horns of his audacity and become recalcitrant against his bishop,"[3] and saw that there was a way of preventing it for the future, by depriving him of the preferment.

When the severance from the deanery was com-

---

[1] Mat. Par., *ad* A.D. 1245, *u. s.*, pp. 660, 661.
[2] *Supra*, p. 254, 255.   [3] Mat. Par., *u. s.*, p. 661.

pleted, the rectory was attached to a prebendal stall, which was first conferred upon Robert de Marisco. The proceeding, however good the result might have been, did not escape censure. It was considered an act of injustice to inflict so great a loss upon the deanery, by the separation from it of a benefice which, from time immemorial, had been held with it. Roger de Weseham was consecrated bishop by the pope at Lyons, in A.D. 1245. And, accordingly, this is to be regarded as one of the repeated acts of papal aggression in England, which roused the spirit of Falk Fitzwarenne, and led to the resistance which caused the precipitate departure of Martin, the collector of the papal revenue, from England.[1] The consecration, it will be observed, took place in the same year of the pope's residence at Lyons, in which the famous council was held, which the abbots and priors of England were specially invited to attend;[2] at which the Emperor Frederick II., the husband of Isabella, the sister of King Henry III., was deposed.

Until the time of the abolition of peculiar jurisdictions,[3] the church of Aylesbury was exempt from the ordinary episcopal visitation, as a peculiar of the dean and chapter of Lincoln. The most illustrious of those who have held this stall is Dr. John Hacket, who, during the sitting of the Long Parliament, made the memorable appeal before the House of Commons on behalf of the cathedral establishments[4]

---

[1] Mat. Par., *ad* A.D. 1245, *u. s.*, p. 659.
[2] Rymer, *u. s.*, vol. i., p. 258; *u. s.*, Rec. ed.; *supra*, p. 199.
[3] *Supra*, p. 34.
[4] Fuller, "Church Hist.," cent. xvi., bk. xi., *u. s.*, p. 179.

## THE PREBEND OF AYLESBURY. 269

on the 12th of May, in A.D. 1641; and who was the munificent restorer of the cathedral of Lichfield, which had been so much injured during the rebellion —of which see, after the Restoration, he was appointed bishop. Nor has the prebendal house of residence at Aylesbury been without an historical resident; for it was occupied for a time by the notorious John Wilkes,[1] who was returned as member of parliament for the borough of Aylesbury, in A.D. 1757. It has at a recent date become the property of the present Dean of Lichfield, the well-known prolocutor of the Lower House of Convocation, who was formerly the Vicar of Aylesbury, and Archdeacon of Buckingham.

Ashridge, where is now the seat of Earl Brownlow, is celebrated as the place in which the Bonhommes were established in the thirteenth century—the "boni viri" or "boni homines" of the early charters.[2] This was a branch of the Augustinian order, and the name has been supposed to be derived from the connexion[3] with the followers of Joannes Bonus, or John Lebon. Their founder, on this supposition, was the son of Mantuan parents,[4] and derived his name from his father, John Bonhomi, and his mother, who was named Bona. He was born in A.D. 1168, and in his early years, to the great sorrow of his

---

[1] Lipscomb, "History of Buckinghamshire," vol. ii., p. 87. Lond., 1831–1843.

[2] Dugd., *u. s.*, vol. vi., pp. 314–317.

[3] H. Spondan., "Ann. Baronii Contin.," *ad* A.D. 1259, sect. ix., tom. i., p. 205. Par., 1659.

[4] H. Wadding, "Hist. Ord. Minorum," *ad* A.D. 1237, sect. xi., tom. ii., p. 432; and Apologia, sect. ii., *ibid.*, ad calc., pp. 447, *sqq*. Rom., 1732.

pious mother, travelled through various parts of Italy as a juggler or comic actor. At last he was visited by a severe attack of sickness, which led to his conversion in A.D. 1208. Subsequently to this, in deep penitence, he retired to the wild country near Cesena; after which he gathered round him a band of followers who made it their work to collect money for alms and other pious uses. The dress which was adopted by them so closely resembled that of the Eremites,[1] that they complained bitterly of the injury which was caused, and a fierce contest ensued which required the intervention of Innocent IV. and of successive popes in order that the question of the habits, which the orders were respectively to wear, might be determined. John Lebon died October 23rd, A.D. 1249.

The foundation was settled at Ashridge by Edmund, Earl of Cornwall, the son of Richard, King of the Romans, who was brother to Henry III. When he was travelling in Germany, while still a boy, with his father, or at a later period of his life more probably, he observed a box, which was described as containing a portion of the sacred blood. Accepting the statement as true,[2] he purchased it, and brought it with him to England, where he bestowed a third part of it upon the abbey of Hayles, in Gloucestershire, which had been founded by his father. After retaining the other two-third parts for a time, he conferred them upon the monastery which he founded

---

[1] *Supra*, p. 46.
[2] Holinshed, "Chron.," *ad* A.D. 1272, vol. iii., p. 275. Lond. 1587.

at Ashridge, at a short distance from his castle at Berkhamstead, in A.D. 1283,[1] and in which he placed the Bonhommes, many of whom were found to answer truly to their name of "boni homines."[2] This precious treasure, as it was esteemed, became a source of much profit from the interest which it excited and the number of persons who came to visit it.

There was but little hope at the first that this foundation would meet with ultimate success, or last for any great length of time. The endowment was small, and the character of the religious whom he placed there at first was unsatisfactory, for some of these conducted themselves but ill.[3] The difficulties, however, which attended their first establishment were surmounted. The church was dedicated by Oliver Sutton, the Bishop of Lincoln, in whose diocese Ashridge then was, at the instance of the founder,[4] in A.D. 1286. And the original endowment was increased by a donation from the founder of the manors and advowsons of Ambrosden and Chesterton in A.D. 1288, in which year also their charter was confirmed by the king.[5] The gift of the founder was rendered a still more profitable acquisition by the appropriation of the titles, which, in the instance of Ambrosden,[6] was effected in A.D. 1334 by virtue of a

---

[1] Leland, "Collect.," *u. s.*, vol. ii., p. 352.
[2] N. Harpsfield, "Hist. Angl. Eccl.," p. 480. Duac., 1622.
[3] Ann. de Dunst., ad A.D. 1283, in "Ann. Monast.," *u. s.*, vol. iii., p. 305. [4] *Ibid.*, p. 363.
[5] Dugd., "Mon.," *u. s.*, vol. vi., p. 515.
[6] Kennet, "Par. Ant.," *u. s.*, vol. ii., pp. 37-41.

previous grant of Pope Clement V.[1] and of Chesterton about the year A.D. 1403.

A colony from the home at Ashridge was settled at Edenton, in Wiltshire, in A.D. 1352. William of Edendon, the Bishop of Winchester at that time, had been a benefactor to the place of his birth, and had founded there a college of secular clergy. And this he was induced to convert into a convent of the Bonhommes,[2] on the intervention of Edward the Black Prince, who had conceived a great affection for the order from what he had witnessed of them in France. This establishment, like the parent foundation, became possessed of large estates.

Edward I. kept the Christmas of A.D. 1290 at Ashridge, and remained there for five weeks.[3] But on another occasion it experienced a very different fortune, for in the troublous time of A.D. 1381 the house was attacked by the mob, which had done other acts of violence in the neighbourhood.[4] It continued to flourish in after-years, and at the period of the dissolution of the monasteries was retained to be of the annual value of £416. 0s. 4d. in the gross receipts. At this time the falsity of the conception which was entertained of the supposed relic was made clear, "for it was perceived to be only honey coloured with saffron, as was shown

---

[1] Kennet, "Par. Ant.," *u. s.*, vol. ii., pp. 202, 203.
[2] Cassan's "Lives of the Bishops of Winchester," *u. s.*, vol. i., p. 187.
[3] Ann. de Dunst., in "Ann. Mon.," *u. s.*, p. 367.
[4] *Ibid.*, p. 417.

at Paul's Cross by the Bishop of Rochester[1] in A.D. 1538."[2]

The Earl of Cornwall died at Ashridge in A.D. 1300. His heart was buried in the conventual church, but his body was taken to the abbey church of Hayles, where it was buried with great solemnity in the presence of the king and of several bishops and abbots whom, by his letters, he had specially invited to attend.[3] As the earl died without heirs, his large estates reverted to the Crown.

The foundation in Buckinghamshire, which is of the highest public importance, and which has exercised the greatest influence, wherever the results of an English education in its noblest ideal have been manifested, yet remains to be described in the notice of Eton College. The origin of its establishment depends in some degree upon the preceding course which had been adopted in reference to one class of the monastic institutions in England. There has already been occasion to mention the attempts of the earlier kings to gain possession of the alien priories,[4] which, from their foreign relations, were deemed to give a reasonable cause for suspicion, and the final acquisition of their revenues by Henry V. in consequence of the action of the Parliament at Leicester in regard to them in A.D. 1414. It was his intention to effect a

---

[1] The bishop was John Hilsey, who had been prior of the Dominican Friars in London.

[2] J. Speed, "Theatre of Great Britain," Bucks, p. 43. Lond., 1611.

[3] Kennet, "Par. Ant.," *u. s.*, vol. i., pp. 483, 484.

[4] *Supra*, p. 64.

T

reformation in the University of Oxford. And he obtained a licence from the pope, who claimed the right of transferring to new objects such benefactions as he might think it desirable to reassign,[1] in order that he might found a college of theologians in Oxford, which he considered would be in accordance with the divine will. To this he proposed that the dissolved alien priories should be annexed; but his intention was frustrated by his death.[2]

Henry VI., who was an infant at the time of his accession, in A.D. 1422, when he came to full age determined to give effect to his father's design, with such variation, however, as he thought fit; which included the abandonment of the proposed college at Oxford, and the substitution of Eton College, and of the allied college of St. Nicholas, his patron saint, which is better known as King's College, at Cambridge, in its place. His early life had been passed at Windsor, from which he must often have looked upon the site of his future college on the opposite bank of the Thames; and it is to the associations of his first years that the choice of this scene for his great benefaction is to be referred. When he assumed the Government into his own hand, as a preliminary step towards the execution of his plan, the king purchased the advowson of the parochial church of Eton in A.D. 1440, with a view to rebuild it on a grander scale, that it might serve the use of a collegiate chapel and

---

[1] "Loci e libro veritatum:" Passages from Gascoigne's "Theological Dictionary," A.D. 1403-48; by J. E. T. Rogers, p. 147, 148. Ox., 1881.

[2] Gascoigne's "Theological Dictionary," *u. s.*, p. 218.

a parish church.[1] There is also a letter of the date of the 12th September in the same year, which contains the appointment of certain persons to treat with the Bishop of Lincoln as proctors for the king, in order that the appropriation of the church might be effected. The rebuilding of the church was commenced, but, however beautiful the design, it did not equal the conception which the king had formed. The evidence of this had been revealed of late years by a document, which had been discovered in the archives of the college, which contains the plan of the collegiate church, with the dimensions altered and enlarged by the hand of the founder himself,[2] which, if carried into effect, would have made it "surpass any cathedral in the kingdom in its dimensions."

The time of Henry's life, in which his mind was directed to this object, in combination with his own character, must forbid other thoughts than those which contemplate the purity of his intention and the simplicity of his motive. It was not to atone for the transgressions of a past life, nor to make amends for the commission of a great crime, but with the single wish to do good, as befitted a king, that he conceived his great design. Nor, again, did this foundation involve the spoliation of others, that the means for its establishment might be procured. It has been seen that the conversion of the revenues of the alien priories

---

[1] Sir Edw. Creasy, "Memoirs of Eminent Etonians," p. 6. Lond., 1876.

[2] "Memorials of the reign of Henry VI."; "Official Correspondence of Thos. Bekynton," by J. E. B. Mayor, vol. i., Introd., p. lxxxiii, note. 1872. Rolls' Ser.

to a similar use had been already contemplated. And some of these, as in the instance of Cogges and Minster Lovell[1] in the present diocese of Oxford, were actually so applied, while the remaining portion of the endowment was provided from other estates which were vested in the Crown. It was, therefore, in order to employ for the best use the time of tranquillity, which was then granted, but which was soon to be replaced by the calamities of a domestic warfare, that this work was undertaken and its foundations laid by the king.

The first charter in favour of the proposed institution was granted in the October of the same year, and it contains an expression of the king's desire to found a college in the parish church of Eton, which was not far from the place of his birth; a description of the persons of whom the foundation is to consist; and a statement of the purpose for which they are to be incorporated; which is according to the usual form, that they shall pray there continually for his health and welfare so long as he lives, and for his soul when he shall have departed this life, and for the souls of his ancestors, and of the faithful departed. The first charter of the actual foundation, which is of the date of A.D. 1441, is found to change the composition of the corporate body in the relative numbers of its members; and it is declared to be "a college to consist of a provost, seventy scholars, ten fellows, ten chaplains, ten clerks, ten choristers, one head-master, one under-master or usher, and ten bedesmen."[2]

---

[1] *Supra*, p. 65.
[2] Schools Inquiry Commission: "Report," *u. s.*, vol. i., app. iv., p. 38.

The first provost who was designated in the charter was Henry Sever, who had been Chaplain to King Henry V., and who was Dean of Westminster and Warden of Merton College. But he never held the office. William of Waynflete, the future founder of Magdalen College, who was named as one of the fellows under Sever, and who was then head-master of the school at Winchester, was induced by the king to become the head-master at Eton, in A.D. 1442; and was appointed provost in A.D. 1443; and when he left his school five fellows of the foundation at Winchester, and thirty-five scholars emigrated with him to Eton, "and became the primitive body of Etonians."[1] They took possession of their new abode, on the Feast of St. Thomas, in this year. Such temporary buildings as were required for their use were raised; but for many years after this the college remained incomplete.[2] King Henry continued to exhibit his interest in the college, and his care for its future welfare; and he appointed the Bishops of London and of Winchester by his letters patent of July 12th, A.D. 1455, his delegates for the correction and improvement of it during his lifetime, with the advice of the provosts.[3] The care taken by Waynflete for the completion of the work did not cease after he became the Bishop of Winchester; a large part of the buildings was finished at his expense; and there is evidence[4] of his participation in the works which

---

[1] Creasy, "Memoirs," *u. s.*, p. 13.   [2] *Ibid.*, p. 14.
[3] Chandler, "Life of Waynflete," ch. iv., in Cassan's "Lives of the Bishops of Winchester," *u. s.*, vol. i., p. 274.
[4] *Ibid.*, pp. 290, 291.

were required up to so late a time as A.D. 1482. Though Waynflete attained a higher position in the bishopric of Winchester and the chancellorship, yet in the provostship of Eton he held that which "is accounted one of the gentilest interests and preferments in England."[1]

As in the instance of Windsor,[2] so in respect of this foundation, when the Act was passed for the dissolution of the chantries and collegiate bodies,[3] an exception was made in favour of "the college of Eton," so that the provisions of the statute did not extend to it, and it retained its former position unaffected by any change.

When the Schools Inquiry Commission was instituted, in the report[4] which was made in A.D. 1868, the income of the college was returned as amounting in the gross to twenty thousand five hundred and sixty-nine pounds. It has since experienced in the appointment of the governing body an alteration of the same kind with that which has affected the original charters in the instance of other schools and colleges.

The history of the diocese of Oxford, which has now been followed from its rudimental state at the mission of St. Birinus to its present organisation, has shown the prominent place which was held at a very early period by the archdeaconries of Buckingham and of Oxford from their connexion with the important

---

[1] Fuller, "Church Hist.," *u. s.*, cent. xv., bk. iv., p. 184.
[2] *Supra*, pp. 249, 250.   [3] 1 Ed. VI., c. 14, s. 15.
[4] Vol. i., *u. s*, app. v., p. 97.

diocese of Lincoln, as well as for their own separate claims. In this respect there is on the part of Buckingham the noble foundation of Eton College; while from the University of Oxford, which occupies the central point of the diocese, there has gone forth at great religious epochs—as those in which a Wycliffe or a Wolsey, a Wesley or a Newman, made their presence felt—an influence of untold importance and of unmeasured extent. In Berkshire, on the other hand, whose connexion with the present diocese is of later date, there is a distinct pre-eminence of its own. The two mitred Benedictine abbeys, during the time of their magnificence, ensured for all within their sphere the first ecclesiastical position. The chapel of St. George, at Windsor, the church of the royal seat, the burial-place of English sovereigns, the religious home of the most illustrious order of knighthood, still retains its own great name.

And, finally, the history of the diocese at large in its united character, and with its wider interests, in connexion with the rest of the English sees, can present an illustration of the important fact, that the Church of England in its present state, is not merely the inheritor of the pre-Reformation Church in this land. It is far more. It is the branch of the Catholic Church in this realm of England, whose continuous life has never been interrupted. Inheritance is suggestive of death. The claims of the Church of England depend upon the survival of its true character in every age, and upon its remaining in every period of its existence essentially one and the same.

# APPENDIX A.

## BISHOPS IN OXFORDSHIRE.

### BISHOPS OF DORCHESTER, AS A WEST SAXON SEE.

| | Date of Accession. A.D. | | Date of Accession. A.D. |
|---|---|---|---|
| St. Birinus | 634 | St. Heddi | 676 |
| Agilberht | 650 | Ætla | c. 676 |
| Wini | 652 | Beda, "Hist. Eccl.," iv. 23. | |
| Leutherius | 670 | | |

| | | | |
|---|---|---|---|
| [St. Aldhelm, Bp. of Sherborne | 705 | [Daniel, Bp. of Winchester | 705 |
| For succession, see "Hist. of Dio. of Salisbury."] | | For succession, see "Hist. of Dio. of Winchester."] | |

### BISHOPS OF DORCHESTER, AS A MERCIAN SEE.

| | Date *u. s.* | | Date *u. s.* |
|---|---|---|---|
| Alheard | [1]869 × 888 | Oskytel | 950 |
| Ceolwulph | 909 | Leofwin | c. 958 |
| Winsy | 909 × 926 | | |

### AND AS COMPRISING ALSO THE SEES OF LINDSEY AND LEICESTER.

| | | | |
|---|---|---|---|
| Leofwin | c. 965 | Eadnoth | 1034 |
| Eadnoth | 965 × 974 | Ulf | 1050 |
| Escwy | 975 × 979 | Wulfwy | 1053 |
| Alfhelm | 1002 | Remigius | 1067 |
| Eadnoth | 1006 | [For succession, see "Hist. of Dio. of Lincoln."] | |
| Ethelric | 1016 | | |

[1] The approximate dates signified by × are taken from W. Stubbs, "Registrum Sacrum Anglicanum." Oxon., 1858.

## Bishop of Oxford at Oseney.

Robert King ... ... 1545

## Bishops of Oxford at St. Frideswide's, or Christ Church.

| | Date *u. s.* | | Date *u. s.* |
|---|---|---|---|
| Robert King | ... 1545 | John Potter | ... 1715 |
| See vacant | 1557–1567 | Thomas Secker | ... 1737 |
| Hugh Curwen | ... 1567 | John Hume | ... 1758 |
| See vacant | 1568–1589 | Robert Lowth | ... 1766 |
| John Underhill | ... 1589 | John Butler | ... 1777 |
| See vacant | 1592–1604 | Edward Smallwell | ... 1788 |
| John Bridges | ... 1604 | John Randolph | ... 1799 |
| John Howson | ... 1619 | Charles Moss | ... 1807 |
| Richard Corbet | ... 1628 | William Jackson | ... 1812 |
| John Bancroft | ... 1632 | Edward Legge | ... 1816 |
| Robert Skinner | ... 1641 | Charles Lloyd | ... 1827 |
| William Paul | ... 1663 | Richard Bagot | ... 1829 |
| Walter Blandford | . 1665 | In union with Berkshire, from | ... 1836 |
| Nathaniel Crewe | ... 1671 | | |
| Henry Compton | ... 1674 | Samuel Wilberforce | ... 1845 |
| John Fell | ... 1676 | In union with Berkshire and Buckinghamshire, from | ... 1846 |
| Samuel Parker | ... 1686 | | |
| Timothy Hall | ... 1688 | | |
| John Hough | ... 1690 | John Fielder Mackarness | 1869 |
| William Talbot | ... 1699 | | |

[1] Nominated on December 22nd, A.D. 1815, consecrated on March 24th, A.D. 1816.

# APPENDIX B.

## BISHOPS FOR BERKSHIRE.

### BISHOPS OF SHERBORNE.

| | Date of Accession. A.D. | | Date of Accession. A.D. |
|---|---|---|---|
| St. Aldhelm | 705 | Eahlstan | 824 |
| Forthere | 709 | Heahmond | 868 |
| Herewold | 736 | Ætheleage | 872 |
| Æthelmod | 766 × 778 | Wulfsige | 883 |
| Denefrith | 793 | Asser | 892 × 900 |
| Wigbert | 796 × 801 | | |

| BISHOPS OF RAMSBURY. | | BISHOPS OF SHERBORNE. | |
|---|---|---|---|
| Æthelstan | 909 | Werstan [1] | 909 |
| Odo | 925 × 927 | | |
| Ælric | ... | [For the succession of bishops, see "Hist. of Dio. of Salisbury."] | |
| Osulph | 942 × 952 | | |
| Ælfstan | 970 × 974 | | |
| Wulfgar | 981 | | |
| Siric | 985 | | |
| Ælfric | 990 | | |
| Brithwold | 1005 | | |
| Herman | 1045 | Herman | 1058 |

### BISHOPS OF OLD SARUM.

| Herman | 1075 | Jocelin | 1142 |
|---|---|---|---|
| St. Osmund | 1078 | Herbert Walter | 1189 |
| Roger | 1107 | Herbert Poore | 1194 |

### BISHOPS OF NEW SARUM, OR SALISBURY.

| Richard Poore | 1217 | [For succession, see "Hist. of Dio. of Salisbury."] |
|---|---|---|

---

[1] For the difficulty as to this name see W. Stubbs, "Registrum Sacrum Anglicanum," *u. s.*, p. 13, *n*.

# APPENDIX C.

List of Endowed Grammar Schools in the Diocese of Oxford: extracted from the Report of the Schools Inquiry Commission, appointed on December the 28th, A.D. 1864, vol. i., app. iv., 37-90; app. v., 96-8, 1868.

| Name of Place. | Founder of School. | Date of Foundation. | Gross Annual Value of Endowment. |
|---|---|---|---|
| **OXON.** | | | £ |
| Bampton | Robert Vesey | 1638 | 36 |
| Burford | Simon Wisdom | 1571 | 368 |
| Charlbury | Anne Walker (by will, 1659) | 1675 | 40 |
| Chipping Norton | (Unknown) | c. 1547 | 17 |
| Cropredy | Walter Colcutt | 1575 | 39 |
| Dorchester | John Fettiplace | 1652 | 10 |
| Ewelme | Earl of Suffolk | 1437 | 1,212 |
| Henley-on-Thames | James I. | 1604 | 304 |
| Oxford | | | |
| 1 Cathedral School | Henry VIII. | 1546 | 60 |
| 2 Magdalen Coll. School | William of Waynflete | 1480 | 216 |
| Steeple Aston | Samuel Radcliffe | 1648 | 29 |
| Thame | Lord Williams, of Thame | 1575 | 659 |
| Watlington | Thomas Stonor | 1664 | 15 |
| Witney | Henry Box | 1663 | 63 |
| Woodstock | Richard Cornwell | 1585 | 68 |

# APPENDIX.

| Name of Place. | Founder of School. | Date of Foundation. | Gross Annual Value of Endowment. |
|---|---|---|---|
| **BERKS.** | | | £ |
| Abingdon | John Roysse | 1562 | 275 |
| Bradfield, St. Andrew's Coll. | Rev. Thomas Stevens, Rector | 1859 | [30. For separate exhibitions] |
| Childrey | William Fettiplace | 1526 | 13 |
| Hungerford | Thomas Sheaff, D.D. | 1653 | 22 |
| Newbury | Unknown | bef. 1677 | 836 |
| Pangbourne | John Breedon | 1685 | 40 |
| Reading | Henry VII. and John Thorne, Abbot of Reading | Temp. Henry VII. | 50 |
| Wallingford | Unknown | c. 1672 | 26 |
| Wantage | From town lands by Act of Parl., 39 Eliz. | 1597 | 585 |
| Wellington Coll. (Wokingham) | By Public Subscription | 1859 | [774. For separate exhibitions] |
| **BUCKS.** | | | |
| Amersham | Robert Chaloner, D.D. (by will, 1620) | 1624 | 190 |
| Aylesbury | Sir Henry Lee (reputed) | 1687 | 607 |
| Beachampton | William Elmer (by will, 1648) | 1653 | 70 |
| Buckingham | Edward VI. (supposed) | Temp. Edw. VI. | 10 |
| Eton | Henry VI. | 1441 | 20,569 |
| High Wycombe | Queen Elizabeth | 1562 | 629 |

# INDEX.

ABBA, early settler in Berks, 224; gives name to Abingdon, *ib*.

Abbot, G., Archbishop, Vice-Chancellor of Oxford, 116; favours Puritan party, 117; suspended, 121; Howson, Bishop of Oxford, one of the five commissioners for, *ib*.

Abbot, C., Lord Colchester, member for University, 175; action of Bishop Lloyd on removal of, to Upper House, *ib*.

Abingdon, original name of, 224; present name of, *ib*.; abbey, history of, 223-31; dissolution of, 236; abbots of, Aldred 229, 230; Ethelhelm, 230; Faritius, 229; Rowland, T., 236; Benedictine chapter at, 231; Chronicle of Abbey, extracts from, 232-35; Guild of Holy Cross, 237, 238; Church of St. Helen, 67, 203, 225, 237; Deanery of, 197

Act books of Diocesan Courts, extracts from, 137-143

Adderbury, apostate deacon crucified at, 52; vicar killed by Parliamentarian soldiers, 135, 136

Adelicia of Louvaine, marriage of, at Windsor, 246; benefactress to Reading Abbey, 240

Advertisements, temp. Queen Elizabeth, 113

Æthelberht, King of Kent, 2, 3

Æthelstan, with successors, bishops of Sunning, so named, 196

Ætla, Bishop, uncertain position of, 10, 15, 281

Agilberht, French bishop, from Ireland, 7; becomes Bishop of Dorchester, 8; is expelled, and purchases see of London, *ib*.

Aldhelm, St., first Bishop of Sherborne, 13, 193

Aldrich, H., Dean of Christchurch, 159; member of Committee of Revision of Book of Common Prayer, 160; designs church of All Saints, 81, 160; character of, 159

Alfred, Archdeacon of Oxford, 31; Alfred, the Little, Archdeacon of Bucks, 254, 255

Alfred, King, born at Wantage, 220; success of, 227; mythical founder of the university, 39, 40, and *n*.; grant of land to Deormodus, 227

Algar, suitor of St. Frideswide, 73

Alheard, styled bishop of Dorchester, 15; death of, 15, 16

Alien priories, two forms of, 63; invaded by Edward I. and Edward III., 64; regranted by Richard II., *ib.*; legally vested in Henry V., 64, 273; grant of certain, to Eton College, by Henry VI., 65, 275, 276

Anna, King of East Angles, receives Kenwalch, 7

Anselm, Archbishop, deference to, by Henry I. in investiture of bishops, 207

Appleford, grant of, to Deormodus, 227; regrant to abbey of Abingdon, *ib.*

Archdeacons, diocesan, appointment of, by Remigius, 30, 31, 255

Archdeaconry of Oxford, early, 31, 34; reconstituted by Henry VIII., 91; present endowment of, 190; of Berks, early notices of, 192, 196; present endowment of, 220, 221; of Bucks, early notices of, 253-255; present endowment of, 265

Architectural Society, Oxford, instituted, 80

Architecture, Saxon, so named, 30; Saxon and Norman, 25-7; Pointed, 65-7; later 80, 82

Armada, Spanish, consequences of, affecting treatment of Romanists, 113

Arundel, T., Archbishop, visits the university, 57; severity of toward Lollards, 59

Ashridge, house of Bonhommes at, 269; colony from, 272; Edward I., visit of, *ib.*; Edmund Earl of Cornwall dies at, 273; church of, 271

Asser, last Bishop of Sherborne, 193, 194

Assingdon, battle of, Bishop of Dorchester slain at, 17, 18

Asterius, Archbishop of Milan, consecrates Birinus, 3

Atterbury, F., dean of Christchurch, 165

Augustine, Archbishop, mission of, 2, 222

Augustinian Friars, at Boarstall, 46; settle in Oxford, *ib.*; influence of, in university, 47; branch of, at Ashridge, 269; *see* Oseney

Aylesbury, vicarage of, 256; rectory of, 266; prebend of, 266; peculiars of, 268; prebendal house of, 269

B.

BAGOT, R., Bishop, 176, 184; Chancellor of Order of the Garter, 178-80; action toward J. H. Newman, 177, 184; translated to see of Bath and Wells, 184; character of, by Cardinal Newman, 177

Banbury, church of, demolished, 80, 150

BANCROFT, J., Bishop, 122; annexes Cuddesdon to see, *ib.*; provides for palace, *ib.*; death of, 123

Bartholomew, St., Hospital of, for lepers, 46, 47; conflicting claims of Oriel College and city of Oxford, 47

Bedingfield, Sir H., guardian of the Princess Elizabeth at Woodstock, 101

Beket, T., Archbishop, present with the two kings Henry at Woodstock, 49; consecrates church at Reading, 241; retires to abbey of Pontigny, 203

Benedictine order, monasteries of, 222, 223; Chapter of, at Abingdon, 231

Bercta, Queen of Æthelberht, 2

Berkshire, origin of name of, 220; united with see of Oxon, 178, 185, 192; Bishop of, so named, 196; independent action of clergy of, 198–201; habits of life of clergy of, 209; see Archdeaconry

Birinus, St., mission of, at Dorchester; state of paganism, 3, 224; consecrated by Archbishop of Milan, 3; royal baptisms by, 4, 5; churches built by, 5; death of, ib.; canonised, 7; memorial of, in abbey church, 6

Boleyn, Anne, marriage of, promoted by Bishop Curwen, 110

Bisham, preceptory at, 62

Bloxham, spire of church of, 66

Bodleian Library, Jews bargain with O. Cromwell for, 134

Bonhommes, boni homines, origin of name, 269; see Ashridge and Lebon

Bradshaw, W., Dean of Christchurch, refuses to admit Vice-Chancellor's notice, 170

Brideoak, R., rector of Witney, confesses Speaker Lenthall, 135, and n.

BRIDGES, J., Bishop, 118–121; residence of at March Baldon, 121

Buckingham, vicarage of; archdeaconry of, early notices of, 254–56; united with Oxon and Berks, 178, 185, 192, 253; peculiars of, 256; see Archdeaconry

Bull, G., Bishop, ordination of, as deacon and priest, by Bishop Skinner, 128

BUTLER, John, Bishop, 173; political writer, ib.

Butler, Joseph, Bishop, born at Wantage, 220

C.

CAMBRIDGE, not a city, reason of, 92

Canterbury, church of St. Martin, 2

Canning, G., candidate for university, opposed by Bishop Lloyd, 175

Canterbury and York, provinces of, contest respecting the extent of, 22, 207

Caroline theology, school of, 168

Ceolred, Bishop of Leicester, 15

Ceolwulph, Bishop of Dorchester, 16

Chamberlain, Rev. T., first to adopt vestments at church of St. Thomas the Martyr, Oxford, 187

Chantries, abuse of, 95, 96; suppressed by Henry VIII., 95; suppression of completed by Edward VI., ib.; exemption in Act, for Windsor, 249, 250; for Eton, 278

Charles I., benefactor to see, 122; escapes from Oxford 129; concessions proposed by, ib.; burial of, at Windsor

250, 251 ; discovery of body of, 251, 252

Charles II., declaration of, from Breda, 146 ; restoration of, consequences of, 146-148

Charles V., of France, declaration in favour of Clement VII., not accepted at Oxford, 56

Cheapside cross, question referred to two universities, 116 ; crucifix for cross, *ib.*; destroyed, *ib.*

Chester, bishopric of, 254, 255 ; *see* Lichfield and Coventry

Childrey, almshouses at, 209 ; leaden font in church of, 27

Churches, consecration of, in diocese, 37 ; number of : Oxon, 35, 36 ; Berks, 197, 198 ; Bucks, 255, 256; *see* Architecture

Cilla, foundation by at Helenstow, 225 ; removal of, *ib.*

Cissa, reputed founder of abbey of Abingdon, 224, 225

Clark, S., ejected minister, 264 ; commentary on Bible of, 264, 265

Clement V., decree of, against Templars, 61 ; assumption of title by, 56

Clergy, sufferings of during usurpation, in cathedral of Christchurch, 131 ; Oxon, 134, 136 ; Berks, 219 ; Bucks, 261, 264 ; action and habits of, *see* Berks

Clewer, vicar of, and Dr. Julius, 190 ; sisterhood at, 220

Cole, Dr. H., preaches in Oxford, 104, 105

Common Prayer, Book of, use of, suspended by Directory, 132 ; faithfulness in use of it during the usurpation, 132, 133, 151; discontinued in Magdalen College, temp. James II., 158 ; proposed revision, 147, 160; frustrated, *ib.*

Commonwealth, cathedral, injury to windows during, 97, 98, 133 ; colleges and chapels uninjured, 132, 133; customs of university u n c h a n g e d during, 132, 133; examination for admission, 133, 134; Maids Moreton Church, injury to, 263 ; Cuddesdon palace burnt, 129 ; Cheapside cross destroyed, 116 ; *see* Clergy

COMPTON, H., Bishop, 149, 150

Conant, J., sufferer after the Restoration, 147

Convocation, disapproves revision of Book of Common Prayer, 160 ; censures Bishop Hoadly, 167, 168 ; silenced, 168 ; debates of, regained, *ib.*

Cornwall, Edmund, Earl of, benefactor to churches of Wallingford, 197 ; founder of house of Bonhommes at Ashridge, 270 ; present at St. Frideswide's, 74 ; death and burial of, at, 273; Richard, Earl of, father of Edmund, 270 ; pleads for Jews, 205

Coventry, Bishop of, 255 ; *see* Chester and Lichfield

Councils, synods : Abingdon, 10, *n.* ; Ænham, 48, *n.* ; Cloveshoo, 10, *n.*; Eynsham, 48, *n.*, 49 ; Hertford, 10 ; Kyrtlington, 48, *n.*; Kyrtling, *ib.* ; Lateran, 231 ; London, 23, 58, 195, 199, 209; Lyons, 55 ; Oxford, 34, 48, 50, 58 ; Reading, 207-209 ; Sardica and Laodicea, 23 ; Trent,

106; Vercelli, 18, 19; Vienne, 61; Winchester, 22; Windsor, 22, 205–209; at place undetermined, 12
Coverdale, M., visits Newbury for T. Cromwell, 210
Cowley, preceptory of Templars at, 61
Cox, R., Dean of Christchurch, at Strasbourg, 95; Frankfort, *ib.*; Bishop of Ely, *ib.*
Cranmer, Archbishop, trial and death of, 98, 105
CREWE, N., Bishop, 149
Cromwell, O., bargains with Jews for Bodleian Library, 134; exhumation of body of, 219
Cromwell, T., assists Henry VIII. in obtaining monasteries, 84; correspondence of Coverdale with, 210
Cuddesdon, origin of name of, 228; vill granted to Abingdon by Edwy, *ib.*; impropriation of, attached to see, 119, *n.*; vicarage and rectory consolidated, 122; church, early notice of, 229; palace, provided by Bishop Bancroft, 122; visited by Archbishop Laud, *ib.*; burnt by Col. Legge, 129; proposed rebuilding by Bishop Paul, 149; rebuilt by Bishop Fell, 150; inhabited by Bishop Lloyd, 176; not by Bishop Bagot, *ib.*; by Bishop Wilberforce, 185; mill, early contest at, 229; Wilberforce College at, 188
CURWEN, CUREN, H., Archbishop of Dublin, Bishop, 110, 111; a favourite at Court, 110; chaplain to Queen Mary, *ib.*; death of, 111

Cynegils, King and son, baptized at Dorchester, 35; death of, 7

D.

DANES, the, 17; burn tower of St. Frideswide's, 74; in Berkshire, 226, 227
Daniel, first Bishop of Winchester, 13
De Coutances, W., Archdeacon of Oxon, made Archbishop of Rouen, 50
De Merton, W., founder of Merton College, 40, 43; important character of statutes of, 40
De Valence, Ethelmar, obtains St. Helen's, Abingdon, 203
Deddington, registers of, during Commonwealth, 137
Directory, the, for Common Prayer, 132, 218, 251
Dodwell, H., nonjuror, at Shottesbrook, 161, 162, 219
Domesday Book: Oxon, 29, 30, 28; Berks, 197; Bucks, 255
Dominican Friars, settlement of, in Oxford, 41, 42; preach to Jews, *ib.*; intercede for Jews at Reading, 205; consequences of this, *ib.*
Donation, form of, to religious foundation, 227, 240
Dorchester, origin of name of, 4; situation of, 23; mission of Birinus at, 4, 5; secular canons of, 5; replaced by regulars, 6, 33, 34; abbot of, deprived, 38; bishopric of, 5; position lost, 14; regained, 15, 16; seat of, removed to Lincoln, 23, 24; church of, 5, 6, 26, 27, 66; peculiar of, 34
Drayton Beauchamp, Richard Hooker, incumbent of, 260

## E.

EDENTON, in Wilts, colony of Bonhommes from Ashridge, settles at, 272
Edmund, St., Archbishop, born at Abingdon, 202; dissatisfied with times, leaves his see, 202, 203
Edward the Elder, assigns various bishoprics, 194
Edward the Confessor, makes Ulph, his chaplain, Bishop of Dorchester, 18; sanctions the united bishopric of Sherborne, 194
Edward I., invades alien priories, 64; keeps Christmas at Ashridge, 272
Edward II., founder of Oriel College, 47; conduct toward Knights Templars, 61
Edward III., seizes alien priories, 64; builds St. George's Chapel, 248; *see* Garter, Order of
Edward IV., begins to build St. George's Chapel, 248; burial of, and of Queen, in choir, 250
Edward VI., provides endowment for see, 96; grants lease of Hook Norton to Duke of Northumberland, 119; founds schools; *see* Chantries
Eleutherius, Lothere, nephew of Agilberht, Bishop of Dorchester, 9
Elfrida builds nunnery at Reading, 238, 239
Elizabeth, Queen, at Woodstock, 101; sends relief to prelates in Bocardo, *ib.*; retains revenues of vacant see, 108, 111, 117, 118; exchanges the estates of endowment for impropriations, 119; treatment of Romanists, 113, 114
Ely, diocese of, formed, 92
Erasmus in Oxford, with Colet and More, 68
Eremites, Friars, 46; contest with Bonhommes, 270
Escwy, Bishop of Dorchester, assists Æthelred against the Danes, 17
Essex, Robert, Earl of, obtains estates of see, 118
Eton College, projected by Henry V., 273, 274; situation of, 274; foundation of, by Henry VI., 274–276; first provost of, 277; Waynflete, head-master, and provost, *ib.*; Etonians, the first, *ib.*; church of, 274; proposed rebuilding by Henry VI., 275, and *n.*; alien priories devoted to, 65, 275, 276; exempted from Act for dissolution of chantries and collegiate bodies, 278; provost and fellows sufferers during usurpation, 135

## F.

FARMER, A., rejected as President by fellows of Magdalen College, 154
Fell, J., Dean of Christchurch, 150; expels Locke from studentship, *ib.*; bishop, rebuilds Cuddesdon Palace, *ib.*; death of, 152; burial in cathedral, *ib.*; character of, 150, 151
Fell, S., Dean of Christ Church, deprived, 131
Five-Mile Act, the, 148
Fonts, leaden, 27
Fox, R., Bishop of Winchester,

# INDEX. 293

patron of Wolsey, 69; founder of Christchurch College, *ib.*; prudence in manner of, *ib.*; portrait of, in hall of college, *ib.*
Fitzwarenne, Falk, resists papal collector, 268
Franciscan Friars, settlement of, in Oxford, 43–46; church of, 46
Frideswide, St., parentage, 73; proposed marriage of, *ib.*; home at Binsey, *ib.*; church of, 26, 30, 73, 74; shrine of, 74, 75; relics of, 74; final burial of, 75; monastery of, founded, 73; surrendered, 76; site of, granted to Wolsey, 77–79; church of, by charter of Pope Hadrian IV., 26; tower of, burnt by Danes, 74; seat of bishop's chair, 94; becomes cathedral of Christ Church, *ib.*; abbess of monastery, deprived, 39; new throne, 188; new font, 82

## G.

GARTER, Order of, founded, 178, 247; chancellorship of, 178–80, 248; lost to Bishops of Sarum, and regained by Bishop Seth Ward, 179; transferred to Bishop of Oxon, 180; prelate of, Bishop of Winton, 248; registrar of, Dean of Windsor, 252
George IV., opposition of, to Roman Catholic emancipation, 175
Gladstone, W. E., character of Bishop Lloyd by, 174
Godstow, visited by Bishop Grosseteste, 38

GOLDWELL, T., nominated bishop, 106, 107; leaves England on accession of Elizabeth, 108
Grosseteste, R., lectures of, in Oxford, 45; visits diocese of Lincoln, 38; preaches at Council of Lyons, 55; deals with rectory of Aylesbury, 267

## H.

HALES, J., the ever memorable, sufferer, at Eton College, 135
Hall, J., Bishop of Norwich, sent to Tower, with Skinner, Bishop of Oxford, and others, 125, 126
HALL, T., reads declaration of indulgence, 157; received as bishop without respect, *ib.*; ordination by, refused, *ib.*; dies in poverty, 159
Hammond, Dr. H., visits Romanists in prison, 120; deprived of canonry, 131; Fell's "Life" of, 151
Hearne, T., nonjuror in Oxford, 163; precursor of modern historians, 163, 164
Hean, unduly delays foundation of Abingdon, 224–226
Heddi, St., Bishop of Dorchester, becomes Bishop of Winchester, 10; translates body of Birinus to Winchester, 5, 11
Henley-on-Thames, church of, Beket window in, 210
Henry I., founds hospital for lepers, 47; Reading Abbey, 238; investiture of bishop, by, 207; death of, at St. Denis, 239; burial of, at Reading, 240

Henry II., visits Reading, 240; Oxford, 48; visits Woodstock, with King Henry his son, 49

Henry III., builds houses for converts from Judaism, 42; visits Reading, 204, 205; treatment of Jews, *ib.*

Henry IV., statute against heretics, 59, 257, 258

Henry V., dissolves alien priories, 64; proposes to found Eton College, 273, 274

Henry VI., *see* Eton; burial of, at Chertsey, and removal to Windsor, 250

Henry VII., tomb, house of, at Windsor, 249; chapel of, at Westminster, 250

Henry VIII., college of, 79, 80; ecclesiastical valuation of, 83; first visitation of monasteries, 84; suppression of smaller foundations by, *ib.*; second visitation, 84, 85; dissolution of monasteries, 85-88; Oseney resigned to, 90; creation of bishopric of Oxford by, 90-93; removal to Christ Church, by, 93-95; Oxford a city by, 92; visit of, to Abbot of Reading, 243, 244; burial place of, 250

Heraclius, patriarch of Jerusalem, visit of, to Reading, 242; consecration of Temple Church by, *ib.*

Herman, Bishop of Ramsbury, forms united see of Sherborne, 194, 195

Heyford, Lower, sufferings of rector of, 136

Hoadly, J., Bishop of Bangor, opposed by Bishop Potter, 167; censure of, by Convocation, *ib.*

Hospitallers, Knights, succeed Templars, 62; dissolved and temporarily restored, 63

HOUGH, J., ejected, 154-156; readmitted President, 158; Bishop, 164

Holliday, B., Archdeacon, deprived of canonry, 131; poems of, *ib.*; suit of, *v.* Styles, 140; son of, 143

Hooknorton, rectory of, 119

HOWSON, J., Bishop, 161; *see* Abbot, G.

## I.

IFFLEY, impropriation of, annexed to archdeaconry, 31, 32; patronage of, 32; church of, 26

Ignatius, St., of Antioch, 11

Ini, King, assigns divided bishoprics, 13; abdicates, 14; treatment of abbey of Abingdon, 225, 226

Islip, chancel of church built by Dr. South, 80; rebuilt, *ib.*

## J.

JAMES II. gives see to S. Parker, 153; appoints A. Farmer President of Magdalen College, 154; S. Parker, 156; Bonaventure Giffard President, 158; full concession of, *ib.*

James, St., hand of, given to Reading Abbey, 239; abstracted, 240; restored, 242

Jewel, J., Bishop of Salisbury, preacher at Sunningwell, supposed builder of the church porch, 216

Jews, early settlement of, in Oxford, 41; Dominicans, care for, *ib.*; house for converts, 42; other houses for, *ib.*;

negotiate with O. Cromwell for Bodleian Library, 134; alleged murder of boy at Lincoln by, 204; pardon of, obtained at Reading, 205
Juxon, W., Archbishop of Canterbury, rector of Somerton, 148; burial of, in Oxford, 148, 149

### K.

KEBLE, J., sermon of, at St. Mary's, Oxford, 182
Kenwalch, King, misfortune and amendment of, 7
KING, R., Abbot of Thame, 93; suffragan bishop, 36, 93; bishop, 90; patent of creation, 93; new patent, 94; house of, 97; death of, and character, *ib.*; monument of, *ib.*; and *n.*, 98
Kirtlington, G. Napper seized at, 119, 120; *see* Councils
Knighthood, conferred by Abbot of Abingdon, 235

### L.

LANFRANC, Archbishop, contest with Archbishop of York, influence of, on diocese, 21, 206, 207; supports Abbot of Abingdon for William I., 231
Langton, S., Archbishop, summons council at Oxford, 50; retires to Pontigny, 203
Latimer, H., Bishop of Worcester, trial and death of, 98–102
Laud, W., Archbishop, born at Reading, 245; rise of, in Oxford, 117; visit of, to Cuddesdon, 122; charge against, for porch at St. Mary's Church, Oxford, 123; benefactor to Reading and St. John's College, 245; burial of, in Oxford, 149
Launton, residence of Bishop Skinner at, 126, 144
Lebon, John, Joannes Bonus, birth of, 269; early life of, 269, 270; death of, 270; followers of, at Ashridge, 269
Leicester, bishopric of, formed, 15
Lenthall, W., Speaker, sequestrator for Oxon, 135; confession of, to R. Brideoak, *ib.* and *n.*
Leofwin, Bishop, united see of Leicester, Lindsey, and Dorchester, 17
Lepers, St. Bartholomew's Hospital for, 47
Leprosy, mediæval, 47
Lichfield, bishopric of, 255; *see* Chester and Coventry
Lincoln, removal of bishop's chair to, 23–25; new minster, 25
Lindsey, *see* Sidenacester
Littlemore Church, 81; retirement to, of J. H. Newman, 184
LLOYD, C., testimony to, of Dr. Pusey, J. H. Newman, and W. E. Gladstone, 173, 174; political conduct, 174, 175; friendliness towards clergy, 176; death of, *ib.*
Locke, J., deprived of studentship of Christ Church, 150
Lollards, the, high support of, 257; statutes against, *ib.*; increase of, 258; persecution of, 257; sufferings of, in Bucks, 258, 259

London, J., commissioner for monasteries, with Leigh and Layton, 86; Warden of New College, Dean of Oseney, 91, 92; death of, in the Fleet, 92
Longland, J., Bishop of Lincoln, first suggestor of Henry VIII.'s divorce, 259; severity of, towards heretics, *ib.*
Lowth, W., Bishop, 172; works of, 172, 173
Lydiat, T., rector of Alkerton, pillaged by soldiers, 136

## M.

Mackarness, J. F., Bishop, 189; successful prosecution of suit by, 189, 190; patronage of, 190
Maids Moreton, church of, 67; injury to church, 263; extracts from, 263, 264; death of rector of, 264
Marriages, civil entries of, in registers, 137; how avoided, *ib.*
Martyr, P., Catherine, wife of, treatment of remains of, 75
Mercia, see of, division by Archbishop Theodore, 15
Methodists, band of, at Oxford, 171, 172; separated, 172
Mill, J., edition of Greek Testament by, 152
Minster Lovell, church of, 67; priory of, 65, 276
Monasteries, brief notices of, 83–87, 222, 223; *see* Ashridge, Abingdon, Oseney, Reading, St. Frideswide's, Henry VIII.
Moss, C., Bishop, benefactor to schools at Wheatley, 173

## N.

Newbury, Reformers burnt at, 214–216; Dr. Twisse, vicar of, 217; Coverdale's commission at, 210
Newman, J. H., Cardinal, first sermon, 181; officiates at St. Clement's, *ib.*; at St. Mary's, 182; at Littlemore, 81; "Tracts for the Times," of, 183; withdrawn by, 184; retires to Littlemore, *ib.*; enters Roman communion, *ib.*
Nonjurors, in three counties, 160, 161; in Oxford, 162–164; at Shottesbrook, 161, 162, 219; penitents, 161

## O.

Oldham, Bishop of Exeter, advice of, to Bishop Fox, 69; portrait in hall of Corpus Christi College, 69
Ordinations, during vacancy of see, 108, 117; during Commonwealth, 125, 126, 128, 129; after Restoration, 144; temp. James II., 157; Presbyterian, 147, *n.*
Oseney, name of, 1; Augustinian abbey of, 87–89; cathedral of, 92; bishop of, so called, 93; bishopric at, surrendered, *ib.*; united with St. Frideswide's, 94; fracas at abbey, 51
Oskytel, Bishop of Dorchester, 16; Archbishop of York, *ib.*; of, 16, 17
Oswald, King of Northumberland, at Dorchester, 4
Owen, J. Dean of Christ Church, works of, 131, *n*; generosity of toward Royalists, 131,

132; removes to London, 148

Oxford, name of, 1; a city by patent, 92; Parliament at, 57; councils at, 48–59; bishopric founded, 91; cathedral, see St. Frideswide; union of three counties in, 178; church expenditure, temp. Bishop Wilberforce, 188; present endowment of see, 190; distribution of clergy, 191; university of, inns anticipatory of, 73; early history of, 39–46; religious character of, 54; prospects of, in future, 55; visitation of, by Archbishop Arundel, 57; by Cardinal Pole, 75, 98, 109; by Parliamentarian commission, 130–134; state of buildings, temp. the Commonwealth, 132, 133; Colleges: Cardinal College, 77; King Henry VIII.'s College, 79, 80; Christ Church Cathedral, 65, 66; staircase of hall, 80, 81, Tom Gate, 81; All Souls', chapel of, 67; Balliol, window in chapel, 116; Corpus Christi, 69; Gloucester Hall, 90, 91, 97, 122, 232; Merton, foundation of, 40, 43; chapel of, 66, 67; New College, chapel of, 67, 133; Magdalen, Waynflete, founder of, 277; chapel of, 67, 133; tower of, 67; see James II.; Oriel, Edward II., founder of, 47; contest with city, respecting St. Bartholomew's Hospital, *ib.*; University, 40, 41; Wadham, Augustinians occupy former site of, 46; churches of, in Domesday Book, 26, 30; All Saints', 81, 160; St. Clement's, 181; St. Ebbe's, 30; of Franciscans, 65; St. Frideswide's, 30; St. Giles's, 65; St. Mary Magdalene's, 66, 106; Martyrs' aisle in, 106; St. Mary the Virgin's, 30, 102, 105, 182, 184; porch of, 81, 123; St. Michael's, tower of, 26, 30; St. Peter's, 30; St. Thomas the Martyr's, 186, 187; Bocardo, 98, 106, 171; Martyrs' memorial, 106

Oxfordshire, becomes part of the extended kingdom of Mercia, 14

P.

PARKER, S., Bishop, 153; intruding President of Magdalen College, 156; death of, 157; descendants of, in Oxford, 163

PAUL, W., Bishop, 149; provides for rebuilding of Cuddesdon, *ib.*

Peckham, J., Archbishop, appointed by Papal encroachment, 208

Peculiars, history of, 34; in Oxon, 33, 34; in Bucks, 256

Peel, Sir R., supported, as candidate for University, by Bishop Lloyd, 174, 175

Penn, W., advocates cause of James II., 155, 156

Pole, Cardinal, returns to England, 101; made Archbishop, 103; visitation of university, 75, 98, 109

Provinces of Canterbury and York defined, 22, 206, 207

Poore, R., Bishop of Sarum, removes chair to Salisbury, 195

POTTER, J., works of, 166, 167; bishop, 166; opponent of Hoadly, 166, 167; consideration for J. Wesley, 170–172; Archbishop, 172
Publicans, origin of name, 48, *n.*; opinions, *ib.*; condemnation of, 49; sufferings of, *ib.*
Pusey, E. B., character of Bishop Lloyd, 173, 174; on Tract XC., 183; treatment of, by Bishop Wilberforce, 186

## R.

RALPH, Archbishop, contest with Roger, Bishop of Salisbury, at Windsor, 246; with Thurstan, Archbishop of York, 207
Ramsbury, bishopric of, 194
Rawlinson, R., antiquary, nonjuror, at Oxford, 163; bishop for nonjurors, *ib.*
Reading, situation of, 238, 239; Benedictine Abbey, founded by Henry I., 238; history of, 239–245; Abbot of, Simon, promulgates sentence against King John, 243; last abbot of, Farringdon, with two secular priests of abbey, executed, 244; meeting of clergy at, 202; visit of Archbishop Beket, 241; of Henry II., *ib.*; of Heraclius, Patriarch of Jerusalem, 242; of Henry III., 204; councils at, 207–209; ancient churches of, 197; church of St. Mary, 81; St. Giles, 245; St. Lawrence, *ib.*; Grammar school, 215; inn, the Cardinal's Hat, *ib.*
Remigius, assists Duke William, 20; Bishop of Dorchester, 21; accused of simony at Rome, *ib.*; saved by Lanfranc, *ib.*; removes bishop's throne to Lincoln, 23, 24; institutes archdeaconry of Oxford, and others, 30; death of, before consecration of cathedral, 25; character of, 23, 24
Ridley, N., Bishop of London, trial and death of, 98–102
Robinson, H., Bishop of Carlisle, ordains clergy during vacancy of see, 117
Roger, Bishop of Sunning, so named, 196
Romanists, executed at Reading by Henry VIII., 244; at Windsor, 213, 214; at Oxford by Elizabeth, 113, 114; by James I., 119–120
Routh, M. J., joint builder of church at Theale, 82; editor of Burnet's "History of James II.," 153, *n.*
Royal touch, by James II., at Bath, 155; Woodstock, *ib.*; previous certificates, *ib.*
Rural Deans, supposed antiquity of, discussed, 35, *n.*; institution of, noticed, 34, 35; in Oxon, 35, 180; Berks, 197; Bucks, 255, 256

## S.

SACHEVEREL, H., opposed by Bishop Talbot, 165
Salisbury, bishop's chair at 195; transference of Berks from see of, to Oxon, 178; and of chancellorship of Order of Garter, 178–180
Sampson, T., Dean of Christ Church, 112; deprived, *ib.*; becomes master of hospital at Leicester, *ib.*

Sancroft, W., Archbishop, nonjuror, 161
Sarum, Old, loses bishop's chair, 195
SECKER, T., Archbishop, Bishop of Oxford, 172; Archbishop of Canterbury, *ib.*; character of, *ib.*
Selsey, mission from, influence in Berks through Hean, 224, 225
Sermons, first, in diocese, of J. H. Newman, 181; J. Wesley, 169
Serf, a, instance of release of, by will, 235, and *n.*
Sherborne, formation and extent of bishopric, 13, 193-195, 226
Sheldon, G., Bishop of London, letter to from Bishop Skinner, 126, 145
Shottesbrook, nonjurors at, 161, 162; church of, 66, 67
Sidenacester, see of, formed, 15; succession of bishops, 17
SKINNER, R., Bishop of Bristol, impeached, 124; translated to Oxford, 123, 124; imprisoned in the Tower, 125, 126; resides at Launton, 126; deprived, 126, 127; diligent in ordaining clergy, 127, 128; and confirming, 128; restored to see, 144; accusation against, and letter to Sheldon in vindication, 126, 145; translated to Worcester, 146; and *n.*
Somerton, Archbishop Juxon incumbent of, 148
Stewkley, Norman church at, resembling Iffley Church, 26
Southleigh, J. Wesley at, 169, 170

Suffragan bishops, 36, 37, 196
Sunning, Sonning, bishops of, so named, 196
Sunningwell, *see* Jewel
Swinbrook, residence and burial at, of Bishop Curwen, 111
Synods, *see* Councils

T.

TALBOT, W., Bishop, 164; supports the union with Scotland, 164, 165; opposes Sacheverel, 165; controversy with Lawrence, *ib.*; translated to Salisbury, *ib.*
Templars, Knights, 60–61; dissolved, 61
Theodore, Archbishop, consecrates Eleutherius, 9; holds a council at Hertford, 10; divides Mercian see, 15; friend of Heddi, 12; leaves see of Wessex undivided, *ib.*; Penitential of, *ib.*
Thomas, Archbishop of York, contest with Archbishop of Canterbury, 22, 205, 206
Twisse, W., incumbent of Newbury, 217; prolocutor of assembly of Divines, *ib.*; retires to Newbury, 218; death of, and burial in Westminster Abbey, 219; exhumation of body and reinterment, *ib.*; character of, 217, 218

U.

ULPH, Bishop of Dorchester, 18; accused of incompetency at Vercelli, 18, 19; saved by King, 19; escapes from London, *ib.*; vacates see, 19
UNDERHILL, J., Bishop, 115; never visits see, *ib.*; state of

diocese, 118; death of in poverty, 115
Uniformity, Act of, 146; statutes repealing, 146, *n.*
Union of Oxon, Berks, and Bucks, in diocese of Oxon, 178, 184, 185, 253

## V.

VISITATIONS, episcopal, of, Alfric, 20; Bagot, 180, 181; Grosseteste, 38, 39; Wilberforce, 185, 187

## W.

WALLINGFORD, origin of name, 197; ancient churches of, *ib.*; benefactions of Edmund, Earl of Cornwall to, *ib.*; ford crossed by Aulus Plautius, 198; by William I., *ib.*; offenders from Oseney captured at, 53
Walsingham, Sir T., examines accused Romanists, 114; recommends Underhill for see, 115
Wantage, King Alfred born at, 220; Bishop Joseph Butler born at, *ib.*; sisterhood at, *ib.*
Ward, S., Bishop of Salisbury, recovers chancellorship of the Garter, 179, 180
Waynflete, W. of, head master of Eton, 277; provost, 277, 278; Bishop of Winchester, *ib.*
Wellington, Duke of, supported on Catholic emancipation by Bishop Lloyd, 175
Wessex, see of, left undivided by Archbishop Theodore, friend of Heddi, 12; divided, 12, 13; associations of Berks and Bucks with undivided see, 193
Wesley, C., student of Christ Church, united with first Oxford Methodists, 171; J., at Christ Church, 169; ordained deacon, *ib.*; first sermon of, *ib.*; fellow of Lincoln College, 170; ordained priest, *ib.*; visits prisoners in Bocardo, *ib.*; is well received by Bishop Potter, 170, 171; mission to Georgia, 172; leaves Oxford, *ib.*; observation on Nonjurors at Oxford, 163
Wheatley, benefactions to school of, 173
Whitefield, G., interview of with the two Wesleys, 172; joins their society, *ib.*
WILBERFORCE, S., Bishop of diocese with present limit, 185-188; first charge of, 185; obtains revival of debates in Convocation, 168; in the cases of Dr. Hampden and Dr. Pusey, 186; diocesan expenditure from last charge of, 187, 188; translated to Winchester, 187; death of 188; memorials of, *ib.*
Wilkes, J., occupies prebendal house, Aylesbury, 269
William I., presents to English sees, 20, 21, 206; appoints Remigius to Dorchester, 20, 22; removes chair to Lincoln, 24; makes Robert D'Oyley, constable of Oxford, 26; deposes Aldred, abbot of Abingdon, 230; appoints Ethelhelm, *ib.*; imprisons Egelwine, Bishop of Durham in abbey, *ib.*

William and Mary, oath of allegiance to, 160

Windsor, grant of by Edward the Confessor, 246; regained by William I., *ib.*; free chapel built by Henry I.; marriage of Henry I., 246; College of St. George founded by Edward III., 247; chapel of, consecrated, 248; rebuilt by Edw. IV., *ib.*; exempted from Act for dissolution of chantries, by Edward VI., 249; tomb-house of, 249–251, 252; royal mausoleum, 252; choir of, royal burials in, 250–252; recent royal marriages, 252; Gospellers, burnt at, 212; J. Mallet, canon, sufferings of, 213; sufferers during usurpation, 135

Wini, Bishop of Dorchester, 8; expulsion of, 9; absent from synod at Hertford, 10

Witney, Bishop Underhill rector of, 115

Wolsey, T., Cardinal, Bishop Fox early patron of, 69; joint papal legate, *ib.*; sole legate, 70; accompanies King and Queen to Oxford, *ib.*; large ideas of for Oxford and Ipswich, 71, 72; consequent suppression of monasteries, 72, 76; effects surrender of St. Frideswide's by Prior J.

Burton, 76; obtains grant of site, 76, 77; founder of Cardinal College, *ib.*; offends king by splendour of and arms over gateway, 89, 90; retirement of to Esher, 90; attainder of, 79; state of college consequent upon this, *ib.*; burial-place prepared by, 249; character of, 71, 72

Woodstock, boy martyred at, 43; Beket at, 49; Beket window in church, 211; extract from register of, 137; extract from parish book of, 155, 156; Princess Elizabeth at, 101

Worton, Over, J. H. Newman preaches first sermon at, 181

Wright, W., Archdeacon of old and new archdeaconry, 91, 108, 109; institutes during vacancy of see, 108; death of, 109; character of, 109, 110

Wulfwy, Bishop of Dorchester, obtains bull in favour of see, 19, 20; death of, 20

Wycliffe, at Oxford, 57; retires to Lutterworth, *ib.*

Wycliffite version of the Bible, Oxford editions of, 59, 60; and *notes*

Wytham, removal of nunnery to, 225

THE END.

www.ingramcontent.com/pod-product-compliance
Lightning Source LLC
Chambersburg PA
CBHW022104230426
43672CB00008B/1272